TERESA OF AVILA, THE HOLY SPIRIT, AND THE PLACE OF SALVATION

Teresa of Avila, the Holy Spirit, and the Place of Salvation

André Brouillette

Paulist Press
New York / Mahwah, NJ

The Scripture quotations contained herein are from the New Revised Standard Version: Catholic Edition, Copyright © 1989 and 1993, by the Division of Christian Education of the National Council of the Churches of Christ in the United States of America. Used by permission. All rights reserved.

All quotations of St. Teresa of Avila are taken from the Kieran Kavanaugh, O.C.D., and Otilio Rodriguez, O.C.D., translation of *The Collected Works of St. Teresa of Avila,* 3 vols. (Washington, D.C.: ICS Publications, 1976–1985, 1987, 2012, 2019).

Cover image by Bill Perry / Shutterstock.com
Cover design by Joe Gallagher
Book design by Lynn Else

Originally published as *Le lieu du salut, une pneumatologie d'incarnation chez Thérèse d'Avila* by André Brouillette by Les Éditions du Cerf copyright © 2014

Library of Congress Cataloging-in-Publication Data
Names: Brouillette, André, author.
Title: Teresa of Avila, the holy spirit, and the place of salvation / André Brouillette.
Other titles: Lieu du salut. English.
Description: New York / Mahwah, NJ : Paulist Press, [2021] | "Originally published as Le lieu du salut, une pneumatologie d'incarnation chez Thérèse d'Avila by André Brouillette by Les Éditions du Cerf, c 2014." | Includes bibliographical references and index. | Summary: "An exploration of the role of the third Person of the Trinity in the works of Teresa of Avila, and its influence on pneumatology, the theological study of the Holy Spirit"—Provided by publisher.
Identifiers: LCCN 2020037163 (print) | LCCN 2020037164 (ebook) | ISBN 9780809153664 (paperback) | ISBN 9781587687365 (ebook)
Subjects: LCSH: Teresa, of Avila, Saint, 1515–1582. | Holy Spirit–History of doctrines—16th century. | Salvation—Christianity—History of doctrines—16th century.
Classification: LCC BX4700.T4 B6913 2021 (print) | LCC BX4700.T4 (ebook) | DDC 282.092—dc23
LC record available at https://lccn.loc.gov/2020037163
LC ebook record available at https://lccn.loc.gov/2020037164

ISBN 978-0-8091-5366-4 (paperback)
ISBN 978-1-58768-736-5 (e-book)

Published by Paulist Press
997 Macarthur Boulevard
Mahwah, New Jersey 07430
www.paulistpress.com

Printed and bound in the
United States of America

Contents

Preface to the American Edition

IT IS A PRIVILEGE for an author to see his or her work translated. A translation is a bridge between two worlds, over time and space. Working now on the other side of the bridge, in the United States, I can see the distance between these worlds, but also the potential for mutual enrichment.

The present book grew out of a dissatisfaction. In the early years of my studies in theology, I was struck by a double lack: the lack of clarity regarding the Christian definition of salvation and the limited role of the Holy Spirit in systematic theology. I started my doctoral studies with an ardent desire to bring a contribution in that regard. As I was looking for an entry point, an intuition came to me to look at these issues through the lens of a spiritual author, namely, Saint Teresa of Avila. By then, Teresa was only an acquaintance, but it seemed that her writings were manifesting the embodiment of life in the Spirit. The intuition was adventurous and original for a systematic theologian (and a bit controversial). The research was properly a quest, and it eventually led to the present book.

Of the many people and institutions who were thanked in the original French edition, I want to highlight two individuals. My own experience of accompanying graduate students has heightened my gratitude for the trust, freedom, and generosity of my doctoral advisors, Professor Anne Fortin and Father Emmanuel Durand, OP, who were then teaching respectively at Laval University (Quebec

City) and the Catholic University of Paris. They modeled, each in their own way, scholarly rigor, love of the Lord, and *cura personalis.*

This book was written in a French-speaking academic environment (between Quebec and France), and relied also, because of its topic, on the abundant Spanish-language literature on Saint Teresa. Therefore, the English-speaking scholarship on Teresa, which has its wonderful distinctive flavor and is less concerned with theology, was not plumbed in its depth.

My thanks go to Paulist Press for having taken the initiative to translate this monograph, in particular Trace Murphy and Donna Crilly. I am happy that this research will find a new audience.

May the words of Saint Teresa and the inspiration of the Holy Spirit lead you to the place of salvation!

André Brouillette, SJ
Solemnity of Pentecost, May 31, 2020

Translator's Note[1]

THE MOST HIGHLY regarded and widely used English translation of Teresa's works is *The Collected Works of Saint Teresa of Avila* (three volumes), translated by Kieran Kavanaugh, OCD, and Otilio Rodriguez, OCD, along with *The Collected Letters of St. Teresa of Avila* (two volumes), translated by Kieran Kavanaugh, OCD. This series of volumes, published by ICS Publications (the publishing house of the Institute of Carmelite Studies, based in Washington, DC), includes all of her major works and several lesser ones. The *Collected Works* was published between 1979 and 1985 and the *Collected Letters* in 2001 and 2007. All quotations from Teresa's works offered here come from these translations. Bibliographic information on these appears in the bibliography.

In the Kavanaugh/Rodriguez translations (as in most critical editions of Teresa's works in various languages), the paragraphs are numbered, making possible easy reference to paragraphs within chapters. This is how her work is typically cited by scholars. Throughout this book, passages will be cited by reference to the title of the work (in shortened form after the first appearance), then the chapter number, then the paragraph number, with the latter numbers separated by a colon, similar to the common method of citing Scripture passages. So, for example, "*Life* 33:5" refers to *The Book of Her Life*, chapter 33, paragraph 5. In the cases of the *Spiritual Testimonies*, the *Poetry*, and the *Letters*, the French editions cited by Father Brouillette number the texts and their paragraphs differently than Kavanaugh/Rodriguez. The translator has taken careful account of this and provided updated references that correspond to Kavanaugh/Rodriguez. Finally, references to *The*

Interior Castle are a bit unique because that work is divided into seven major sections (on the first through seventh "mansions"), as well as chapters and paragraphs. These references follow the format of shortened title, then mansions number as Roman numeral, then chapter number, then paragraph number. Thus, *Castle* I:2:17 refers to *The Interior Castle*, first mansions, chapter 2, paragraph 17.

Introduction

The Holy Spirit fascinates and eludes us. The Spirit is God acting in the world, present everywhere and yet invisible. The Spirit has spoken through the prophets, in Jesus Christ, and still whispers today in the heart of every human person.

Salvation is omnipresent in Christian discourse and theology, especially the figure of Jesus Christ, the bearer of salvation. This is not without difficulty at times, because the mediation of salvation by Christ raises many questions and opens infinite horizons to theological research. Furthermore, the very definition of salvation—of the individual believer and of the people of God as a whole—remains open.

While neither the Spirit nor salvation are easily understood, they come together in the figure of the saint. Led by the Spirit, the saint shows both humanity and the church what salvation—accomplished, grounded, and lived—looks like. The saint testifies in his or her flesh to the mystery of an encounter in history between the gift of God's own self and a welcoming human will. They may speak at times in clumsy words, limited by their context and the inherent fallibility of any language that tries to articulate the inexpressible, but it remains true that they offer important insights that ought to be received, both by the church and by theology.

It is in this fragile place of human words, at the intersection of God's action in the Spirit and a salvation welcomed and made fruitful, that the present theological reflection is situated. What is salvation? What role does the Spirit play in God's saving work? At the heart of the singular experience of Saint Teresa of Avila, this question played out long before we could ask it today.

CONSIDERING SALVATION, IN SEARCH OF THE SPIRIT: CONTEMPORARY THEOLOGICAL ADVANCES

Theological research in pneumatology and soteriology during the last several decades has been abundant. Moreover, the great movements that have shaped contemporary theology have left their mark on the scholarly work done in these fields. This abundance makes it impossible to offer an exhaustive history in a few pages. But it seems important to explain briefly the context of our own research. Thus, after having defined *grace* and *salvation,* we will identify the milestones and main issues of theological research first in soteriology, then in pneumatology.

Grace and Salvation

Dealing with the topics of grace and salvation is challenging in more ways than one. Besides the intrinsic complexity inherent in the fact that grace has been the subject of many theological controversies over the centuries, the difficulty is increased by trying to define the terms.[1] In general, grace is understood as a free gift of God to the human person, a gift that originates in the love of God.[2] It counteracts sin and makes one free. It is oriented toward salvation and accomplishes sanctification through participation in the life of God. This God communicates himself in grace,[3] in a trinitarian perspective. Grace introduces the human person into something new: a new relationship, a new creation,[4] in which the Son plays a central role in sharing his place in God's own life with the human person.[5] These few elements already give some sense of the broad horizon of the question of grace and suggest its many ramifications. But we still need to attempt a definition.

Otto Hermann Pesch offers a definition of grace that links it closely with salvation. Grace, he writes, is

> the gratuitous, unexpected, inconceivable gift of God's love to humanity, a gift that brings salvation by allowing the human person to share in the divine life, by helping the person to understand resistance to God as a sort of locking oneself up within oneself, and by triumphing over this resistance through liberation.[6]

Here, grace as a gift is not without effect, since a relationship is formed that is said to take the form of participation in the divine life. Grace is also understood as salvation, knowledge (being made "to understand"), and victory-liberation. Pesch's definition particularly emphasizes the essential role of grace in salvation.

For her part, Eva-Maria Faber defines grace as "the very essence of divine solicitude toward humanity, incarnate in Jesus Christ and communicated in the depths of human nature as a gift of the Holy Spirit; it also sums up the relationship that is established through this gift between God and the human person, who needs grace even in order to respond to grace."[7]

Faber's definition emphasizes the relational quality of grace, as the movement of God's love toward the human person, which invites the person into a relationship and is its condition sine qua non. Faber also emphasizes the trinitarian dimension of grace, which is made concrete in Christ and communicated as a gift by the Holy Spirit.

In light of these two definitions, we can essentially define grace as *the gift of God that establishes or strengthens the relationship between the human person and God.*[8] This "gift of God" can be considered both from the perspective of created grace—it is *a gift* that God gives—or from the perspective of uncreated grace—the gift given by God is *God's own self.*[9] Speaking of grace primarily as a gift highlights the *gratuitous* character of the divine initiative, which is reiterated by the fact that it comes first in "establishing" a relationship between the human person and God. The presence of God through grace in the individual is not limited to a singular moment; rather, it creates a relationship that is intended to endure. Although our purpose here is not to develop a theology of grace, our work is fraught with such questions since it addresses the problem of salvation and therefore the way it is given by God and received by the human person.

For salvation, we propose the following definition: the state of an individual or a people brought into an intimate relationship with God that is marked in a permanent way by the unfolding of new life. Salvation is therefore not a moment or a single event (though it may be punctuated by these); it is, rather, a state, which necessarily has a beginning. Moreover, salvation is not only an individual reality, contrary to the way it is often understood. The collective dimension of salvation is, in fact, primary in the unfolding revelation of the mystery of God in the Bible: it is a people that God chooses, a people that God saves.[10] This state, individual or collective, is marked by the establishment or deepening of a relationship with God. This relational component makes clear the connection between grace and salvation; grace is the means whose hoped-for end or purpose is salvation. The relational state of salvation introduces a new, permanent life, not just a static gift; like all relationships and all life, salvation is inscribed with an orientation toward growth for the one who lives it. This definition is meant to be descriptive since it does not indicate by what Christic mechanism salvation is carried out.

We should note that this definition distances itself from a purely liberationist or redemptive perspective that would present salvation as being freed from a state of loss that is connatural to being human. For example, the *Petit Robert* dictionary defines salvation thus: "In the Judeo-Christian and Buddhist religions, eternal happiness; being saved from the natural state of sin and from the damnation that would result."[11] According to these terms, salvation would be the negation of a natural state of sin and damnation. This is clearly not in keeping with the Christian conception of salvation. Moreover, Christian salvation cannot be limited to a kind of "eternal happiness" (even though one may desire that); salvation passes by way of the cross and therefore cannot ignore the reality of suffering.

The Legacy of Historical Controversies on Justification

The legacy of the theological controversies of the sixteenth century and their ecclesial consequences weigh heavy on the contemporary understanding of salvation. Relying on various Pauline writings, Martin Luther understood salvation as *Rechtfertigung* (justification), the reinstatement of a right relationship with God by the sole fact of the believer welcoming the offer of divine grace, that is, by faith (*sola fide*).[12] Justification is a concept of salvation modeled on a juridical relationship; the human being who deserves, in all justice, to undergo punishment for sin is freely ransomed by Jesus Christ, who took upon himself the penalty that the person deserved.[13] This identification of Christian salvation with justification has marked subsequent Protestant theology up to our own day.

The influence of the controversy about justification driven by Lutheran theology is not limited to the Protestant world. The Council of Trent responded by offering its own interpretation of salvation that involves faith and also works, the latter being signs of the believer's acceptance of Christ's offer of salvation. That is what is developed in the *Decree on Justification*.[14] This decree represents a rare magisterial document that defines the way in which Christ saves. However, the conception of salvation it offers is strongly marked by its historical context, viewing the question through the prism of justification.

Despite the historical importance of the justification debate,[15] we must not lose sight of the fact that salvation, even in its theological conceptualization, is not limited to the concept of justification. Justification and salvation are not interchangeable; justification is just one concept among many that explain salvation. The Bible—and following it, the fathers of the church—deploy a wide variety of concepts to describe salvation.

A Diversity of Scriptural Images of Salvation

Flowing from the establishment of the École Biblique in Jerusalem (1890), that of the Pontifical Biblical Institute in Rome (1909), and the publication of Pope Pius XII's encyclical *Divino afflante Spiritu* (1943), the study of Scripture in the Catholic context received a new vigor in the twentieth century. This reappropriation of the biblical heritage led to renewal in the way of doing theology, by considering the Bible not merely as the source from which to draw support for predetermined theological convictions, but as its own distinct object of inquiry.

On the question of salvation, a thorough consideration of the Bible allows us to appreciate the great diversity of images and perspectives it offers. For example, in the Pauline writings alone, Joseph Fitzmyer identifies ten different images of salvation: transformation (*metamorphoô*), new creation (*kainè ktisis*), redemption (*apolytrôsis*), liberation (*eleutheria*), reconciliation (*katallagè*), justification (*dikaiôsis*), sanctification (*hagiôsynè*), glorification (*doxa*), expiation (*hilastèrion*), and salvation (*sôtèria*).[16] This collection demonstrates that justification is one concept among many that carry important theological posterity. These various concepts are not merely synonyms; each one deploys its own nuances and imagery.

The plurality of images of salvation in the Bible—and we still have only mentioned a few of the most eminent—already suggests the intrinsic difficulty of expressing in a univocal manner the way that salvation happens. More positively, we could say that this plurality expresses the creative power that salvation holds, a power that diffracts into a multitude of concepts.

Patristic Renewal: Reflection on Salvation

Renewed interest in patristic theology in the mid-twentieth century—illustrated by, among other things, the publication of the *Sources Chrétiennes* series beginning in 1942—opened new horizons for theology.[17] In the nineteenth century, the use of historical tools by scholars like Adolf von Harnack to understand the evolution of dogma made it possible to develop a theological genealogy that understands the dogmatic statements inspired by the fathers of the church in the contexts of the controversies in which they emerged.

In the first phase of reception of this research, patristic soteriology was divided into a Greek branch and a Latin branch. The former, it was said, emphasized the pneumatological dimension, the divinization of the believer, and uncreated grace, while the latter lingered on created grace and the "juridical" dimension of salvation. Thanks to a more serene and careful examination of the thinking of the various fathers, these oversimplified categories can now be disregarded. In this sense, Jean-Pierre Jossua's book *Le Salut, incarnation ou mystère pascal* is representative of the turning point that took place in the second half of the twentieth century, allowing for a more careful consideration of the uniqueness of theological thinking by the various fathers.[18]

Studies in recent decades have sought to highlight the specificity of the contributions of individual fathers of the church, or even those of other ancient writers who were previously considered heterodox in some ways.[19] This attention to the theology of each author in his own context offers a more nuanced understanding of their work than was previously offered in textbooks and which acquired an almost dogmatic status. This renewed look offers a glimpse of a wide variety of approaches to the question of salvation: the relationship to biblical images, the understanding and articulation of the incarnation and the paschal mystery, the role of the humanity of Christ, the divinization of the believer (in Maximus the Confessor, for example), even the inconclusive reflections on the notion of ransom (in Gregory of Nazianzus and Gregory of Nyssa).

Like a biblical bouquet, salvation is expressed by the fathers in manifold ways. The question of the Incarnation, for example, is approached by these writers in diverse ways and opens a space that allows for significant dialogue.[20] Finally, the fathers remind us of the importance of the biblical witness and the difficulty of creating a narrow system to understand the question of salvation.[21]

Understanding Salvation in Christ

Devotional images common in the nineteenth century generally offered a sorrowful vision of Christ accomplishing the work of salvation. In this way, art reflected the emphases of the theology of that epoch. In the twentieth century, theological discourse on Christ's paschal event developed a deeper awareness of the death/resurrection dyad. This perspective, insisting on the inseparability of Christ's death and his resurrection in the theological consideration of his mission, became normative for contemporary theology.[22] We see this expressed especially in images that present Christ as simultaneously crucified and victorious.[23] Christological and soteriological reflection of recent decades maintained a close orbit around this particular pole, while paying limited attention to the incarnational pole.

However, beyond agreement on the centrality of death/resurrection in the event—that is, the advent—of salvation, we find a plurality of approaches regarding the way Christ "effects" salvation. Drawing from biblical sources and from those of the tradition, Bernard Sesboüé summarizes this plurality by presenting the figure of Christ as mediator of salvation under ten modalities.[24] The first five are "descending" concepts: Christ the revealer (salvation through revelation), the victor (redemption), the liberator, the divinizer, and the justice of God.[25] These are followed by four "ascending" concepts: the sacrifice of Christ, expiation and propitiation through his suffering, satisfaction (the only concept among these that belongs only to tradition, with little grounding in Scripture), and substitution/solidarity. Finally, Sesboüé concludes with the concept of reconciliation and forgiveness. This set of concepts covers well the various christological dimensions of soteriology and allows for contrasting approaches.

Beginning in the 1960s, at the same time theological studies were taking greater account of the human sciences,[26] the emergence of liberation theology—developed from the political theology pioneered by Johann Baptist Metz—offered a new vector to christological and soteriological questions: liberation. The concept of salvation as liberation is already present in the Bible—in both the Old and New Testaments—but liberation theology was a paradigm with renewed consideration of the social and collective impacts of Christian salvation. Rejecting a vision of salvation as only an eschatological projection of individual reward (heaven), liberation theology instead emphasized rootedness in concrete reality—with consequent calls to change this reality—as well as the collective dimension of salvation, echoing the accents of the Old Testament's Book of Exodus. While some aspects of liberation theology have been criticized,[27] it is clear that its call for dialogue between the discipline of theology and a *praxis* of transformation of the world from a soteriological point of view of liberation has left its mark in the church and theology and constitutes an important milestone in the understanding of salvation.[28]

In summary, the paschal and liberationist inflections of twentieth-century theological discourse highlight the fact that the understanding of how Christ effects salvation is still evolving and has not been exhausted.

New Questions: The Salvation of Non-Christians

The Second Vatican Council's Declaration *Nostra aetate* (1965) marked a turning point for the Catholic Church and, in turn, for the whole of Christian theology regarding the understanding of other religions. Reflecting the patristic idea of *semina Verbi*,[29] the document recognized the "ray of Truth"[30] (*radium Veritatis*) that other religious traditions reflect, as well as God's universal plan of salvation.[31] As a declaration, *Nostra aetate* did not develop a complete Christian soteriology that takes non-Christians into account. The task of thinking in a fresh way about the mediation of salvation—Christ as Savior, the role of the church, of faith, of baptism, and so on—fell to theologians.

Thirty years later, the International Theological Commission's text "Christianity and the World Religions" (1997) provided a good description of the state of the question and useful guidelines for interreligious dialogue that respects the distinctiveness of Christianity. It was also at this time that theologian Jacques Dupuis—Belgian Jesuit, longtime missionary in India, then professor at the Gregorian University—wrote the landmark book on the subject, *Toward a Christian Theology of Religious Pluralism*.[32] Acknowledging that the central question of a theology of religions was christological, Dupuis tried to think theologically, in conversation with mostly Anglo-Saxon authors such as Paul Knitter, John Hick, Mark Heim, and the like, about how to reconcile the unique and universal character of Christ. His exploration of the intersection between the Divine Word and the human existence of Jesus, or between the Logos and Christ, with the aim of developing theological models, attracted the attention (and criticism) of the Congregation for the Doctrine of the Faith.[33] The latter also published the declaration *Dominus Iesus*, "On the Unicity and Salvific Universality of Jesus Christ and the Church" (2000), with the aim of guiding research on the theology of religions in a Catholic perspective.

Beyond interfaith dialogue, the christological and soteriological challenges of the theology of religions are far from being resolved. It must be remembered, however, that this is a Christian question, since it is an attempt to provide a conceptual articulation of the universality of the offer of salvation; the presence of God in different persons, cultures, and religions; and the essential character of Christ as Savior. In doing so, questions are addressed to Christology today that had seemed to be settled by Chalcedon. But upstream—epistemologically—there is also the question of what "salvation" *is*. What kind of salvation are we talking about, even on the Christian side, when we engage in interreligious dialogue? This imposes a certain urgency on the need for soteriological reflection.

Trinity and Spirit

The Trinity Revisited

The past few decades have also been rich for trinitarian theology. In addition to the contributions of the biblical and patristic renewals, new approaches have unfolded, including the aesthetic approach—illustrated by the work of Hans Urs von Balthasar—and narrative theology.[34]

But it is undoubtedly the contribution of Karl Rahner that marked, in the 1960s, a turning point that changed the context in which all other theologians addressed the topic. In his work *The Trinity*,[35] Rahner questioned certain commonly accepted axioms in trinitarian theology. Within the framework of the relationship between the immanent Trinity and the economic Trinity, Rahner proposed the fundamental axiom, "The 'economic' Trinity is the 'immanent' Trinity and the 'immanent' Trinity is the 'economic' Trinity."[36] In other words, it is through the action of God in the world that we can understand God's nature and being. Rahner rejected the idea that God's action *ad extra* is unrelated to his eternal essence.[37] On the contrary, starting from the Incarnation of the Son, Rahner shows that each Person of the Trinity has its own mode of subsistence and of presenting itself to the world that is more than simply an "appropriation" of a characteristic of the one God.[38] By thus reversing the traditional perspective that starts from *De Deo uno* and moves to *De Deo trino* and by opening the door—through the specificity of the Incarnation of the Son, which reveals something of the very being of the Trinity—to a differentiation in unity, Rahner created a space for theological research in which many scholars have worked. And we follow them.

The Spirit Reconsidered

At the same time, renewed attention to the person of the Holy Spirit has emerged in theological discourse and in the life of the church. This interest continues to the present day.[39] One masterful response to Rahner's challenge, without necessarily being in complete agreement with him, is Yves Congar's *I Believe in the Holy Spirit*, which touches on various dimensions of the new consideration of the Spirit: the Bible, the fathers (of the East in particular), but also the contemporary life of the church.[40]

The Catholic renewal of exegesis has included a greater interest in the figure of the Holy Spirit. Congar's work is clearly marked by this. One of the most original perspectives in this field is that of the French Redemptorist theologian and biblicist François-Xavier Durrwell. His theological work is deeply scriptural in nature, and some of his later works relate directly to the question of the Spirit, offering new and clear insights.[41]

The patristic renewal noted above has included, in the context of pneumatology, a renewed contact with the theology of the Christian East, where the Spirit occupies a more prominent place than in the West. The orthodox theologian Paul Evdokimov brought the accents of the Eastern tradition clearly to the attention of Western theologians.[42] The *filioque* issue takes up a lot of attention, but it is only one part of the intersection of theological universes that have evolved independently for centuries. The reception of these different perspectives on the Holy Spirit, beyond the literal resolution of theological differences, constitutes an interesting theological development.

Returning to Congar, the most surprising aspect of his work is the way it takes into account the ecclesial experience of the charismatic movement—in which the role and activity of the Holy Spirit has a central place—that emerged after the Council. It was to the credit of a classical theologian like Congar that he would let himself be challenged theologically by a phenomenon that was at that point relatively new in the life of the Catholic Church, particularly on subjects like "baptism in the Holy Spirit" or the gift of tongues.

Though Congar's work on the Holy Spirit has a notably encyclopedic character, other theologians have also embraced pneumatology in their theological enterprise. Jürgen Moltmann, for example, presents an "integral pneumatology" in his work *The Spirit of Life*.[43] The relative neglect of the Spirit that marked Western theology for centuries can now be considered a thing of the past.

At the Confluence of the Spirit and Salvation

It is at the confluence of multiple branches of systematic theology that our research takes place. The developments and issues raised above are immense and constitute worlds in themselves. Our contribution will therefore depend on them while exploring new ground. One of the original features of our contribution will be consideration of the work of an author with an approach that is more spiritual than systematic, a distinctive strategy that raises new questions.

SPIRITUAL TEACHING AS A THEOLOGICAL PATH

The question of the use of spiritual texts in systematic theology is the subject of debate and caution. Before approaching this issue on a solid footing, we must define the essential terminology we will be encountering since several terms are polyvalent and even problematic.

Defining Terms: *Experience*, *Mystical*, and *Spiritual*

The concept of *experience* is problematic. The German language has the words *Erlebnis* and *Erfahrung* to designate what, in English, would only be the word *experience*.[44] *Erlebnis* is constructed from the word *Leben* ("life") and designates an experience as an event (*Erlebnis*) that one lives. Something happens. *Erfahrung* also signifies experience, but it implies that one learns something from it. The English expression "an experienced person" (or someone who "has experience") also refers to this reality of a multitude of experiences (*Erfahrungen*) that constitute knowledge. Experience is what counts, just as the repeatable experience (*Experiment*) does in the context of science. Spiritual experience, then, is a kind of *Erlebnis* that one lives, but it is also experience as a singular event at the heart of existence.

A consideration of Spanish also sheds light on the uniqueness of experience. There we find a distinction between *experiencia* and *vivencia*. The word *vivencia* expresses a sustained, existential (lived) state of being that is shaped by a set of discrete experiences (*experiencias*). *Vivencia* is close to *Erlebnis* by its character of existential experience, but it is different in that it does not refer to a singular experience but rather to a state or condition. Unfortunately, the English language does not have an equivalent word that can account for a continuous state of this kind; it is necessary to fall back on the term *life*, or, in some cases, *experience*.

In the context of spirituality, Sylvie Robert offers a detailed definition of the Christian spiritual experience as a "relationship experienced by a subject with the God of Jesus Christ."[45] With its emphasis on relationship, this definition suggests the proximity between grace and spiritual experience. Robert also emphasizes that spiritual experience extends through time; as a relationship, it goes beyond any single event. Given that our research is located within the context of Christianity, the spiritual experiences we explore here will be considered in a Christian perspective.

Keeping in mind the relational and personal character of experience, it is not easy, without resorting to a neologism, to distinguish between experience as a singular event or as an existential continuum. We will make sure as much as possible that our meaning is clear according to the context. That being said, for Teresa of Avila, the singular experience is generally transmitted in the form of a narrative, while "ongoing" experience (made up of singular events, but also of reflections and judgments) is generally delivered in the form of teaching. This distinction will reduce the possible ambivalence of the notion of experience.

Another ambiguous term is *mysticism*.[46] As a noun, it is sometimes used in a sense similar to that of *spirituality* (e.g., "Ignatian mysticism") to denote all the phenomena, interactions, and ways of acting that have to do with one's relationship with God. This can go so far as to cover a whole historical spiritual movement (e.g., "German mysticism"). As an adjective, *mystical* suggests an extraordinary character—a mystical grace or experience with an irreducible character that goes beyond the common experience of most believers. That being said, some authors tend to broaden the scope of the adjective *mystical* to make it synonymous with *spiritual* or even *Christian* (speaking, e.g., of the "mystical life" to designate an altogether common spiritual experience).[47] This expansion reflects a laudable concern—and a theological decision—not to restrict the experience of God to extraordinary events or to a small, chosen elite. However, for the sake of clarity, we will reserve the use of the adjective *mystical* to spiritual phenomena (favors, visions, and so on) of an extraordinary kind.[48] This does not imply a judgment on the universality of access to the experience of God; but this question will be developed in due course and cannot be resolved by an overly broad use of the term *mystical*.

In addition, we will generally avoid the term *spirituality*. To refer to the whole of the singular spiritual experiences recounted by Teresa as well as the guidance she offers, we prefer the term *spiritual teaching*. As we see in *The Book of Her Life* (hereafter referred to as her *Life*), the didactic dimension of Teresian teaching is strongly marked by her own spiritual experiences, experiences that she describes in narrative form. The interrelationship—and inseparability—of testimony and teaching is clear in a book like *The Interior Castle*, which brings into play various spiritual experiences of Teresa—described in the third person—in a structured unit that is highly pedagogical. The choice to use the term *teaching* to cover the whole of what she says also echoes her own conception of her writings, even the very personal ones, which she understands to be not merely the sharing of personal experience, but rather sharing an experience that, received from an Other, is intended, sometimes against her will, to be shared in order to help others experience God. In this sense, her teaching is experiential and existential both in its content and in its aim, since she seeks to guide others through a process of learning that is not only intellectual (understood) but also incarnate (experienced, put into practice). However, this Teresian experience is not delivered raw; it is shaped by her ways of expressing it, though as transparently as possible.

A final word on what we mean by *spiritual.* From a theological point of view, this adjective engages the whole of life in the Spirit, whether under the Spirit's guidance or as a search. As used in this work, the word suggests a conception of a trinitarian God who is open to relationships with human beings.

The Challenge of Using Spiritual Teaching as a Source for Systematic Theology

Even in an era of interdisciplinarity, academic nomenclatures abound, with each field seeking rigorously to define its content and method, but not without disagreements and inflections. Theology in its various meanings is no exception. The traditional study of *dogmatic theology* aims to produce a discourse that gives a faithful account of the Christian faith as it is expressed in the Scriptures and the tradition of the church under the regulation of dogma.[49] However, because this presupposes a mindset shaped by a faith and its doctrine, it becomes limited in cultural contexts where faith is no longer presumed. In this sense, *systematic theology*—a theology carried out within a "system"—attempts to address ethical and doctrinal questions through theological reflection, while not hesitating to question dogmatic normativity when appropriate.[50] Today, *systematic theology* is a more common term than *dogmatic theology* in the North American context. A third distinct term is *fundamental theology*. This, attentive to dogma and eager to work with a system, takes seriously the anthropological foundations of the act of believing and considers statements of faith in relation to them. Karl Rahner's *Foundations of Christian Faith* is emblematic of this approach.[51] In doing so, contemporary theology—systematic or fundamental—takes account of the experience of believing in its approach to its object of study, an approach that was for centuries not considered to have a place in theology.[52] Exploring the faith experience of a saint is therefore not incongruous in the light of current theological studies.

The fissure between theology, as an academic discipline, and spirituality, as a description of Christian spiritual experience, gradually occurred in the Middle Ages and had crystallized by the sixteenth century.[53] By this time, it was easy to distinguish theological texts from spiritual texts, a distinction that previously could not have been made with such clarity. Literary production of the biographies of or spiritual writings by saints, for example, was mostly ignored by theology and left instead to the field of spirituality, which was considered of lesser importance. However, with the contribution of the historical sciences, then through contact with the various methods of literary hermeneutics, a properly spiritual field of investigation has gradually been established as an academic discipline within theology, albeit on the margins of systematic theology. This is known as *spiritual theology*, which has its own methods, criteria, and currents, having also forged links with dialogue partners within the university that are different from those of systematic theology. Its object of study is the Christian spiritual experience, as it is expressed in spiritual writings as well as in other sources.[54]

We could therefore hastily conclude that the task of spiritual theology is the study of spiritual writing, but that would be to disregard the renewed interest within systematic theology of accounts of the experiential dimension of faith. This consideration was born from a development endogenous to systematic theology. As Sylvie Robert notes,

> It has been by listening to its times, fulfilling its task of thinking in dialogue, paying attention to essential dimensions of faith, and not merely reflecting on spiritual experience itself, that contemporary theology has found it impossible to overlook the experience of belief. It does not have to turn its back on theology in order to be "spiritual theology." It is by fulfilling its task of reflecting on the nature of God, bearing "the responsibility of faith from the point of view of truth," that it takes account of, and offers a place within its field to, the experience of faith.[55]

It is clear that the respective a priori that are presumed by systematic theology and spirituality, even spiritual theology, have evolved in recent decades. A body of work like that of Hans Urs von Balthasar, for example, weaves links between the experience of God and academic theology, refusing to keep these two fields hidden from one another.[56]

Is it therefore legitimate for systematic theology to take spiritual teaching as one of its sources? Because it wants to be attentive to Christian experience, yes. However, it considers this material from a perspective that is different from that of spiritual theology. Systematic theology keeps in mind the normative reference of dogmatic theology, and it is therefore in a more distanced relationship to experience, while spiritual theology opts for proximity to experience, even if that means downplaying dogmatic normativity.[57] A systematic theological approach to a spiritual text therefore calls for different methodological assumptions.

Moreover, it is the questions posed to the text that will determine disciplinary approach. In this sense, our research, while relying on spiritual texts, is fully in line with the systematic orientation of theology by the questions it raises, which are mainly pneumatological and soteriological. The results will therefore need to be put in dialogue with key figures of the theological universe mentioned above.

The choice to study the work of a particular spiritual author is not arbitrary; it was imposed by the very subject of this research. Indeed, approaching the Spirit in theology is not an easy task. Various studies have been carried out from a biblical or patristic point of view, and as far as Teresa is concerned, the most relevant passages have been noted by skillful commentators. However, the Spirit is not easy to grasp head on. Presuming the Spirit's action,[58] one can, however, study it more broadly than through textual material alone.

A narrative account of life in the Spirit, even that of a canonized witness, obviously does not bear the same type of normativity as other sources of systematic theology, such as Sacred Scripture or conciliar teaching. Despite the individuality of all experience of God and the a fortiori nature of accounts of it, one can legitimately assume that her narrative displays the role of the Holy Spirit from an original angle.[59] One can thus hope that a theological approach to spiritual texts will offer new perspectives, just as the biblical and patristic renewals of the middle of the last century or the emergence of the human and social sciences in theology in the last decades of the century have changed the way of understanding and practicing theology. This means ascribing a value to the faith experience of key figures that not only is more than that of everyone else but is even canonical.

Joseph Doré, in his time, illustrated well the intrinsic theological relevance of a spiritual author like Teresa of Avila, despite her not being a "professional theologian." In his introduction to Michel de Goedt's work on Teresian Christology, Doré wrote,

> Since, on one hand, she is "of Jesus,"[60] she has something to tell us about Jesus....But since, on the other hand, her authority in matters of doctrine has been recognized at the highest levels, her audience is not limited solely to the domain of spirituality; she deserves to be heard also on a strictly theological level.[61]

The decision by the Vatican in recent decades to bestow the title of "Doctor of the Church" upon various saints known for their spiritual teaching[62] gives these saints, in addition to the recognition already acquired by their holiness of life, the aura of an official ecclesiastical magisterium. This certainly merits the interest of the systematic theologian.

TERESA OF AVILA, THE HOLY SPIRIT, AND SALVATION

Choosing Teresa of Avila

The audience for Teresian teaching today is very broad and goes well beyond the world of Carmel. Teresa's writings are available in various editions and translations.[63] This is a sign of the relevance of her teaching; our contemporaries still pay attention to what she had to say more than four centuries ago and remain challenged by it.

A Doctor of the Church, Teresa is traditionally depicted in Christian imagery in the company of a dove, suggesting that she was inspired by the Holy Spirit. This ecclesial perception of Teresa as an inspired writer makes a deeper exploration of her thought on the Holy Spirit all the more fitting. In addition, the diversity of her writings—which include autobiography, letters, and didactic works—and the interweaving, even within individual texts, of experience and theological reflection offer fertile ground for a nuanced and distinctive consideration of God's action in the Spirit. Finally, on the question of salvation, her role as both writer and founder opens, beyond the matter of her own personal salvation, a window on the prospect of the salvation of others.

The Life and Work of Teresa of Avila

Born in 1515, Teresa learned to read and write at an early age. She would carry these interests with her throughout her life. At the age of twenty, she left her father's house and entered the Carmelite monastery of the Incarnation in Avila. As a young nun, she became ill and nearly died in 1539. She remained sick for three years, until she was, she believed, healed by the intercession of Saint Joseph. In 1554, when she was thirty-nine years old, seeing an image of Christ scourged initiated a conversion in her; she rejected her own religious lukewarmness and decisively undertook anew the way of prayer. In 1560, after the mystical betrothal and the grace of transverberation, a vision of hell marked the beginning of a path that led her to a career as a foundress, starting in 1562, with the establishment of the monastery of Saint Joseph. Twenty years, many writings, and fifteen monastery foundations later, on the evening of October 4, 1582, Teresa, en route to Avila, died at Alba de Tormes.

In parallel with the growth of the Carmelite reform, Teresa engaged in an intense literary activity. In addition to thousands of letters (of which more than four hundred remain extant), various writings and a few highly consequential works make up this diverse corpus. Most important among them are *The Way of Perfection,* the *Constitutions,* her *Life, Meditations on the Song of Songs, The Book of Her Foundations* (hereafter, *Foundations*), and *The Interior Castle.*

Even during her lifetime, several of her writings circulated widely. Most of them were published in 1588 by Luís de Leon, a well-known Augustinian monk and poet. A biography of Teresa, written by a Jesuit named Francisco de Ribera, appeared in 1590. Teresa was beatified in 1614, then canonized on March 12, 1622, with, among others, Ignatius of Loyola and Francis Xavier. On September 27, 1970, Pope Paul VI proclaimed her a Doctor of the Church, the first woman to obtain this recognition, a few days before bestowing the same honor upon Saint Catherine of Siena.

Between Life and Teaching

Teresa's writings are notable for the concern for accuracy that she displays, in a combination of humility and self-assurance. On one hand, she acknowledges a discrepancy between what she perceives and her ability to articulate it. On the other hand, she is also capable of asserting with great vigor, and in opposition to mediocre scholars (*medio letrados*), certain strong theological convictions. Her teaching is at times truly magisterial. Teresa speaks from experience, referring to sources of authority (books and others) only to help her formulate her thoughts or to address anticipated doubts.[64] This leads Eulogio Pacho to observe that "perhaps no other spiritual master of the time gives, as much as Teresa, such an impression of writing on the sidelines of scholarship and research, with an intentional absence of citations. Her primary and constant source is her own human and spiritual experience."[65] Tomás Álvarez discerns Teresa's "typical theological approach," which consists of starting from the empirical data to arrive at doctrinal conclusions.[66] However, although rooted in her own experience, the Teresian approach is more than a mere personal report of what happened; the mystical graces (or "favors") are embedded in an original theological construction[67] that Castro describes as "authentic spiritual theology."[68] De Goedt writes that, unlike John of the Cross, whose mystical graces and spiritual teaching are generally unrelated, "with Saint Teresa... the mystical graces become the source of spiritual doctrine."[69] Castro follows in the same vein when he writes,

> It is not a question of isolated experiences of the mystery of God, but of a global and growing perception of this mystery, the formulation of which is endowed with more harmony and internal coherence than what is offered to us by many theologians who, lacking the deep experience [*vivencia*] of what they speak, perceive

> the history of salvation from a distance, without entering existentially into the dynamics of its realization.[70]

While Castro's judgment regarding theologians may be too reductive and may also exaggerate the distinction between spirituality and dogmatic theology, his praise of the intellectual coherence of Teresian teaching is correct.

The mystical graces that Teresa recounts have a pedagogical function, often inaugurating for her a turning point or new progress. They strike the imagination before introducing the reader to material that is often less spectacular but that has universal value. Teresian teaching does not point down an inaccessible path, since Teresa always takes care to remember that it is not mystical graces that ensure salvation,[71] but charity.[72]

The link between her experience and her teaching is also clear in the fabric of most of her important writings. Her *Life*, *The Way of Perfection*, and *The Interior Castle*—in the case of the latter, even under the thin literary veil of experiences narrated in the third person—each intertwine accounts of personal experience, advice, exhortation, and thanksgiving. Personal experience is offered as the source and validation of the teaching given. Against her own will, in response to the direction of confessors and religious superiors, Teresa shared her experience in the form of teaching. This is why one of her first important writings, *The Way of Perfection*, was clearly addressed to her sisters at Saint Joseph monastery.[73] It is in a concrete ecclesial context, then, that her writings emerge; her experience is intended to benefit others. As she neared death, exhausted and traveling out of obedience, she exclaimed that it was as an *hija de la Iglesia*,[74] a "daughter of the church," that she had lived.

The Milestones of Teresian Research

Teresian research is abundant. The *Bibliografía sistemática de Santa Teresa* (2008) lists almost thirteen thousand bibliographic entries on various Teresian subjects, from critical editions to articles to monographs.[75] The body of texts and studies available to researchers is impressive. We must note, in particular, the pioneering work of Father Silverio de Santa Teresa, who, at the beginning of the twentieth century, published an extensive critical edition of Teresa's texts and important historical documents concerning her life. In recent decades, the work of Father Tomás Álvarez has also been monumental; in addition to historical and theological works, he is responsible for facsimile editions of the best manuscripts of Teresa's primary works.[76] Teresiologists also rely on an excellent concordance of her writings,[77] a Teresian encyclopedia that is both historical and theological,[78] and many works of historical research. It is in the Spanish-speaking world—Teresa's own—that many of these studies have been produced. If the progress of Teresian research is mainly due to historical and theological work, other perspectives have also opened up new avenues—most notably, literary[79] and feminist[80] studies. Thus, for example, Felicidad Bernabéu Barrachina's notable 1963 article, which proposed Teresa's Jewish ancestry as an explanation for certain features of her literary style.[81] Interest in Teresa has not been limited to clerics or spiritual theologians alone.

Among all this literature (which is far too vast to try to give an exhaustive account here), we will focus on identifying the essential milestones with regard to three major theological topics: Christology, the Trinity and the Spirit, and finally, grace and salvation.

From Spirituality to Christology

Until the 1970s, Teresa of Avila, mystic and reformer, was mainly considered from the standpoint of prayer, about which she was considered an expert. Already during her lifetime, she chose to share her interest in prayer with her sisters and beyond. The form and content of Teresa's works, which give pride of place to prayer, in the form of narratives and advice, encourage such a reading.

However, the 1978 publication, of Secundino Castro's doctoral thesis, *Cristología teresiana,* quickly gave a christological inflection to scholarly understanding of her work.[82] The development was so sudden that three years later Augusto Guerra could write, "Christology is the most important theme [in Teresa's writings] and the one upon which Teresian spirituality must be supported. Until the publication of *Cristología teresiana*...it was generally accepted that the central question was that of prayer. Today, no one is defending this position."[83] In terms of francophone research, the major contribution to Teresian Christology has been Michel de Goedt's *Le Christ de Thérèse de Jésus,* published in 1993.[84] To these monographs one can add the important article by Tomás Álvarez, "Jesucristo en la experiencia de Santa Teresa."[85]

From the literature on Teresian Christology, several important results emerge.

First, the ubiquity of the figure of Christ in Teresian spirituality. This ubiquity is not vague; it is, rather, that of Christ in his "most sacred humanity" (*humanidad sacratísima*), thus displaying a very real concreteness. Castro thus emphasizes that the summit of "configuration to Christ" (*cristologización*) can be found in the mystical marriage, which takes place with the humanity of Christ and not by the intervention of the Word.[86] Teresa's deep-rooted christocentrism and vigorous theological positions have been the occasion for much debate against those who advocate the need for an abandonment of Christ's humanity in order to progress spiritually.[87] Beyond theological controversy, this Teresian emphasis on Christ in his humanity also reflects the primacy that Teresa accords to her own experience in the elaboration of her teaching. It is an experience that involves sight, hearing, and the flesh as well, and it ensures that this teaching is marked with the seal of concreteness.

Second, the paschal nature of the Teresian conception of Christ. Teresa's Christ is the risen Christ, who has passed through death and entered into glory.[88] The prevalence of the Johannine *yo soy* ("I am") in the words that Christ addressed to Teresa contributes to this characterization.[89] Of the four Gospels, John's is the one that most clearly presents Christ as already glorified, even in his earthly life. The phrase "I am" that appears regularly in this gospel echoes the "I Am Who I Am" (Exod 3:14), the self-identity that the Lord offered to Moses in the episode of the burning bush; in this way, the evangelist suggests the divine nature of Jesus. For Teresa, then, the person of Jesus Christ is always seen in the light of Easter.

Third, the importance of christological visions. Such visions punctuated the entire Teresian journey. At first, they were experienced in a relationship of exteriority: a vision of the angry

Christ[90] that led Teresa to recover herself spiritually; an image of the scourged Christ that distressed her (*Life* 9:1). From an initially distanced relationship, the visions then evolved relationally, from courtship (*ir a vistas*) through betrothal (*desposorio*) to marriage (*matrimonio*). The relationship to Christ structures the evolution of Teresa's spiritual life and thereby provides her with a key to understanding—and teaching—the possible stages of this growth, as we see in *The Interior Castle*.[91]

Fourth, the close relationship with the Word of God. Christ often presents himself to Teresa in the form of word(s)—and even as "a living book" (*libro vivo*) (*Life* 26:5). More broadly, she has a subtle relationship with the biblical text.[92] First of all, she encountered it—prior to the prohibition of vernacular versions of the Bible[93]—and she knew it, in particular through Ludolph of Saxony's *Vita Christi*, a very popular work in her time.[94] Her prayer was nourished by it; she noted that she often used a book to help her pray (*Life* 4:9; *Way* 17:3). When Christ speaks to her personally, it is often in a style and vocabulary of the New Testament; the one who speaks to her follows in the path of biblical revelation.[95] Moreover, the biblical structure being so familiar to Teresa, it also becomes a hermeneutic structure for understanding herself. This existential relationship can be read par excellence in the figure of Saint Paul, whom Teresa echoes both explicitly[96] and implicitly.[97]

In addition to the theological importance of Teresian Christology, at the level of the history of Teresian study this new wave of work signals a properly theological inflection of Teresian research.

The Trinity and the Holy Spirit

In terms of research on the Trinity, Rómulo Cuartas Londoño's monumental work *Experiencia trinitaria de Santa Teresa de Jesús* is certainly the most significant recent contribution to the question.[98] Cuartas Londoño strives to read Teresa's whole experience of the trinitarian life by paying particular attention to the role of the Holy Spirit—which translates into the experiential schema of "Spirit–Son–Father," rather than the traditional "Father–Son–Spirit"—and puts it in conversation with contemporary theology, represented by Hans Urs von Balthasar, whom he cites frequently, but also Karl Rahner, Walter Kasper, Jürgen

Moltmann, and Bruno Forte.[99] Cuartas Londoño's work explores the place of the Trinity in Teresa's thought by considering all the principal points, first through a spiritual biography (first part), then a consideration of the three Divine Persons (second part), and finally the Teresian confession of her "trinitarian experience" (*experiencia trinitaria*), marked strongly by doxology[100] (third part). This is what Cuartas Londoño identifies as the originality of his thesis.[101] The book concludes, notably, with a consideration of trinitarian indwelling. Cuartas Londoño's work is dependent on Angel María García Ordás's thesis, *La persona divina en la espiritualidad de Santa Teresa,* published in 1967, which took up the personalism of contemporary theologians like Juan Alfaro to think theologically about the Divine Persons as they appear in Teresian teaching.[102]

It has to be said that the Holy Spirit is a topic too often ignored in Teresian research. Teresa herself rarely refers to the Holy Spirit, although she does at some pivotal moments. Cuartas Londoño accurately describes the general situation when he writes, "We must begin by expressing our agreement with Teresiologists who assert that Teresian pneumatology is more implicit than explicit and that references to the Holy Spirit in Saint Teresa's writings are limited in comparison with the superabundance of Christological experiences and ample allusions to the Father."[103] But he quickly adds that "while we agree, it is clear that in all believers, and especially in Teresa, whose path of perfection is contemplative prayer, we must recognize the particular action of the Holy Spirit."[104]

The various Teresian allusions to the Holy Spirit and the visions in which the Spirit specifically has a place have been analyzed, many final words of books by Teresian commentators are inspired by them,[105] and the importance of the Holy Spirit has been underlined,[106] but, as Jesús Castellano notes, "an exhaustive study on the Holy Spirit in the mystical experience of Teresa of Avila does not exist."[107]

Why does Teresa say so little about the Holy Spirit? One reason, based on her historical context, may be fear of the suspicion of heresy through association with the *Alumbrados,* the Spanish movement of "enlightened ones" who engaged in questionable mystical practices.[108] After all, Teresa had been threatened with denunciation to the Inquisition.[109] But Castro believes that the relative absence of the Spirit in the Teresian corpus is attributable primarily to the supreme importance she gives to Christ:

> Although the person of the Spirit is present in Teresa's writings, this is not as much as is sometimes suggested nor as much as one might hope. The reason, in my view, is that Christ captured her attention entirely, completely absorbing the mind of Teresa. It follows from this that several images and symbols that, in the New Testament, represent the Spirit are applied by Teresa to Jesus Christ.
>
> However, as we have said, there are many allusions to the Spirit, and the Spirit remains thoroughly integrated in her thought.[110]

Teresa's inattention to the Spirit, however, should not be attributed entirely to this omnipresence of the figure of Christ. We can also see in her relative silence an indication of the particular nature of the Holy Spirit.

In a chapter on Teresa's "experience of the Trinity" (*vivencias trinitarias*), Castro explores several interesting lines of thought, more impressionistic than systematic, but highly fruitful. Here, we note two of them, which we will come back to later in our work. The first concerns the place of Christ and of his humanity within the Trinity. Castro observes that, for Teresa, it is Christ in his humanity who is present within the Trinity.[111] Teresa's christocentrism therefore shaped her conception of the Trinity. In a second insight, Castro recalls the salutation with which Teresa begins many of her letters: a wish for the grace of the Holy Spirit. He sees in this "a sort of paschal greeting; like Christ, she [Teresa] intends to communicate the Spirit. This fact, in our judgment, is very significant, since it indicates that in this gift she sees concentrated all the goods that one can desire for her relatives and friends."[112]

Even more striking than the fact that Teresa sees in the grace of the Spirit the concentration of all the gifts one could hope for is the very posture of Teresa; she adopts that of the risen Christ, who is both inhabited by and the bestower of the Holy Spirit. It is a signal that what is seen of the Spirit cannot be reduced to knowledge, but dwells in the very heart of Teresa's existence.

We should not forget to mention the comparative trinitarian studies done by Michael Strucken on Ignatius of Loyola, Teresa of Avila, and John of the Cross,[113] and by Giuseppe Ferraro on John of the Cross, Teresa of Avila, Thérèse of Lisieux, and Elizabeth of the Trinity.[114] Their comparative methodology makes it possible to articulate the specificity of Teresa's contribution in a systematic way.

In summary, although the primary allusions to the Holy Spirit in the Teresian corpus have been addressed by various scholars, research remains to be done on the specific mode of action of the Spirit that goes beyond conventional observations.

Grace and Salvation

The angle of approach to the question of *grace* in Teresian research is through the descriptions of her experience that she offers in her writings. Teresa sometimes uses the word, but more often we understand her thought on grace by applying theological concepts to her words, which are more often figurative in nature. This allows us to consider several important questions about Teresa's theology of grace. Is this gift universal or specific? How is it received? Does the end state—the state of grace—require a welcome, or is it the conscious realization of what already inhabits the human being? Does the established relationship imply divine presence? Is this presence the presence that is within all things, or is there a specific trinitarian indwelling?

In a 1967 article, José Cristiano Garrido sought to articulate the Teresian experience of grace using scholastic categories, but with more attention to the existential dimension (*vivencia*) than the didactic dimension—even in the expression of what she believes—of her writing.[115] Garrido observes that Saint Teresa distinguished the "natural" presence of God in everything that exists (even despite sin) from God's loving presence through grace[116]—for example, in trinitarian indwelling. For example, she expresses her singular experience of an all-encompassing presence of God using the metaphor of a sponge.[117] Contrasting the state of grace to the state of sin, Teresa, anticipating the metaphor of the central dwelling place of the castle of the soul, says that the soul in a state of sin does not reflect the beauty of God, but that God always remains in the human person, giving it existence.[118]

However, for the soul in a state of sin, even good works do nothing to gain eternal glory.[119]

Twenty years later, Miguel Maury Buendía took up the topic and summarized the state of the question.[120] On the Teresian experience of grace, Buendía noted that not all subjective perception belongs to the order of mystical experience.[121] But, taking account of the position of various commentators, Buendía defended Teresa against those who have accused her of having a limited or poor understanding of grace. In the end, Buendía adopted the suggestion of Efrén de la Madre de Dios, that rather than having to fit Teresa's words in one or the other scholastic alternative, there could be an elusive key that systematic theology struggles to express in adequate formulas.[122]

The question of *salvation* is related to that of grace. The notion of salvation can also be approached in a multitude of ways, including by way of grace (being saved by grace, the state of grace, and so on). Like the broader subject, the question of salvation in Teresian teaching has received little study. We will now consider two instances in which it has.

First, the work of Jean-Marie Laurier enters directly into the dogmatic dimension of salvation by considering the theology of justification.[123] Laurier points to Teresa's existential synthesis as a response to the historical unilateralism of Lutheran and Tridentine theologies of justification[124] regarding the question of God's saving action and the types of human response to it.

Despite an approach that some scholars have questioned, Laurier offers a meticulous consideration of Teresa's *Life*, *The Way of Perfection*, and finally *The Interior Castle*, which he develops extensively as "witness-synthesis." Seeking to reconcile conflicting theologies, he finds support in Teresa's image of the castle and its central light—representing God—seeing it as a way of avoiding a dichotomy between created grace (a gift of God) and uncreated grace (the Giver himself).[125] It is interesting to note that in his development of the final image of the soul according to Teresa—in the seventh mansions of *The Interior Castle*—Laurier, after three sections on the trinitarian life, mystical marriage, and deification, offers a fourth and final section on identification with Christ the servant and the ecclesial value of works.[126] Thus, at the summit of the Teresian theological vision, the question of salvation in its apostolic dimension is prominent.

The apostolic dimension of Teresa's life reveals the *ecstatic* dimension of salvation as a desire for the salvation of others. In his book *L'Idéal apostolique des Carmélites selon sainte Thérèse d'Ávila*, Emmanuel Renault judiciously explores the entire question, based as closely as possible on Teresa's own words. Renault skillfully demonstrates that Teresa introduced into the heart of Carmelite spirituality an apostolic—even missionary—dimension, alongside the contemplative dimension.[127] Like Castro's contribution in Christology, Renault's work corrected the purely spiritual understanding of Teresa's achievement by recognizing fully, and at the same level, the apostolic dimension aimed at the salvation of others.[128]

THE PLAN OF THIS BOOK

Question, Hypothesis, and Thesis

What can be said about salvation? What can be said of the Spirit? Does the Spirit save? These are the basic questions that have inspired this research. They fall within the theological fields of soteriology and pneumatology.

Faced with the diversity of ways to understand salvation theologically and the sparseness of theological consideration of the Holy Spirit, looking carefully at the corpus of a great spiritual master like Teresa of Avila seems to offer a promising way forward because of the insights from both the experiential and the narrative points of view it offers. To ask such questions, a theologian must often make use of tools and methods borrowed from literary analysis, in order to open a text and allow it to speak.

To pneumatological and soteriological questions, analysis of the Teresian texts offers answers that are trinitarian ("pneumato-christological") and "inhabitational." Two interconnected themes emerge. First, salvation as *divine indwelling in a place*, emphasizing the *incarnational* nature of salvation. Second, *the Holy Spirit as "incarnator" of salvation*, emphasizing the *dynamic* nature of salvation (which is pneumatological and indissociably trinitarian as well).

In this study, we will make frequent use of the notion of incarnation. We will use it first in the sense of the historical and unique Incarnation of the Son of God made flesh (when we use it in this sense, it will be with a capital letter *I*). But this work of the Spirit is also replicated analogically in a broader movement or dimension that we will speak of as incarnational (and when used in this sense, it will be with a lowercase *i*).[129]

Method and Outline

The three-part movement of this work unfolds in five chapters. Chapters 1 and 2 represent a first section, in which we focus mainly on some texts from Teresa's *Life.* These texts—chapters 32 to 36 and 38 of her *Life,* as well as the beginning of her *Foundations*—recount a turning point of her life: while a fervent nun already experiencing certain mystical graces, she received the project of founding a new monastery, which would become Saint Joseph. This story brings into play several concepts that, discerned by a hermeneutical approach of a semiotic nature, bring new insights on the question of the role of the Holy Spirit in salvation. The heuristic role of the original semiotic reading of these texts will be mentioned only briefly; we offer the fruits without detailing the process of maturation. In fact, various approaches to literary analysis will be put to use, not limiting our investigation to only one of them.

We have made the choice, for these two chapters, to be attentive to the text itself and for itself, introducing historiographic elements or references to secondary literature only with extreme parsimony. Our bias here is to let the texts speak for themselves, not to make judgments about orthodoxy or to draw connections with contemporary theology.[130] It is not with the yardstick of the Teresian interpretive tradition nor even that of the entire Teresian corpus that we read these texts. Attention to the narrativity of events in this story, therefore, lends similar weight to factual elements as it does to mystical experiences and the metaphors and images related to them; we receive them *prima facie* as elements of Teresian discourse.

The initial working hypothesis—subsequently confirmed—was that by rigorously analyzing these texts, a specific concept and structure of *the relationship of the Spirit to salvation* could be discerned and that this could be, in a second stage, synthetically confirmed by a review of the entire Teresian corpus.

Chapters 3 and 4 form the second section of this work. Here, the insights gleaned by textual analysis in the first two chapters are considered systematically, with an eye toward all of Teresa's writings and in an effort to integrate the contributions and questions of contemporary secondary literature on Teresa. Although these two chapters are closely connected, chapter 3 focuses on describing a "dynamic of the Spirit," while chapter 4 seeks to consider the place of salvation in terms of trinitarian indwelling and incarnation. It is important to note that this reading will not be done in the context of the "spirituality of Carmel," that is, by taking into consideration the work of John of the Cross, Thérèse of the Child Jesus, and Elizabeth of the Trinity, among others. Without denying possible interconnections, both contemporary and posterior, Teresa will be analyzed for herself and in her own context.

In a third section, chapter 5, we attempt a synthesis of the Teresian proposition of *salvation incarnated by the Spirit in the human person.* This final chapter summarizes the Teresian insights by gathering them into a tight systematization, evoking biblical themes and developing certain ramifications for contemporary theological reflection. This is where we will confirm the theological fruitfulness of contemporary exploration and analysis of Teresa's texts.

Beyond the interest a systematic theologian may have in this subject, this research offers Teresiologists an original reading of the salvific dynamic of the Spirit as it can be understood from Teresa's writings. In doing so, we develop original insights that shed new light on the teaching and experience of Teresa of Avila. Also novel for Teresian studies is our approach of considering the center before then expanding to the whole. Indeed, beyond monographs of a historical, sociological, or literary nature, theological works on Teresa adopt either an ascending approach, considering the linearity of her evolution,[131] or a descending approach, considering her work in its maturity and presenting it synthetically.[132]

Moreover, while not pretending to be an exhaustive summary of our topic, this book offers new perspectives that will assist in the preparation of such a summary on the Spirit and salvation in Teresa's thought.

Chapter 1

A Place for God

The Story of the Foundation of Saint Joseph Monastery

TERESA WROTE. Through her writing, she spoke to her readers. Like the prayer that bursts through the words addressed to God throughout the text, a word is given to the reader to hear, who then becomes a listener. Her writing is marked by a breath that gives life to the words she uses to tell the story of the inspired events she experienced. This breath can be sensed by the reader throughout the account.

This chapter and the next are an act of reading. We will read the texts in themselves and for themselves. Through the story's images, narrative framework, events, asperities, and hesitations, an underlying coherence points to something beyond the account itself. The passages we consider below are both distinct stories that can be understood even outside the context of the broader narrative. Our reading approaches the text alone, leaving aside for now the interpretative tradition that will be considered later with the rest of the Teresian corpus.

The narrative of the *Life* seems at first glance to be purely descriptive. Unlike *The Interior Castle,* where Teresa describes events in a more systematic framework—and in the third person—here we find a more straightforward account of sequential events, although certain shifts in time call for careful reading. Teresa is not as consciously pedagogical in her *Life* as she is in *The Interior Castle*, but this allows her account to be more open, because her concern is to tell the story chronologically.

The texts chosen here describe salvific events. They include images of the Spirit, the Incarnation, and salvation, among others. It was reading these texts that suggested the working hypothesis with which this work is taken up—that is, in Teresian thought, the Spirit is the "incarnator" of salvation, the one through whose action salvation takes flesh. It is with this question in mind that our research has scrutinized the Teresian corpus to understand salvation and the role that the Spirit plays in it.

The first story we consider describes a key moment in Teresa's life, one that led to her founding of Saint Joseph, the first monastery of the Carmelite reform.[1] The transition from concern for her personal salvation to an apostolic expansion of this concern—through the foundation of monasteries and the ministry of writing—happens here. A second, parallel account, that of the foundation of the second reformed monastery, Medina del Campo,[2] will echo the first and marks the inauguration of a series of new foundations that would occupy Teresa until the end of her life.[3] Teresa's vocation as a founder is rooted in these two important events.

PRESENTATION OF TEXTS

Chapters 32 to 36 of *The Book of Her Life*

Teresa recounts the events that led to her founding the monastery of Saint Joseph in Avila, in 1562, in chapters 32 through 36 of her *Life*. While a first redaction of this text was written in 1562, in response to a command by Father Pedro Ibáñez, the present text is the result of a revision and expansion she did in 1565.[4] The *Life* is not simply an autobiography in which Teresa narrates the events of her life sequentially. Some important events are developed in considerable detail, while some fairly long periods are summarized in just a few words. Teresa also offers her readers[5] various opinions on prayer and spiritual gifts, and she regularly addresses God as well, to offer a petition or to give thanks. One of the titles Teresa used to refer to this work was *De las misericordias de Dios* (On the Mercies [or Favors] of God).[6]

The section we consider here is no exception. These five chapters cover a little over two years, starting with the initial impetus for the founding of Saint Joseph and ending with its accomplishment. These chapters constitute a well-defined unit. However, they also include various stories of seemingly secondary incidents. These latter stories are, in fact, integral parts of the general framework of the foundation story and must not be treated simply as dregs that disturb its purity. Many of these elements throw a different light on the subject of our work.

The Beginning of *Foundations*

In a second step, we will consider the beginning of Teresa's *Foundations* as an expansion upon and a response to the story of her *Life*. The founding of the monastery of Medina del Campo in 1567 marked the inauguration of a new stage in Teresa's career as founder. The first three chapters of *Foundations* narrate the events that led to the foundation of this second reformed monastery. This was not just an accident or a repetition of what she had done with Saint Joseph in Avila; it is marked by a unique context and unique set of people, though of course it also bears a real relationship with her work in the first foundation.

Foundations covers, in its present form, a period that extends from the conception of the monastery of Medina (in 1566) to that of Burgos (1582), the final Teresian foundation. Against her own will, Teresa began writing it in August 1573.[7] The first chapters certainly date from this period.[8] This redaction therefore takes place six or seven years after the fact and approximately eight years after the completion of her *Life*.

One Story in Two Acts

These two selected moments represent a turning point in Teresa's life and the meeting place of two of her major writings. Her description of the foundation of Saint Joseph comes near the end of her *Life*,[9] while *Foundations* picks up after that,[10] describing the second foundation (Medina). The founding at Medina is not in a purely sequential relationship with the one at Avila, since Teresa could well have chosen to confine herself to her "little dwelling corner for God" (*rinconcito de Dios*) (*Life* 35:12). *Another* impetus set in motion a new foundation, which was followed, in turn, by others.[11] But the fundamental impetus was the *same.* An analysis of Teresa's accounts of these two episodes will reveal a number of similarities, suggesting a similar salvific character. As for Teresa herself, it is during this period that she attains an apostolic and spiritual maturity, and her apostolic activity as founder and writer[12] unfolds on a large scale. This step is not only an existential hinge; it also reveals important links between salvation, the Holy Spirit, and the Incarnation.

FROM HELL TO SAINT JOSEPH: A FIRST FOUNDATION (*LIFE* 32—36)

The Story of the Foundation

*A Vision of Hell (*Life *32:1–3)*

The starting point of the story of Teresa's foundation of Saint Joseph is her dramatic first vision, which was of hell.[13] The significance of this vision in her life cannot be overstated. Here we find the unexpected starting point of a path that would lead her to a career as a writer and founder. Furthermore, this vision crystallized for her the question of salvation, which frightened her—because of her sin—and became a reference point throughout the rest of her journey. This vision, which she would remember vividly thereafter, included the first appearance of many images of salvation that we will encounter again—often more developed—later.

In her vision, Teresa saw hell, and very specifically as the place prepared for her by the demons that she had, she said, "merited because of my sins."[14]

Teresa's account places this vision within the context of her relationship with God. She first mentions the long period (*mucho tiempo*) of receiving favors (*mercedes*) from the Lord (*Life* 32:1), then, more immediately, the fact that she was in prayer at the time of the event (*estando un día en oración*) (*Life* 32:1). The context is therefore one of an intimate and positive relationship with the Lord. At the very moment when she felt herself in hell, she understood (*entendí*) that it was indeed the will of the Lord that she had this vision (*quería el Señor*). This mention of the will of God comes up regularly in this account, emphasizing that it was God who guided her to contemplate this *place that was not of God.*[15]

This vision's relationship to time is notable: it happened "suddenly," without warning. It lasted only very briefly (*brevísimo espacio*), but it left an indelible mark on Teresa, which she never forgot.[16] It reminded Teresa of her past experience of intense physical pain (*Life* 32:2) during her first years in the monastery, at a time when she had seemed near death (*Life* 5:9). It also opened the way to subsequent visions that would complement this original vision of hell on certain points (*Life* 32:3). Furthermore, she knew that what she was experiencing represented something that went on "without end and without ever ceasing" (*Life* 32:2), a place without hope.

The vision of hell was fundamentally the experience of a "place" (*lugar*) where Teresa found herself "put" (*metida*; *Life* 32:1), a place prepared by the demons and not by God. It was a place lacking in space; she uses the words "cramped" (*estrecho*) and "confined" (*angosto*) to describe this nonplace (*Life* 32:1). As if that were not enough, the walls "closed in on themselves and suffocated everything" (*Life* 32:3). There was a lack of air. There was no room to sit or to stand up (*Life* 32:3). Teresa compares the entrance to this place to a long and narrow alley and then to "an oven, low and dark and confined" (*Life* 32:1), accentuating the crushing walls of the place. The space in this place constricted, shrinking whatever was there: "I felt myself...crumbling" (*Life* 32:2).

This vision, then, was an intensely bodily experience for Teresa. She experienced her body in a place that was smothering, a place that tended toward annihilation. Her body's senses played an important role. Sight, in particular, was active, although in this place "there was no light, but all was enveloped in the blackest darkness," and yet "everything painful to see was visible" (*Life* 32:3). The floor of this place seemed to be covered with "dirty, muddy water," inhabited by "putrid vermin" (*sabandijas malas*; *Life* 32:1). Smell was also involved; Teresa wrote of a "foul stench."[17] Although this experience of hell came in a vision, Teresa remarked that "the Lord wanted me actually to feel those spiritual torments and afflictions, as though the body were suffering" (*Life* 32:3). Teresa's whole being was involved.

Beyond the sensory experience—already disturbing—the bodily experience of hell was also an interior experience. Teresa even comments that the very real physical sufferings she had experienced in the past "were all nothing in comparison with the ones I experienced there" (*Life* 32:2). The heart of this experience was, Teresa wrote, "a fire in the soul that I don't know how I could describe" (*Life* 32:2). The two points of comparison by which she tries to describe this "fire" are the sensory experience of this vision of hell and her past experience of physical suffering.[18] She describes this interior fire as an intense feeling of despair, as well as of being burned,[19] that has no end.[20] Her soul seemed to be being destroyed from within.[21] According to Teresa, it was this interior experience of pain (*pena*) that produced fear, even more than the things she saw.[22]

Ultimately, Teresa considered this vision of hell to be a great gift because the Lord showed her the place from which she had been freed by divine mercy (*Life* 32:3), thanks to having seen hell "with my own eyes" (*Life* 32:3), by an engagement of her whole being, beyond all that she had previously heard, thought, or read.

This vision of hell, which put Teresa in the place of nonsalvation par excellence, the nonplace of God, but which God wished her to visit and to experience the unimaginable sufferings, is the unexpected starting point of the story of Teresa's foundation of the first reformed monastery. While this place was not God's, it was not Teresa's place either, since she was spared from it, saved, by God. This vision therefore has a different purpose, inscribed in itself, but elusive at first sight. While the vision itself was dramatic, so was the abrupt transformation that it brought about in Teresa, though the connection between the vision and the transformation would not become clear until later. This transformation would soon launch her on the path of a deep attentiveness to the salvation of others.

*A Triple Transformation: Personal, Apostolic, and Foundational (*Life *32:4–8)*

Teresa's vision of hell brought about in her a decisive triple transformation: a personal fruit, an apostolic fruit, and the fruit of a foundational set of desires (*Life* 32:4, 6, 7–8). This transformation takes place under the mode of *reception*; just as she *received* the vision, she also *received*, like unexpected gifts, the fruits that shaped her transformation. This transformation was like the tail that follows a comet; in time, Teresa would understand and accept not only the experience but also its consequences.

First, the personal fruit developed in two ways: she lost her fear of the difficulties of life (*tribulaciones y contradicciones*), and she developed a desire to undergo them as a way of giving thanks to the Lord who had set her free (*Life* 32:4).

Second, Teresa's awareness widened to become oriented toward the salvation of others, an apostolic fruit. This basic orientation toward others, already present initially in her propensity to promote prayer, would become the leitmotif of her existence. Even more profoundly, it marked a radical turning point from self-consideration—especially in her relationship with God—to the primacy of others. She felt great pain (*grandísima pena*) for souls who were lost, "especially the Lutherans."[23] A spiritual pain, like an absence of joy, echoed the loss of salvation by some souls. Paradoxically, Teresa writes that she "gained" or "won" (*gané*) this pain.[24] Then, in a section oriented completely toward action, she says she felt "great impulses" (*ímpetus grandes*) to help (*aprovechar*) souls, even if doing so would mean suffering many deaths herself.[25] This pain and desire are important. On the one hand, the "extraordinary pain" felt by Teresa indicates that this desire was deeply inscribed in her; she was affected in her person by the loss of souls. She was marked by her visceral adherence to the divine plan of salvation because she identified with the divine point of view, beyond simply the sphere of the consideration of her own salvation, by widening the horizon to the salvation of others to which she could not be indifferent. On the other hand, her desire to act to help souls would be the leitmotif of her apostolic commitment, a motive that would also be found in the story of the establishment of the series of foundations.

Finally, Teresa's experience of the vision opened up in her a set of desires, expressed by her repetition of the verb *desire* (*desear*); she writes in quick succession of her *desire* to do for God all that she can possibly do, her *desire* to do penance in order to merit all the good bestowed on her by the Lord,[26] and her *desire* to flee from people and withdraw completely from the world. This is the foundation of desires that would mark Teresa's life, even if not all of them would be realized in the ways she articulates (*Life* 32:7–8).

In this transformation, the deepening of personal desire and apostolic desire may seem at first to be rather disconnected. But connection between these fruits will become clear in their subsequent actualization in Teresa's life. Despite the strength of these desires, she initially took up no program of action, nor even considered one. The triple transformation we have described suggests an action in the horizon of salvation, an action that would fundamentally engage Teresa's whole person. Already the complementary dynamic of self-emptying, through the vision of the non-place of hell and the interior experience of pain, and of desire, as a movement that carries toward action, are lived under the impulse of another, namely, God, as Teresa makes clear at the beginning of her narrative. The incarnation of a possible action remains in shadow.

*Into Action: Personal Response and Apostolic Initiative (*Life *32:9–10)*

Having noted the fruits of the transformation Teresa experienced, we now consider the ways her response to the gift took the form of concrete action. There are two. Teresa first seemed to initiate the movement of a personal response: "I was thinking about what I could do for God." She concluded that the most fitting response was one of greater fidelity, embracing more closely her call to religious life and following the rule with the greatest possible perfection. Teresa's first response to the broad challenge that had been presented to her, then, was individual in nature. But two difficulties immediately presented themselves: the frequent outings that the nuns went on and the fact that the more rigorous observance of the primitive rule was no longer followed.[27] Thus, even Teresa's desire for individual action was thwarted by institutional circumstances. She seemed to be at a dead end (*Life* 32:9).

It was at this point that the apostolic dimension of her response emerged, but not on her own initiative. During a conversation among a group of a few of the nuns at Incarnation, one of them raised the question of whether it might be possible for them to establish a monastery where they could live as discalced nuns (*Life* 32:10). The movement of inspiration was therefore subtle, prompted by the innocuous comment of another person. Thus, just as with the triggering event of the vision of hell, it was a prompting from outside herself—in the first case by a vision, and now by an idea expressed in a comment—that set Teresa down the road she would follow. This comment from a fellow sister, whose name was María de Ocampo,[28] ignited a burning desire in Teresa. She discussed such a project with her companion, Guiomar de Ulloa,[29] a widow, who began to make plans for the house's income[30]—plans that Teresa later realized were naive and unrealistic (*Life* 32:10). In a sense, it was a grace that she failed to recognize the greatness and the difficulty of the enterprise. But not everything was in place for Teresa yet because her comfort and satisfaction with her living conditions at Incarnation caused her to continue to hesitate. She felt at home there and liked her room very much.[31] Despite this personal resistance, Teresa and her companion decided to entrust this question to God in prayer (*Life* 32:10).

*Divine Confirmation of the Mission (*Life *32:11–12)*

Confirmation from the Lord came in the form of a vision. Teresa described it like this:

> One day after Communion, His Majesty [*su Majestad*] earnestly commanded me to strive for this new monastery with all my powers, and He made great promises that it would be founded and that He would be highly served in it. He said it should be called St. Joseph [*San José*] and that this saint would keep watch over us at one door, and our Lady at the other, that Christ would remain with us, and that it [the monastery] would be

> a star shining with great splendor. He said that even though religious orders were mitigated one shouldn't think He was little served in them; He asked what would become of the world if it were not for religious and said that I should tell my confessor what He commanded, that He was asking him not to go against this or hinder me from doing it. (*Life* 32:11)

This paragraph's structure and style—in the original, it is a single sentence written in a style that seems hurried and inelegant—suggests the gush of a single breath, even as she remembered and described the vision[32] years after the fact. With its striking divine promises, it served not only as a confirmation of the divine origin of the initial inspiration, but even included a precise description of the supernatural significance of the proposed project, while providing strong assurances of God's support of the establishment of this monastery and of its future flourishing.

Like Teresa's initial vision of hell, this vision came to her abruptly, while she was praying. It marks another turning point, in the sense that what it conveys, notably in the form of promises, exceeds what could have been hoped for. This vision goes beyond the mere topic of the establishment of a monastery, addressing more generally the role of religious life in the world. It is also notably detailed, particularly in the way it directs Teresa in the procedure to follow with her own confessor.

The annunciatory nature of this vision is threefold. First, it is a message that offers not just information or inspiration, but a *command* from Christ. It calls for action. The verb *mandar* (to command) is the first verb Teresa uses in describing it. She mentions nothing at all about what she saw, but only what she heard; it is not until in the following paragraph that the reader learns that it was a vision, when it could have been an "audition."[33] Second, this act of speaking announces an action: the establishment of a monastery and its name, both a supernatural action and an action of the nuns. Finally, Teresa is personally directed to an action by the words she hears. Thus a structure begins to take shape here—a seeing/hearing that leads to a telling—that we will encounter again.

The impact of this vision on Teresa is striking, and it would be decisive for what lay ahead. "This vision had such great effects, and this locution the Lord granted was of such a nature, that I couldn't doubt it was from God,"[34] she declared (*Life* 32:12). However, it included a "severest pain" (*grandísima pena*) because she understood in it how much the foundation of this new monastery would "cost" her, including her own well-being at Incarnation. But the Lord spoke to her many times about this endeavor, in such a way that she could see that it was God's will and could therefore overcome her hesitations (*Life* 32:12).

*Negotiations, Opposition, and Waiting (*Life *32:13—36:4)*

At first, everything seemed to come together easily for Teresa's project. Aware that there was more to the project that simply natural interest, her confessor told her to speak to her superior about it. This was done by Teresa's companion, Guiomar, and the provincial praised the project. Teresa and Guiomar also discussed the question of income and number of nuns the new house should have. When Friar (later, Saint) Peter of Alcántara was consulted on the project, he strongly encouraged them (*Life* 32:13).

However, when word of the plans became known in Avila, a "great persecution" broke out that snuffed out the support they had received, even among "people of prayer" (*gente de oración*) and including that of the provincial who had previously offered encouragement and cooperation. Guiomar was even refused absolution because she was considered to be the cause of scandal, which a priest obliged her to remove. The Lord remained faithful, consoling Teresa and assuring her that many saints who had founded religious orders had experienced worse persecution. So at a time when her internal resistance was quelled, the external resistance was intense (*Life* 32:14–15).

In the midst of this opposition, Teresa and her companion consulted a local Dominican priest, Father Ibáñez, whom she called "a most learned man" and "a very great servant of God." This consultation marked a turning point in the story. After listening to them explain the whole affair (not sharing Teresa's revelations with him but offering only the "natural reasons" that motivated their enterprise), Ibáñez told them to come back to him a week later, asking for their assurance that they would follow his instructions at that time. He later confided to Teresa that his intention was initially to discourage them from their enterprise, since "it seemed to him as it did to everyone to be foolish." But after taking time to consider the project beyond the clamor of the crowd, he decided that it truly would be in the service of God and that he should not abandon her. And so prayerful discernment of the project caused him to shift from an initial, reasonable opposition to confident support. It was a complete reversal—a kind of conversion—that was to be confirmed over time. So when Father Ibáñez met them again eight days later, he told them that while the property (*hacienda*) they had chosen was small, they had to put some trust in God. The wind was changing, which was to be confirmed later. They even bought the house that would become the cradle of the new monastery (*Life* 32:16–18).

Yet, the external resistance did not stop. Indeed, two movements were pushing Teresa at the same time. On the one hand, a strong external opposition. Her provincial opposed the foundation, and her confessor told her to abandon the project;[35] the nuns at Incarnation were offended that she wanted a stricter enclosure (*Life* 33:2); and there was opposition to the possibility that the new monastery would have no income, though the ancient rule called for that to be the case (*Life* 35:2–3). On the other hand, strong signs of divine confirmation consoled her. God supported her in her difficulties (*Life* 33:2) and made love grow in her to such a degree that she desired trials and persecutions;[36] Saint Joseph (*Life* 33:12), Saint Clare (*Life* 33:13), and Our Lady[37] each appeared to her; and Christ spoke to her,[38] as did the Holy Spirit.[39] Travel and providential presences also marked this path: her stay of several months in Toledo (*Life* 34); the visit of a *beata* of her order, a future founder, who revealed to her that the primitive monasteries had no income;[40] the providential illness of her brother-in-law;[41] and the survival of Peter of Alcántara.[42] In the meantime, Teresa remained steadfast in her abandonment to God.

*The Fragile Achievement (*Life *36:5–6)*

The final divine confirmation of Teresa's desire was the successful foundation of Saint Joseph monastery. For Teresa, this accomplishment took two concrete forms: the new nuns took their habits and the Blessed Sacrament was installed in the chapel.[43] A house had become a monastery. The importance of recognizing the installation of the Blessed Sacrament as the clearest expression of the completion of the monastery's foundation is notable.[44] Here, one can recognize an echo of Christ's promise to Teresa that he would live among the nuns of this house (*Life* 32:11). Teresa therefore insisted on the inhabitation of this place—by the nuns, but also by Christ. The monastery only has meaning as an inhabited place. In this sense, she fulfilled her desire to separate herself from everything and to live in a stricter enclosure (*Life* 36:5). At the new monastery, the people who entered it would become its foundation by their example (*Life* 36:6). Teresa was insistent that this monastery was not merely her own project, but God's, which was expressed especially through the scrupulous attention paid there to obedience.[45] She wrote that if it had been pointed out to her that there was the slightest imperfection in this foundation, she would willingly have "left a thousand monasteries, let alone one" (*Life* 36:5). For her, this project was from start to finish God's rather than her own.

As this project reached its accomplishment, Teresa wrote that seeing it happen was for her "like being in glory," or in heaven (*como estar en una gloria—Life* 36:6). It is notable that inhabited "glory" (being *in* glory) is a key image of salvation. Her joy overflowed—she wrote that she was "so intensely happy that I was as though outside myself"—because the Lord had used her as an instrument for this work (*Life* 36:6). In the context of a narrative that had its origins in a vision of hell and was subsequently confirmed in a vision, Teresa's "being in glory" represents a first instance of sanction, following the project's realization, by what semiology would term the *sender*. But this achievement remained fragile and would soon come under heavy assault.

*Subsequent Tribulations: Three Obstacles (*Life *36:7–23)*

Three obstacles against the young monastery of Saint Joseph would emerge.

First, once external resistance to Teresa's effort was overcome, the origin of that resistance was unmasked as she waged a final "spiritual battle" with the devil[46] that led her into a state of spiritual desolation that caused her to doubt her obedience and the future happiness of the nuns (*Life* 36:7–8). She questioned both the origin of the project (whether it was her own will or obedience to the will of God) and its purpose (the well-being of the nuns who would eventually live in this monastery). This was one of the most difficult moments in Teresa's life (*Life* 36:9). This temptation presented itself as a simulacrum, an inverse image of the vision of hell, with its absence of God; she was unable to pray and forgot all that God had told her during the previous two years "as though it had never been" (*Life* 36:7). Echoing elements of Teresa's vision of hell, the devil reminded her of the smallness of the house (*casa tan estrecha*) compared to the larger and more pleasant home she was leaving behind, even to the point of "despair" (*Life* 36:8). She found herself in a state of desolation, darkness (*tinieblas*), and "anguish...like that of someone in the death agony" (*Life* 36:8). In a sense, this interior experience of opposition by the devil—the not-God—validates, or confirms, Teresa's efforts; the one who opposes God opposes this project inspired and willed by God, by mimicking aspects of the initial vision but giving them a negative value. But this ruse was thwarted by "a little light" from the Lord that helped her see the truth and unmask the lies the devil was using to try to frighten her (*Life* 36:9). God delivered her from the torments of this temptation (*Life* 36:11).

Back on firm ground interiorly, Teresa promised before the Blessed Sacrament to do everything possible to establish herself in this monastery (*Life* 36:9). In other words, she promised the one who founded and dwelt in the heart of the monastery—Christ present in the Blessed Sacrament—that she would live, like him and with him, in that place. After this, "the devil fled instantly" (*Life* 36:10), leaving her calm and content (*sosegada y contenta*), a state of mind she maintained thereafter (*Life* 36:10). This perpetual peace and contentment, granted before the Blessed Sacrament on the first day of the foundation of Saint Joseph, constitutes a second confirmation of Teresa's understanding of God's will.

However, a new obstacle quickly materialized. Exhausted from the conflicts, Teresa was ordered by her superior to return immediately to the monastery of the Incarnation to explain her actions (*Life* 36:11). Teresa did so to her superior, then to the provincial, then to all the assembled sisters (*Life* 36:12–14)! Reassured, the provincial promised her that "if all went well," she could return to live there once the tumult in the city had calmed (*Life* 36:14).

Alarmed by the new foundation of poor nuns with no income, the civil authorities and the people of the town had begun to buzz (*Life* 36:15–16). The mayor and city council consulted with leaders of other religious orders, and there was talk of suppressing the monastery (*Life* 36:15). The attacks reached a crescendo, and Teresa clearly saw the hand of the devil in them (*Life* 36:19). A temptation then appeared in the form of a compromise on poverty. Her opponents allowed that if the monastery were to accept income, the foundation would be allowed to continue (*Life* 36:19). Teresa had decided to accept this condition as a compromise, in order to bring the controversy to a close, but as she prayed, the Lord told her not to accept any income, even for an initial period, and the deceased Peter of Alcántara, who had written to Teresa on this subject when he was still alive and since his death had already appeared to her several times in a glorified body, now appeared and insisted to her that she not follow such a course (*Life* 36:20). She therefore stuck firmly to her original intention and refused any compromise on the poverty of this foundation (*Life* 36:21). After many negotiations and troubles, the city calmed down and the provincial allowed Teresa and some companions to go and live with the other nuns already at Saint Joseph (*Life* 36:23).

*Final Confirmation and Epilogue (*Life *36:24–29)*

Upon arriving at the new monastery of Saint Joseph,[47] Teresa approached the chapel:

> Before entering the new monastery, while in prayer outside the church, being almost in rapture [*arrobamiento*], I saw Christ who seemed to be receiving me with great love and placing a crown on my head and thanking me of what I did for His Mother.
>
> Another time while all were at prayer in choir after compline, I saw our Lady in the greatest glory clothed

> in a white mantle; it seemed she was sheltering us all under it. I understood how high a degree of glory the Lord would give to those living in this house. (*Life* 36:24)

This presentation of a crown by Christ was for Teresa the final confirmation of her efforts. By noting that in the second vision, which happened sometime later (she does not offer specifics about when), the mantle of Our Lady covered the nuns of Saint Joseph, Teresa includes her daughters in this great confirmation of God's will being accomplished by this foundation.

She also saw confirmation in the fact that so many of the people of Avila who had previously opposed the foundation came around to supporting it. Among those who had persecuted the nuns of Saint Joseph, many began to express support and give them alms; those who had disapproved began to approve; and little by little, they abandoned their lawsuit and recognized the new monastery as the work of God (*Life* 36:25). Teresa was finally happy to be living among such detached souls (*Life* 36:26). The Carmelite monastery of Alcala, founded by María de Jesús, was also favored by the Lord (*Life* 36:28).

Teresa concludes her account by offering a strong warning and a defense of the spirit of Saint Joseph, as well as a reminder that she sees this monastery as a place of salvation, though one among others: "Those who think the life [at Saint Joseph] harsh should blame their own lack of spirituality [*espíritu*] and not what is observed here...; they should go to another monastery where they can be saved in a way conformable to their own spirituality [*espíritu*]."[48]

In these concluding words of the story of the founding of Saint Joseph, Teresa restates the important elements of this event: the monastery as place, a place of salvation to which some are called, a place of a certain *espíritu*—a spirit, a spirituality, an impulse, a conviction that lives in and animates the women who live there and the monastery of Saint Joseph as a whole.

An Integral Experience of Salvation

We have explored the narrative of the founding of the monastery of Saint Joseph. But within the thread of this story, various important moments emerge that shed light on the concept of salvation. These moments become instances of individual realization of salvation, both for Teresa and for others. We will explore them in terms of Teresa's personal salvation, then of the personal salvation of others, before tackling the question of the vision of the glorified body.

*Teresa's Personal Salvation (*Life *33:14–15; 34:9)*

An important element to add to this soteriological dossier is Teresa's striking vision of the Virgin Mary and Saint Joseph.[49] It took place in a context in which Teresa was feeling that she lacked the means necessary to carry out the mission entrusted to her. The burden she bore seemed too heavy for her:

> My Lord, how is it You command things that seem impossible? For if I were at least free, even though I am a woman! But bound on so many sides, without money or the means to raise it or to obtain the brief or anything, what can I do, Lord? (*Life* 33:11)

Teresa was acutely aware of her lack of capacity to carry out this project. She was a woman, poor, impeded, and lacking in the necessary resources to carry out the task at hand.[50] Hence her cry to the Lord.

Then she experienced a vision of Saint Joseph, who encouraged her; an audition[51] of Christ who scolded her a bit; and a vision of Saint Claire, who assured her of her support.[52] Following these, she experienced this significant vision:

> On one of these same days, the feast of the Assumption of our Lady while at a monastery of the order of the glorious St. Dominic. I was reflecting on the many sins I had in the past confessed in that house and many things about my wretched life. A rapture came upon me so great that it almost took me out of myself. I sat down; it still seems to me I couldn't see the elevation or hear Mass, and afterward I had a scruple about this. It seemed to me while in this state that I saw myself vested

> in a white robe of shining brightness, but at first I didn't see who was clothing me in it. Afterward I saw our Lady at my right side and my father St. Joseph at the left, for they were putting that robe on me. I was given to understand that I was now cleansed of my sins. After being clothed and while experiencing the most marvelous delight and glory, it seemed to me then that our Lady took me by the hands. She told me I made her very happy in serving the glorious St. Joseph, that I should believe that what I was striving for in regard to the monastery would be accomplished, that the Lord and those two would be greatly served in it, that I shouldn't fear there would ever be any failure in this matter even though the obedience which was to be given was not to my liking, because they would watch over us,[53] that as a sign that this was true she was giving me a jewel. It seemed to me she placed around my neck a very beautiful golden necklace to which was attached a highly valuable cross. This gold and these stones are incomparably different from earthly ones. (*Life* 33:14)

This vision began as Teresa was reflecting on her past sins; its context, then, was her consideration of nonsalvation. But she was suddenly pulled out of her reflection and taken to another place, beyond sight or hearing (she "couldn't see the elevation or hear Mass"), not because those senses would not be involved, but because they were so overcome.[54] Seeing and hearing nothing outside herself, something happened deep within Teresa, the agents of this action becoming clear in the course of it. The central message of this vision was Teresa's awareness of being cleansed of her sins. In addition to bringing relief to a recurrent anxiety she bore, this assurance of salvation strengthened her confidence in her ability to carry out the work that had been entrusted to her; being in this place of friendship with God, she could hope to serve as someone who helped open its doors to others. Teresa also entered a place of delight and glory; she was thus already present in the eschatological place and was receiving, in a sense, a down payment on the reward that awaited her.

Later, anxiety about being in a state of grace returned to

Teresa (*Life* 34:10). On one occasion, as she prayed for one of her acquaintances, that he would become even more committed in his service of God, she became grieved at the thought of being "at enmity [*in enemistad*] with God." Although she had received great spiritual graces, Teresa feared being in a state of mortal sin, preferring even to die than to live a life in which she was not sure whether she was (spiritually) dead.[55] The Lord then gave her the assurance of being personally in a state of grace: "Then I understood [*entendí*][56] that I could truly be consoled and certain that I was in grace because a love of God like this, and those favors and sentiments His Majesty gave me, could not exist harmoniously with a soul in mortal sin."[57]

It was because of the gifts of God in her—not by the merit of her deeds—and by the words of the Lord that Teresa could be assured of her salvation. In subsequent considerations of this question of the state of grace and personal salvation, rather than doubt, which would return her to her sinful condition, it was praise for the gift of God that would prevail.

*The Personal Salvation of Others (*Life *34:19)*

An explicit concern for the salvation of others is common in Teresa's work. One of the prominent examples concerns one of her sisters, María de Cepeda. The story comes four or five years after the fact.[58] Teresa's brother-in-law had suddenly passed away, without having had time to confess, which had caused Teresa great anxiety (*mucha pena*). She was then told, while she was praying, that her sister would die like her husband and that she should go see her to help her prepare for it. Without revealing to her anything of this supernatural information, Teresa visited her sister and instructed her to confess frequently, which she did. So when her sister suddenly died a few years later, she had recently been to confession. Here we find, succinctly, a pattern already seen: a word from God, Teresa's anxiety for a soul in danger, then an invitation to action in the context of prayer.

Teresa took great joy (*gran alegría*) in learning the circumstances of her sister's death. Moreover, the Lord appeared to her a few days later, when she was receiving Communion, wanting her to see him carry her sister to glory (*Life* 34:19).

This episode shows how the question of salvation—whether for herself, for another individual, or for others in general—marked Teresa's life and thought. A pattern is recognizable, including a discreet inspiration (word, pain, and invitation to action in prayer), a response by Teresa, and accomplishment confirmed in a supernatural way, in the form of a vision of Christ.

*The Glorified Body (*Life *36:20)*

Teresa does not describe in detail the entry into heaven of her dead sister María, although she says Jesus showed her María's ascent into glory (*Life* 34:19). In another vision, however, she saw Father García de Toledo carried by the angels into great glory, even though he was still alive at the time.[59]

However, Teresa writes with particular intensity about her visions of Peter of Alcántara "in his glorified body" (*cuerpo glorificado—Life* 36:20). The glorified body is the way Teresa visually experienced the presence of a person who had died and entered into the glory of heaven,[60] similar to the manner of Christ in his Easter apparitions.[61]

In the context of her reflection on the question of income for the new monastery, Teresa describes an apparition of Peter of Alcántara, in which he spoke sternly with her.[62] She then recounts other recent appearances of the same man, who had recently died:

> I had already, two or three times since his death, seen him and the great glory he possessed; so I wasn't frightened. Rather I rejoiced greatly, for he always appeared in his glorified body, filled with great glory; it gave me a powerful feeling of glory to see him. I recall that the first time I saw him he told me, among other things, about how sublime his joy was and how the penance he had performed brought him fortune in that he had gained such a reward. (*Life* 36:20)

Teresa also relates one of these apparitions of Peter of Alcántara more briefly in *Life* 27:19. Here she clearly connects the person she experiences in the apparition to the same man before his death and at the time of it. Her vision of his glorified body put it in continuity with his terrestrial existence: he spoke, he intervened in human affairs, he was corporeal. This visible face of salvation achieved was not discontinuous with the rest of human existence. He told Teresa that the "reward" he had received was related to the "penance" he had done while he lived (a point she repeats in *Life* 36:20). On the other hand, in their similarity to the apparitions of the risen Christ and accompanied by markers of divinity (including glory), the glorified body also expresses salvation as a gift from God.

Conclusion

These stories, which are part of Teresa's great narrative of the foundation of Saint Joseph, reveal that at the very heart of the genesis of the great Teresian apostolic enterprise, the personal dimension of salvation is crucial. We see it in Teresa's anxiety about her personal friendship with God. We see it in her preoccupation with the salvation of others, a preoccupation nourished and confirmed by God. We see it in her visions of the achievement of salvation by other individuals; they are inhabited by glory, by God himself, as expressed in their bodily reality. These individual experiences of salvation enrich the depth of view of the apostolic plan of salvation at work in Teresa.

The Emergence of the Spirit

The Spirit is not very prominent in the principal structure of Teresa's story, at least not in an explicit way. But two passages embedded in this structure help us understand the Spirit's work and language. This exploration will also provide points of support for broader consideration of the issue in the context of the cross-sectional analysis that follows.

*The Spirit of God Recognized (*Life *33:7–11)*

The arrival of a new rector at the Jesuit house in Avila prompted some very important paragraphs on the role of the

Spirit in Teresa's work, but also on her relationships with her confessors and their perception of God's work in her.

After Teresa's confessor forbade her to continue her involvement in matters concerning the founding of Saint Joseph (*Life* 33:1), she ignored the subject for five or six months (*Life* 33:7). Her confessor's pusillanimity meant that Teresa had to stifle her "spirit" (*espíritu—Life* 33:7) since she continued to experience "great spiritual impulses" (*grandes ímpetus de espíritu*). The Lord told her one day that this state of things would soon come to an end, which brought her great joy (*me alegré mucho—Life* 33:8) because she thought this meant that she would die soon.[63] Instead, it was because of the arrival of a new rector, who instructed Teresa's confessor "that he should let the spirit of the Lord work [*obrar*]";[64] she welcomed this because "at times it seemed with these great spiritual impulses that my soul couldn't even breathe" (*Life* 33:8). Indeed, another Breath took over, which was the reverse of the *suffocation* she experienced in her vision of hell.

When opening her soul to this rector whom she had never met, Father Gaspar de Salazar, Teresa, noting that she usually felt uncomfortable in such a circumstance, writes, "[I] felt in my spirit [*espíritu*] I don't know what....For it was a spiritual joy [*gozo espiritual*] and an understanding within my soul that his soul would understand mine and mine would be in harmony with his; although, as I say, I did not know how such an experience was possible" (*Life* 33:9). Teresa thus anticipates the joy of the Spirit in knowing that the Spirit would be understood. This would be confirmed later. When the Lord asked Teresa to resume the monastery project, she spoke about it to her confessor and the rector. Father Salazar, who, Teresa said, had a special gift for the discernment of spirits (*conocer espíritus—Life* 33:10) "never doubted the project was from the spirit of God, for through much study and prayer he considered all the consequences" (*Life* 33:10). The confessor, Baltasar Alvarez, SJ, then gave her permission to do everything in her power to carry out the foundation.[65]

This important milestone in Teresa's story sheds light on the place of the spirit/Spirit (*espíritu*) in it in more ways than one.[66] First, there is *Teresa's spirit*, an animated meeting place between the Holy Spirit and her. This is where she feels impulses, joy, and sometimes pain. Second, there is *the rector's spirit*, the place where he discerns various *spirits*, the movements that agitate the soul and whose origin must be carefully weighed. Finally, there is *the Spirit of the Lord*, the Spirit of God, who acts.[67]

This passage allows us to identify some characteristics of the action of the Spirit of God in Teresa. In the order of action, we see the idea of movement and impulse, often quite strong: Teresa writes of "my spirit...moving with such great impulses of love" and that "it seemed with these great spiritual impulses that my soul couldn't even breathe," and she comments that when the Lord guides a person, "he makes them run rather than walk with measured step" (*Life* 33:7, 8, 9). But the most prominent sign of the Spirit's presence is joy (*gozo*), to which Teresa, significantly, gives the adjective *spiritual*. As for the orientation of the action, in this case, the Spirit is pushing to continue the enterprise of the foundation. Thus, in all simplicity, through this story of Teresa's relationship with the rector of the Jesuit house in Avila, we glimpse the Spirit working.

*The Language of the Spirit (*Life *34:17)*

Another aspect of this story introduces the question of the "divine language" that the Holy Spirit seemed to speak to Teresa (*Life* 34:17). This is an important passage, even in the broader context of the entire Teresian corpus, because her writings include so few explicit references to the Holy Spirit in instances other than conventional ones (liturgical references, epistolary greetings). This inclusion comes while she is staying in Toledo with a prominent figure of the city, Doña Luisa de la Cerda, and she meets an old acquaintance, Father García de Toledo, who shares her complete devotion to serving the Lord. Teresa had once asked the Lord to make this man, whom she considered "good," to be "very good" (*Life* 34:8).

Teresa wrote that at an earlier encounter with Father García, her soul and spirit felt the love of God that burned (*ardía*) in him. Through these exchanges, a new fire (*nuevo fuego*) seemed to push Teresa to desire to serve the Lord with renewed fervor (*Life* 34:15). And so here at the threshold of this vision, we find, very subtly, even before the Spirit is mentioned explicitly, one of the characteristic signs of the Spirit: fire.[68]

During the course of her encounter with him, Teresa realized the great favors the Lord had unfolded in his life. She gave thanks for this, blessing the Lord for answering her prayer:

> While with the deepest joy [*gozo*] I was contemplating that soul, it seems the Lord wanted me to see clearly the treasures He had placed in it. Seeing the favor [*merced*] He granted me in that He used me [*por medio mío*], as a means though I found myself unworthy to be such—I had higher esteem for the favors the Lord granted this soul and considered them more my own than if they had been given to me. I praised His Majesty upon seeing that He was fulfilling my desires and had heard my prayer, which was that the Lord awaken [*despertase*] persons like these. My soul being then in such a state that it couldn't bear so much joy, it went out of itself and was lost, so the more to gain. The reflections were forgotten, and while I was hearing that divine language in which it seems the Holy Spirit was speaking, a powerful rapture [*arrobamiento*] came over me which almost made me lose my senses, although it lasted only a short while. I saw Christ with awesome majesty and glory showing great happiness over what was taking place. Thus He told me and wanted me to see clearly that He was always present in conversations like these and how much He is pleased when persons so delight in speaking of Him. (*Life* 34:17)

Teresa perceived that the Lord had showed her that her prayer was decisive in the spiritual growth of Father García. She was for him an instrument of salvation. The fact that the help she sought for someone else had been given seemed to Teresa to be more important than the graces she herself had received, a sign that her vision was becoming more apostolic. The shift of her attention toward other people who would, as a result, pay more attention to God caused Teresa to praise God. In this way, Teresa recognized the reach and the effectiveness of her personal action.

This is when the floor, so to speak, dropped from under her. Teresa's narrative shifts immediately from describing her action done for others and for God to the receiving, as a result, an action of God in herself. She first notes—not once, but twice—the state of great joy in which she was immersed, and which marked the height of the emotional dimension of her experience. It was in this state that Teresa's soul "went out of itself." It was a dramatic experience and introduced her into a register of gains and losses: the loss of rational reflection, but the gain of listening to the language of the Holy Spirit; almost a loss of the senses, but the gain of the vision of Christ in majesty who offered her approval and encouragement.

The language of the Spirit heard by Teresa was speechless language. She recounts not a single word spoken by the Spirit. The nature of the Spirit's language becomes clear in what accompanies it in Teresa's description: "a powerful rapture" (*gran arrobamiento*) that "almost made me lose my senses" for a short time. This rapture was marked by both movement and by joy, completing what was revealed of the Spirit's action with the Spirit's language.

On the other hand, this language of the Spirit led to the vision of Christ marked with divine attributes: majesty and glory. The Holy Spirit, who was "speaking," was not seen. But Christ would not only be seen; he will be heard too. He is the Image and the Word of God.

In her narrative, Teresa opens a fascinating window on a trinitarian action of God in her. She first reveals who it is that hides behind the most dazzling manifestations of the divine presence that she describes with words like *joy, rapture,* and *glory*: it is the Holy Spirit. At the height of her being taken outside of herself, the figure of the Holy Spirit is revealed as the vehicle—the "language"—with which God speaks. And what God speaks would be both seen and said: Christ in glory and majesty addresses words to her. The language that the Holy Spirit *seemed* to speak thus leads to the face of the glorified and speaking Christ. *The Spirit is therefore the one who introduces Christ, the face of God, but also the one in whom and through whom Christ speaks.* The imprint of the language of the Spirit spoken in Teresa here helps to discern the Spirit's presence and action in other places, thanks to the signs that are manifested.

Teresa's attempt to put a finger on this divine language that the Spirit seemed to speak in the context of a mystical experience makes it possible to understand the manner in which the Spirit communicates—the Spirit's language. This is an important hermeneutic key provided by Teresa to discern the action of the Spirit toward human beings in a trinitarian framework, with regard to the Word of God who is Christ.

CROSS-SECTIONAL ANALYSIS

Having looked in a linear fashion at the story of the founding of Saint Joseph, then having taken a closer look at some particularly important moments of this story, the next level of analysis is more transversal. In this section, we will first consider Teresa's bodily experience and the role of a place for God, both in connection with the incarnation. Second, we will reread the account of the foundation of Saint Joseph in a biblical key, drawing out several aspects and offering a deeper theological understanding. Finally, by considering the elements of the main dynamic at work in Teresa in relation to this project, we will understand better the discreet presence of the Holy Spirit in action.

Two Places of Incarnation

An Experience of the Body

The term *incarnation*, which is central to this study, invites us to take seriously, even by its very etymology (*in-carne*), the experience of the body that emerges in the chapters of Teresa's work under consideration.

First, a spiritual experience of the body is omnipresent. In the context of her mystical experiences, Teresa experiences the body in tension; she is sometimes "out" of her own body (*Life* 33:14), yet at the same time has sensory, bodily experiences with great acuity. The experience of the senses is paramount in the consideration of Teresa's relationship with God. During her encounters with God, Teresa sees and hears. This experience of the senses is not unilateral, since from the start, her senses perceive what can be seen, heard, and tasted, but on the other hand, they are experienced in terms of loss: her sight is blurred, her senses are paralyzed. Surprisingly, the register of loss or absence does not suggest a lesser experience; on the contrary, this emphasizes the intensity of what happens, its sudden character, and the "otherness" of its origin. Her vision of hell is emblematic of a divine event in which Teresa's whole body was involved: sight, smell, touch, hearing. She also feels pain. Teresa's body, then, is deeply interwoven in her experience of God.

Second, her experience of the body has more than a spiritual dimension; it is also kinetic. She is set in motion. Teresa was called to move (sometimes hurriedly), to go great distances. And yet at times, she was forbidden to go to a place. She experienced in her body the fatigue of following Christ.

Finally, she experienced the body transformed. First as a glorified body—Teresa has the opportunity to see glorified bodies on several occasions. But also as a eucharistic body, a subtle presence.[69] The links between these dimensions of the transformed body will be highlighted in chapter 38.[70]

A Place for God

The theme of space, of *place*—in the image of the house, for example—comes up repeatedly in Teresa's writing. It is an aspect of her vision of hell, where space is lacking, constricted, and she feels it shrinking.[71] In fact, hell is primarily presented not as a state, but as a place. In contrast, the place of God, suggested in some contexts to be small or narrow, is for Teresa large; one can breathe there and live easily. Taking a view unlike the gospel image of the "narrow way" (Matt 7:14), Teresa considers that, on the contrary, the way that leads to God is wide, royal, and full of confidence, while it is the path that leads away from God that is narrow and subjects the traveler to the continual risk of being annihilated (*Life* 35:13).

What will come as a counterpart to the inaugural vision of hell is the project of another place, totally incarnate, but ordered to another space. It is not simply an inversion of the place of hell, but an original place. Teresa constantly returns to the house (*casa*)[72] that she wants to and eventually does establish; she seeks it, prepares it, finds it too small. This latter complaint earned her a rebuke from the Lord.[73] This place she pursues is not primarily hers; it is God's place. Teresa herself, in the midst of difficulties, one day cried out to God, "Lord, this house is not mine; it was founded for You" (*Life* 36:17). Through Teresa, the Lord prepared a place for himself, as becomes clear in the vision recounted in *Life* 32:11, where Jesus says he will "remain with" the nuns of Saint Joseph, and in the fact that it is the installation of the Blessed Sacrament that marked the inauguration of the new monastery. Once is was established, Teresa could not live in the new house herself for several months, since she was forced to return to the monastery of the Incarnation. So the place she had so longed to establish was first of all the Lord's and also that of the new nuns; it was a place of and for others.

When she finally was able to inhabit this place, Teresa spoke of Saint Joseph monastery as a "little dwelling corner for God" and God's "paradise." In a passage where narrative, desire, prayer, and experience are juxtaposed, Teresa proclaims the importance of this new monastery to the Lord:

> It was so important, as regards the business of this holy house, for me not to have delayed a day longer that I don't know how I might have brought things to a conclusion if I had then stayed on there. O greatness of God! Often I am amazed when I consider how particularly His Majesty wanted to help me found this little dwelling corner for God. I believe this is what it is; it is an abode [*morada*] in which His Majesty delights [*se deleita*], for He once said to me while I was in prayer that this house [*casa*] was a paradise of delight [*deleite*] for Him. (*Life* 35:12)

Saint Joseph is not a place like any other. Teresa's vocabulary about it—little dwelling corner, house, abode, paradise—launch us in various directions. Between "little dwelling corner" and paradise, all the tension between the physical smallness of the place, its insignificant material, and its inhabitation by God unfolds. Paradise (heaven) is God's place par excellence, the place of his delight, a place inhabited by the saints, while the *rinconcito*, the "little dwelling corner," is no place special, but great because it is "for God." The guest thus conforms the place to himself to make it truly his.[74] As for this *morada* (abode) in which God takes delight, it has a very subtle meaning as Teresa writes about it: it represents the interior place at the heart of the human person, where God dwells.[75] Both the question of place and of the body will play an essential role in the further development of Teresa's incarnational soteriology.

A Biblical Story?

Teresa's close relationship with Sacred Scripture is a central element of her intellectual and spiritual formation. She learned to read at a young age in the family home, which had a small library,[76] and she had always loved literature. As a young nun, Teresa used writing to help her prayer, and she avidly read various contemporary spiritual authors in Castilian, including John of Avila and Francis Borgia, among others. The publication of the Index of Prohibited Books in 1559 meant that Teresa lost access to these authors, as well as to vernacular editions of biblical texts, causing her great turmoil. However, the Lord promised her on this occasion to give her "a living book" (*Life* 26:6). It was around this very time that she lost her access to so many of these written texts that she began her writing career in earnest.[77] At the same time, the most familiar mode for Christ to make himself known in Teresa was through words (*hablas*) addressed to her, often using language much like that of the Bible.[78]

Reading the five chapters in which she describes the period between the conception of the idea of the foundation of the monastery of Saint Joseph and its final realization reveals a typical biblical structure. How much of this biblical character is conscious? The question is not so much about the biblical, and even properly evangelical, character of the Teresian story. By expressing her experience in biblical categories, Teresa reveals another dimension of her intellectual makeup.

We can recognize two poles of the scriptural subtext of the foundation of Saint Joseph. We will consider each in turn.

The Incarnational Pole

The similarities between the story of the founding of Saint Joseph monastery in Avila and the stories of Christ's childhood, found mainly in the Gospel of Luke, are striking. But since they are not apparent through direct or indirect citation, they are not noted by most Teresiologists. The narrative appropriation of the story of the Incarnation opens the door to other, more implicit types of appropriation.

The will of God at the heart of Teresa's account of the foundation of Saint Joseph monastery was made clear in an annunciation,[79] following the vision of hell and the transformations it brought about in her. The resemblance between the annunciation to Mary and the vision of Christ confirming the project to Teresa is striking.

Like the angel Gabriel, who arrives and speaks to Mary (Luke 1:28), Christ (after Teresa had received Communion) entrusts to Teresa a command and promises. After clarifying the object of the visit—for Mary, the birth of a son; for Teresa, the establishment of a monastery—the visitor provides the name that will be given to the fruit of the promise: Jesus in one case, Joseph in the other. Then the eminent significance of the event is revealed: the child "will be great, and will be called the Son of the Most High" (Luke 1:32), and the monastery "would be a star shining with great splendor" (*Life* 32:11). Finally, God's role in what is to come is made clear: Mary hears that "the Lord God will give to him the throne of his ancestor David" (Luke 1:32), while Teresa is told that Saint Joseph "would keep watch over us at one door, and our Lady at the other, that Christ would remain with us" (*Life* 32:11). The Lord had to do more to convince Teresa than Gabriel did for Mary, because Teresa mentions that the Lord spoke to her of these things several times to show her clearly that it was his will (*Life* 32:12). The parallelism between these two stories of "annunciation" signals that it is not accidental.

The project entrusted to Mary was to create within her a space for God (Luke 1:31). The creation of a divine space is also the project entrusted to Teresa; the words of Christ are to the effect that he himself will live with the nuns. With the promise that both Saint Joseph and the Virgin Mary would be with them, it is clear that the space Teresa was invited to create is a home, and one in which the Holy Family would dwell.[80] She was to inhabit a new space, a "very small" house, "so small that it didn't seem to be adequate" (*Life* 33:12); just like in Bethlehem, Mary put the newborn baby in a stable "because there was no place for them in the inn" (Luke 2:7). The poverty of the stable will find an echo in the confirmation of the poverty to which Teresa aspires for the new monastery[81] that she receives in a vision of Saint Clare.[82] The humble circumstances of the Savior's birth in Bethlehem is also echoed in the "deep secrecy" (*Life* 36:3) in which the immediate preparations for the establishment of the new monastery were wrapped.

The Lukan flavor of Teresa's story is also found in the collaborators involved in her enterprise. Teresa speaks of the friar Peter of Alcántara, whom she consulted very early on in the project (*Life* 32:13), in words that bring to mind Simeon, who came to the Temple in Jerusalem, prompted by the Holy Spirit, since he had been promised that he would see the Lord's messiah before his death (Luke 2:26–27). Saint Peter, then, is "this saintly man" whom the Lord seemed to have kept alive in order to allow him to accomplish this final task, to convince the bishop of Avila to take the monastery under his jurisdiction, since he was only in Avila for a few days, already very sick, and would die just a few weeks after Saint Joseph's foundation was accomplished (*Life* 36:2).

Furthermore, the visit of the *beata* named María of Jesus, at that point in Toledo, to Teresa of Jesus,[83] was echoed in the visitation of Mary to Elizabeth (Luke 1:39–56). All of these women are in the process of childbirth (either real or figurative). Teresa said the Lord made María hear about her and then travel seventy leagues to meet her. The same year, and in the same month, the Lord inspired María with the desire to found a reformed Carmelite monastery. This "blessed woman" (*Life* 35:2) spent a fortnight with Teresa. Inspired by an apparition of Our Lady, she had gone to Rome to obtain the necessary authorizations for the foundation. During their time together, they talked about the ways they would establish their monasteries. María of Jesus informed Teresa that before the bull of mitigation, Carmelite monasteries were forbidden to have income (*Life* 35:2), which Teresa had been unaware of but wanted for her own monastery. The bearer, like

Teresa, of a project inspired by God, María of Jesus subsequently founded the convent of Imagen in Alcalá (*Life* 36:28).

We can also recognize a sort of "Magnificat" that Teresa addressed to the Lord, in the context of her talks with Father García de Toledo.[84] Teresa felt great joy (*grandísimo gozo*) at seeing the soul of her friend and the treasures that the Lord had given him (*Life* 34:17). Despite Teresa's unworthiness, the Lord condescended to use her to give his favors (*mercedes*—*Life* 34:17). She thanked the Lord for having fulfilled her desires and heard her prayer (*Life* 34:17), expressing intense joy and delight (*Life* 34:17). This moment of thanksgiving reflects the joyful atmosphere, the gratitude to God, the humility or unworthiness of the chosen servant, and the orientation toward others also present as elements in the Magnificat of the mother of Jesus (Luke 1:46–55).

The joy that dwells in and transcends Teresa's story, despite her struggles, recalls the joy that shines through in the Gospel of Luke.

In the story of the annunciation to Mary, the Holy Spirit is the means by which the promised reality will take shape (Luke 1:35). But Teresa's story seems at first glance to lack this element. However, both in its structure and in its content, as well as in the irruption of the Holy Spirit in an event at the heart of the narrative, one can recognize the Holy Spirit playing the same role in Teresa's story as the Spirit has in Luke's; in Teresa's narrative, the identity of the divine agent is unmentioned, the Holy Spirit occupying the place left, narratively, empty.

Other elements of Jesus's childhood stories, found in the Gospel of Matthew, are also reflected in Teresa's story and reinforce the gospel imprint. First, the gift of a jewel, given to Teresa first by Our Lady (*Life* 33:14) and later by Christ, is a gesture that resembles that of the wise men to the child Jesus (Matt 2:11). This image of the adoration of the magi can also be recognized in a central element of Teresian mysticism—that of eucharistic adoration in the presence of the Blessed Sacrament. The installation of the Blessed Sacrament was for Teresa an essential element in the establishment of the new monastery. It was a sign of the presence of Christ in the midst of the sisters. The monastery became a place of worship, where first the nuns and then, more broadly, the people who lived in the area came to worship Christ. This gesture of adoration inscribed in the "birth" of the monastery therefore echoes that of the magi at the birth of Christ.

Another very strong reference to Matthew's Gospel is Teresa's exile to Toledo (*Life* 34–35). On Christmas eve (significantly), Teresa received an order from her provincial to go to Toledo to console a recent widow, an important woman of the kingdom.[85] "The Lord told me to go" (*Life* 34:2), Teresa wrote. The realization of the monastery's establishment project was at stake (*Life* 34:2). Like Joseph warned by the angel (Matt 2:13), Teresa, like so many other great biblical figures, took the road that led her temporarily away from the land of promise, into exile.

What does the presence of such an evangelical structure in Teresa's story tell us about the founding of Saint Joseph? First, it is a project of incarnation, an image of the Son of Man's coming in human flesh to earth.[86] As with the begetting of the Son of God in Mary, the task was to create a space for God. Not a royal temple, such as the one Solomon built, but a humble place—the body of a poor virgin, a manger at Bethlehem, a little house in Avila. A joy like that of the first chapters of Luke shines in this part of Teresa's story, but the difficulties and exile we read of in that Gospel are also there. Finally, the strong Lukan aspects of Teresa's story invite us to discern there the active presence of the Holy Spirit, bringing about incarnation for the purpose of salvation.

Seeing this story as one of incarnation allows us to liken Teresa to the figure of Mary, a woman who accepts that the Word becomes flesh in her and thus contributes, at the risk of her own well-being, to the salvation of humanity. The founding of Saint Joseph is not just any event; it is properly a story of incarnation in which God acts and is made present through human cooperation in view of the salvation of others.

The Paschal Pole

A second strong evangelical pole of Teresa's story is the paschal one. In her account of the foundation, the figure of Christ's passion intervenes forcefully at the end of the journey, when the monastery finally exists, although it is threatened. At the time she departed for Toledo, the Lord had promised Teresa a "cross" (*Life* 35:8). Because it was time for the election of the prioress at

Incarnation, she assumed that her cross would be to take on this position. This was not to be the case; rather, the promised passion materialized later.

Once the foundation of Saint Joseph was accomplished (*Life* 36:5–6), Teresa entered this passion through a great "spiritual battle" (*Life* 36:7), as at Gethsemane (Matt 26:36–46; Mark 14:32–42; Luke 22:40–46). It was one of the most difficult moments of her life (*Life* 36:9), since her deeply held convictions were under attack. She experienced an anguish that was like "the death agony" (*Life* 36:8). Eventually the attack ended and peace returned (*Life* 36:10).

However, that peace was short-lived, since she was ordered to leave Saint Joseph and to give an account of her activities, first to her superior, then to the provincial (*Life* 36:11–12). Teresa thought at that point of the trial of Christ (*juicio de Cristo*), and she took joy in suffering something for Christ (*Life* 36:12). After facing her provincial, she was ordered to stand before an assembly of all the nuns as well (*Life* 36:13). Then it was the civil and religious authorities' (the mayor and the city council, leaders of religious orders) turn to judge that it was necessary to suppress (*deshacer*)[87] the monastery, since it would cause harm (*daño*) to the city (*Life* 36:15). According to Teresa, given how "furious" these people were, it is surprising that this threat of suppression was not carried out immediately (*Life* 36:15). This long lawsuit (*gran pleito*) went to the royal council (*Life* 36:17). At a time when everything seemed lost, Teresa surrendered herself to God: "Lord, this house is not mine; it was founded for You" (*Life* 36:17).

Just as Jesus faced unreasonable accusations in his trial, so Teresa noted with liveliness and good humor the ridiculous fears for harm upon the city that her opponents voiced:

> I was startled by...how everyone thought—I mean those opposed—that this house could be so harmful to the city. There were only twelve women and the prioress (for there were to be no more); and they were living such a strict life. If the house were harmful or a mistake, it would be so for these women; but that it would be harmful to the city didn't make sense. But the adversaries found so many reasons for opposing it that they did so in good conscience. (*Life* 36:19)

The phrase "twelve women and the prioress" called to mind Christ and his apostles all the more directly because it was not the number of those present at the Saint Joseph monastery at that time, but rather the maximum number of nuns envisaged by Teresa.[88] Moreover, Teresa herself was not living there during this storm. Thus, not only does Teresa identify herself in a certain way with the person of Jesus, but she saw her sisters in the place of the disciples in this passion.

After the temptation to accept income and then final negotiations, the city calmed down (*Life* 36:23), Teresa was able to move into Saint Joseph (*Life* 36:24), and the people (*pueblo*) even developed a devotion for this house (*Life* 36:25). Out of the threats and trials, a redemption emerged; having passed through the risk of death, life was renewed.

This appropriation of the passion marks a passage for Teresa from appearing in the narrative as a figure of Mary to one of Christ. This shift in literary configuration indicates that Teresa understood herself narratively in light of their example, thereby marking a construction of her own identity through the reception of another. Something new takes shape in Teresa that is expressed through this configuration.

Conclusion

This exploration of the evangelical elements of Teresa's narrative helps us better understand both Teresa herself and the meaning of the events she reports. The relation of these events to the gospel text is not to be found simply in references to it (explicit or otherwise) or even in Teresa's adoption of a biblical structure, but more in the harmonics that these elements provide, resulting in rich music.

What it means to participate in the work of salvation by following—and identifying with—Christ emerges magnificently through the presence in her narrative of the two major poles in the history of salvation in Jesus Christ, which we can identify in contemporary terms as the Incarnation and the paschal mystery (death/resurrection). By viewing and expressing the experience of the origin and birth of the monastery of Saint Joseph through this double prism, Teresa highlights the salvific dimension that was already visible in the very object of the story: the creation of a place where people are saved (*Life* 36:29). Thus, Teresa places herself in the context of Christ's work of salvation.

Of these two poles, the predominance of the incarnational dimension, from a largely Lukan perspective, reveals the accent she gives to the work of salvation.[89] Furthermore, the Lukan flavor of this story suggests the importance of the role of the Holy Spirit in this process, even though there are few explicit mentions.

The Presence of a Discreet Agent: Elements of a Dynamic

We have seen how the presence of the Holy Spirit is revealed in several aspects of Teresa's narrative. By reconstructing a certain dynamic of Teresian action in the foundation of the new monastery, we can discern another dimension of this divine presence.

An Event in Context

The content of Teresa's initial vision of hell introduced salvation as one of the principal themes of her narrative. Special mention should be made of the circumstances in which this vision occurred. It happened while Teresa was praying, as did many of her other important visions. This characteristic immediately suggests a sacred context that is oriented by nature to openness to the divine word and action.

The vision of hell happened abruptly, unrelated to what she was doing or thinking, seemingly from nowhere. This "sudden" character of divine intervention would come up again and again with Teresa.[90] This characteristic suggests a gesture of creative action on the part of God.

From Desire to Consent, Beyond Resistance

In response to the irruption of God, a desire emerged in Teresa to extend God's incarnation. She did not ignore her numerous desires (to do more, to help souls, and so on); they became action.

While the direction they would take her was not clear at first, their apostolic character was.

The first place of the incarnation of desire in the concreteness of existence was in Teresa herself, in her full consent to this desire. Of course, there is no guarantee that a person will act upon their desires, even clearly authentic ones. Teresa's internal resistance to acting upon her desire, to making it incarnate, was very real—she was comfortable in the monastery of the Incarnation, she foresaw potential obstacles, and so on. Such resistance, which would subsequently diminish, had to first be overcome in order for it to be welcomed, that it might take on, through Teresa, flesh and life.

Several instances of confirmation of the divine origin of Teresa's desire supported this. For Teresa, the journey toward the incarnation of desire was made of commitment and dispossession.[91] It took commitment because she had to make great efforts, face trials both internal and external, and take many steps in order to accomplish it (though one must avoid here a kind of voluntarism that says everything depends on one's own efforts). It took dispossession because at the heart of vigorous commitment of oneself is gift; it is from another that the desire had arisen, it was this other who animated it, and it was from this other that the realization would be tested. This dispossession also implies consent to weakness. Not only did Teresa receive her desire from another, but she also received from the other the capacities she needed to carry out this project.[92] These capacities ranged from assurance about her personal salvation to access to financial or spiritual help. Teresa, though resolutely committing to this project, commented several times that she was poor, a woman, of little value, *ruin.*[93] In other words, everything was given to her, from the desire to the ability to implement it. Teresa's desire was entirely gift[94]—received, welcomed, and shared.

The disinterested consent to the desire of another is also seen in Teresa in the great importance she gave to obedience. This was for her the guarantee that her efforts to establish Saint Joseph were not for herself, but for God and God's will. She remained attentive to obedience to her confessor and also to her superiors, even when she could not inform the latter of the imminent realization of the monastery (*Life* 36:5).

The initial strength and enthusiasm of the desire were also supported by a certain (providential) blindness that helped her to overcome some of the obstacles and protected the momentum of desire. Thus, on the question of whether the monastery ought to have had an income, Teresa writes that the amount she and her companion had been planning would have proven not to have been enough, but their desire at the time made them think that it was sufficient (*Life* 32:10).

The external resistances, which were numerous and sometimes quite strong, did much to obstruct progress toward the fulfillment of the desire. Some impasses had to be circumvented (thus the opposition of the provincial, which made sure that the monastery of Saint Joseph would fall under the authority of the bishop), while other resistances vanished. Teresa, as the principal bearer of the desire, had to be continuously reinforced in her desire through her relationship with the one who instilled it. Her force of consent and adherence is seen as a movement of abandonment to the divine inspiration disclosed.

The Involvement of Others

Teresa's efforts to establish Saint Joseph monastery were about more than herself and God. The apostolic aim of the salvation of others, which was the purpose of the effort, directed her from the start beyond this simple two-party relationship. In fact, another person was part of Teresa's original inspiration for the effort. Let us recall the role played by a fellow sister, whose idea of founding a monastery seemed to crystallize the desire that Teresa carried in her. Following that, Guiomar's continued support for the project offered Teresa human comfort in a way that softened the impact of the resistance that others put up.

The most obvious example of someone else being affected in a way that contributed to the desired project is Father Ibáñez. He experienced a complete reversal in his stance toward Teresa's idea, from a reasonable opposition to vigorous support that never waned thereafter.[95] Moreover, his reversal also took the form of a renewed commitment to prayer that was, of course, a way to salvation.[96] The source who had brought about his reversal was thus personally leading him toward the overall goal of the Teresian project, that of salvation.

Another important "other" that both had an effect upon and was affected by Teresa's project was the populace of the city of Avila. The fierce opposition with which they greeted the founding of the monastery culminated in an effort to suppress it. But little by little, the residents of Avila allowed themselves to be affected by this new place and went there to pray and to help the community of sisters with their alms. The turnaround was complete, much to the surprise of those concerned.[97]

The central role of others in the process leading to the incarnation of Teresa's desire points to a certain dispossession on the horizon of this desire on the part of the subject itself. The desire that Teresa receives is not for herself—she aims at the foundation of a monastery for others—but even more, others must be inspired by the same source to allow the project to take shape, and they are themselves affected by it, as if by a collateral benefit, even if this project is not intended for them. This dispossession, in the fragility of the desire, reminds us as well that Teresa's project was not simply hers, but that it was indeed the project of Another.

An Agent Hidden but Present

The story of the genesis of Saint Joseph and the highlights we have considered above allow us to understand better the Holy Spirit's role in the work of salvation.

In Teresa's experience of the vision of hell, both the context of the appearance of the vision (in prayer) and the suddenness of its occurrence (suggesting a creative event) point in the direction of a divine impulse that is startling.

The desire instilled in her as a result of the experience was a movement of inspiration that would motivate her relentlessly, becoming a force of advancement, even in the face of great difficulties. As a source of inspiration, the Spirit worked in others who were able to help advance Teresa's work, softening their opposition or shifting their opinions entirely. The Spirit also acted as a sort of veiling agent, when a certain degree of blindness to all the contours of a situation might have helped Teresa to avoid discouragement. One might think here not only of the inadequate plans for income that Teresa reports, but also of the vision of hell, which Teresa considered to be a great gift, despite the dreadful things she experienced in it. A creative spirit, the Holy Spirit ensured the (sometimes surprising) passage between two stages, as between the vision of hell and its consequences in Teresa's life.

Finally, the final—and futile—attack by the devil, once the monastery of Saint Joseph was established, made clear all the power deployed by the Spirit to carry out this new enterprise.

Another way we recognize the unexpected work of the Spirit is at the level of the signs of the Spirit's activity or presence in Teresa: joy, peace, glory. Obviously, one can think here of the signs of the Spirit described in the letters of Saint Paul or in the Gospel of Luke. A certain divine milieu is then sketched that encompasses both the visions of Christ as well as the other spiritual favors Teresa experienced. These signs reveal the Spirit's presence even when she doesn't mention the Spirit explicitly.

Elements of a Dynamic of Incarnation

The dynamic of incarnation initiated by the Spirit can be schematized in the following way:

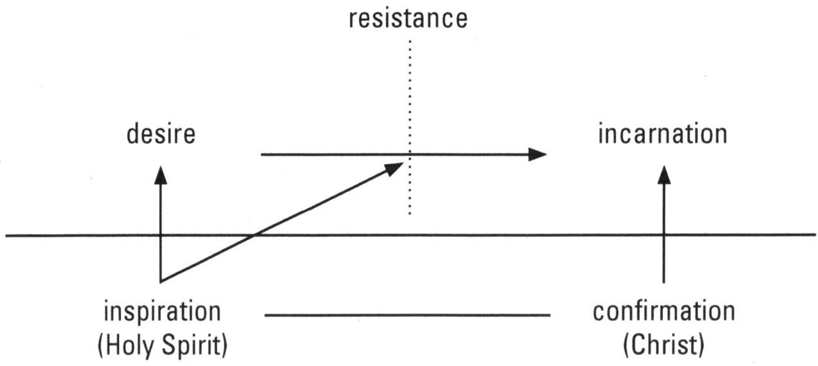

The inspiring source is the Holy Spirit, acting within both the desire of the subject and the occasions of resistance that would stand in the way of the realization (incarnation) of this desire. These elements of resistance can prevent this incarnation if one relents before them, but they can also be overcome, if one's will is strong enough. It is Christ who, as the face of God, comes to confirm the incarnation, both in the form of confirmation to the desire[98] and in the effective realization of the project.[99] The strong link between impulse and confirmation, between the Spirit and Christ, reveals the unity of the source, but also that the Spirit acts in the world in a manner parallel to the Spirit acting in Christ in a trinitarian framework in view of the incarnation of salvation. This initial sketch will be developed more systematically in chapter 3 in the context of the entire Teresian corpus.

FROM DISARRAY TO EXPANSION: A HISTORY OF THE FOUNDATIONS (*FOUNDATIONS* 1—3)

The account of the foundation of the monastery of Medina in the first chapters of *Foundations* is an echo of that of Saint Joseph recounted in the *Life*. This second foundation is not simply a repetition of the first effort. Indeed, Teresa had not envisaged a subsequent foundation, and she was very happy at Saint Joseph, leading the life of prayer she had desired. A new impulse—new without being unusual at first—intervened that would launch Teresa along the path of a series of foundations. The dynamics that emerged in this activity reinforced and completed the initial dynamics of Saint Joseph.

This second milestone in Teresa's apostolic thrust comes five years after the founding of the monastery of Saint Joseph. She recounts it at the beginning of *Foundations*, composed in 1573.

The situation described by Teresa in the first paragraphs is paradisiac.[100] She was living among holy and pure young women,[101] the virtue of obedience was prized (*Found.* 1:3–4), and the Lord was well served in this monastery (*Found.* 1:2). There were thirteen nuns, the number Teresa had chosen as the limit for the house (*Found.* 1:1), marking the completeness of the initial project. At the time she was writing, Teresa already suspected that it would be the quietest years of her life (*Found.* 1:1).

Within this idyllic situation, though, the seeds of future development were planted. First, an intuition to the effect that the great riches that the Lord had given these nuns were to be for a purpose (*Found.* 1:6). She notes that what later came about "never passed through my mind" (*Found.* 1:6). Second, she recounts her growing desire (*deseo*) to contribute to the good of souls, to help all enjoy (*gocen*) the great treasure she had found (*Found.* 1:6.). But her soul seemed bound (*atada*); the favors that the Lord had given her in those years were very great, but, she wrote, "I thought that I was not putting them to good use" (*Found.* 1:6), since she only served the Lord with her poor prayers and by encouraging her sisters to do the same (*Found.* 1:6).

A New Call

*The Triggering Event and Its Consequences (*Foundations *1:7–8)*

A thunderclap occurred for Teresa with the visit to Saint Joseph of Father Maldonado, a Franciscan missionary who worked in America. He was, she said, motivated by the same desires for the good of souls as she was, but he was better able to put them into action. Teresa wrote about his brief visit: "He began to tell me about the many millions of souls that were being lost there for want of Christian instruction, and before leaving he gave us a sermon, or conference, encouraging us to do penance" (*Found.* 1:7).

Teresa's reaction to this visit is dazzling:

> I was so grief-stricken [*lastimada*] over the loss of so many souls that I couldn't contain myself. I went to a hermitage with many tears. I cried out to the Lord, begging Him that He give me the means to be able to do something to win some souls to His service, since the devil was carrying away so many, and that my prayer would do some good since I wasn't able to do anything else. (*Found.* 1:7)

This immediate dual reaction of grief for the loss of souls and the desire to win them is precisely the same apostolic fruit of her earlier vision of hell (see *Life* 32:6). In both cases, grief was the negative side of Teresa's affective response to an absence, a void. Desire was the positive side of her affective response to the absence, marked by the hope that the void could be filled; it was thus oriented outwardly, toward others, the future, through action. This similar double reaction—a desire for salvation that led to the founding of Saint Joseph and that which marked the beginning of a series of foundations—reinforces the relationship between these two narratives, despite the few years that separate both the two events and Teresa's narration of them.

It is however notable that Teresa's reaction here immediately aims at the salvation of others, whereas after the vision of hell, her concern was initially personal before taking an altruistic turn. We can recognize here both a purification of Teresa's desire, directed toward others, and the assuagement of her fear for her own personal salvation.

Returning to the story, after expressing her envy for those who could work at the task of actively saving souls for love of the Lord, Teresa notes that when she read the lives of saints, she felt greater devotion and envy about their work converting souls than she ever did about the martyrdoms they suffered (*Found.* 1:7). The primacy of others again asserts itself.

Having experienced this longing and offered her cry to the Lord, the response was immediate: "Well, going about with such great affliction, while I was in prayer one night, our Lord represented Himself to me in His usual way. He showed me much love, manifesting His desire to comfort me, and said, 'Wait a little, daughter, and you will see great things'" (*Found.* 1:8).

Teresa was convinced that these words were true and came from God, but she could not understand at the time what these "great things" to come would be (*Found.* 1:8.). This first response effectively presented itself as an invitation to hope and to desire with confidence. Teresa no longer had to be turned toward herself (her grief) but could be attentive to whatever it was that she would "see."

*A Project Proposed by Another (*Foundations *2)*

Six months later, Teresa learned that the father general of the Carmelite order was going to come from the order's Rome headquarters to Spain (*Found.* 1:8; 2:1). It would be, in her eyes, a providential event (*Found.* 2:1). She was afraid he would be displeased with her, since the foundation of Saint Joseph was not done under the auspices of Carmelite obedience,[102] and she knew that he could even go so far as to order her to return to the monastery of the Incarnation (*Found.* 2:1).

During the father general's visit to the monastery of Saint Joseph in Avila, Teresa bore her soul to him, giving him "an account of my soul and of almost my whole life" (*Found.* 2:2). The general was pleased with what he saw: "a portrait [*retrato*], although an imperfect one, of the beginnings [*principio*] of our order" in which the primitive rule was preserved in all its rigor (*Found.* 2:3). It was he—in another instance of another person playing a key role in Teresa's carrying out God's plan—who gave her the key to the divine project that awaited her:

> And with the desire he had that this beginning go forward, he gave me very extensive patent letters, so that more monasteries could be founded, along with censures to prevent any provincial from restraining me. I did not ask for these, but he understood from my way of prayer that my desires to help some soul come closer to God were great. (*Found.* 2:3)

Next, it was the bishop of Avila who intervened to help obtain the necessary permission to open new discalced Carmelite monasteries in his diocese (*Found.* 2:5). This was needed because, although the father general wanted the new monasteries to be created, he told Teresa that in order to avoid opposition from within the order (*halló contradicción*), she needed the approval of local provincials to move forward (*Found.* 2:5). Teresa thus received the help of two prominent figures (the father general and the bishop) to carry out the project that Christ had asked of her.[103] In the case of the Carmelites, although the initiative for new monasteries had come from the father general, Teresa took up the project and quickly pushed it farther with him. After a few days of prayerful consideration, Teresa saw a need for the establishment of new monasteries of discalced Carmelite men, in addition to the new ones for women, and she wrote to him explaining why (*Found.* 2:5). The father general received the idea favorably, providing her with authorization for the establishment of two (*Found.* 2:5). Teresa then found herself with the problem that she knew of no Carmelite brother or even layman interested in taking up such a work, nor did she have a house available or a means of obtaining one. But armed with the necessary authorizations and good wishes of those in authority, she proceeded with courage and hope that the Lord who had given one part of what she needed would also provide the rest (*Found.* 2:6).

*A Successful Foundation Despite Obstacles (*Foundations *3:1–10)*

The work of establishing the second monastery of discalced Carmelites, in Medina del Campo, demonstrated its providential character. Teresa first engaged the help of the Jesuits of Medina in obtaining the permission of local civil and ecclesiastical officials, permission that she obtained before she had either a house or even the money to buy one (*Found.* 3:1–2). It was then that a young woman who had been unable to enter Saint Joseph, because of lack of room, asked Teresa to allow her to enter the new monastery (*Found.* 3:2). The dowry she brought was not enough to purchase a house, but it did allow them to rent one. As word spread in Avila about the new monastery, negative judgments did, too (*Found.* 3:3). In Medina, a property in poor condition was found and could be purchased with no surety, but they had to live in the rented house while it was being repaired (*Found.* 3:3). However, on the way to Medina, Teresa learned that a community of Augustinians in that town would oppose the new monastery (*Found.* 3:4). Father Heredia, an ally of Teresa in Medina, told her of a house he had made an agreement to buy that would be sufficient temporarily (*Found.* 3:6). It was in fact in a sorry state, but since Teresa and her companions arrived at night, they didn't fully realize it at first (*Found.* 3:8). The owner provided tapestries to hang on the walls to make the place acceptable as a chapel, so that in the morning a Mass could be celebrated and the Blessed Sacrament installed, which marked the taking possession of the new monastery (*Found.* 3:8–9). It was therefore a successful foundation, despite its share of obstacles, thanks to helpful collaborators.

*A Final Attack and Its Resolution (*Foundations *3:10–18)*

At the same time as the new foundation, Teresa was seized with virulent internal doubts. Now seeing the building in daylight, she became troubled by the lamentable state of the place the Lord in the Blessed Sacrament would be housed, particularly at such a troubled time for the church (*Found.* 3:10). Even more painfully, the entire enterprise began to seem impossible; Teresa was conscious only of "my lowliness and my powerlessness," and she was pained by the idea that her companions would have to return to the monasteries they had just left (*Found.* 3:11). This attack was similar to the one Teresa had experienced following the founding of Saint Joseph: doubts about mistakes and failure, especially in the eyes of others (*Life* 36:7). Because of her dismay, she also feared that what the Lord had promised to accomplish would now never come to pass; she even began to think that what she had thought she had heard God communicate to her in prayer has in fact been an illusion (*Found.* 3:11). Although it was difficult and harsh, this last assault of the devil—after the foundation—seemed to fade away. Teresa was consoled by the presence of the Blessed Sacrament in the chapel and by the people of the town who began to come to visit it there (*Found.* 3:12–13). A merchant invited the sisters to live temporarily on the upper floor of his house, and a neighbor offered her help in getting repairs and construction started for the new monastery. Teresa's anxiety receded, regular recitation of the office began, and the prior of the Carmelite monastery began overseeing repairs.[104]

A Simple yet Surprising Dynamic

Certain elements of the dynamic presented here are clear. First, the initial situation, with the foundation of Saint Joseph accomplished, was idyllic, but under the varnish of success, certain irrepressible desires began to emerge in Teresa. The impact of Father Maldonado's visit is surprising. After all, the things he talked about were probably not new to Teresa; we know that she had already been preoccupied, for example, about the salvation of Lutherans. Moreover, the priest's visit seems to have been brief and rather unremarkable, yet it was the catalyst that set in motion something significant.

The question arises of the identity of the provider of the inspiration for all of these events—in semiology, the sender. We know that Christ intervened to give assurance of the divine origin of the inspiration—a form of formal confirmation, even though the details of what was to come were not yet unveiled—but the figure inspiring the entire movement is hidden. However, by the effectiveness of action displayed, by the discrete nature of the activity, and by divine confirmation, one can recognize the presence of the Holy Spirit.

Understanding the details of the divine plan came slowly. Even the confirmation offered by Christ, which Teresa took as a promise, did not allow her to know what lay ahead.

Another remarkable element of this dynamic is the direct transition within Teresa from desire to consent. No trace of resistance emerged in her. Nothing stood between her desire—the divine origin of which became clear only after the fact—and her active (not merely passive) consent, expressed in a request to the Lord. Such absence of resistance in her, unlike during the founding of Saint Joseph, was probably due to her greater intimacy with the Lord, who was therefore able to dispel more readily any occasions of doubt or resistance. That being said, this absence of personal resistance also played a role in the way events played out, since the external obstacles that materialized seemed to melt without difficulty before God's will, despite the threat that some of them seemed to pose.

Foundation and Foundations: A Movement in Two Acts

The two stages of the genesis of the Teresian apostolic project that we have just analyzed include important similarities between them, despite notable differences in time and circumstance. The similarities of the modus operandi that emerge in these two episodes suggest that the same agent animates them both and that the two stages share the same origin.

In both cases, an unexpected triggering element, connected to the theme of salvation, marks a starting point. In the case of the founding of Saint Joseph, the vision of hell played this role. For the inauguration of the subsequent series of foundations, it was a conversation with Father Maldonado about the loss of souls in the Americas. The consequences of both these events, however, were not ones that would have seemed to have flowed obviously from their sources.

Teresa's reaction to the triggering elements is the same in both cases: first pain or tears, followed by wanting, or even asking, to be able to do something for the salvation of souls. The first part pulled her into herself while the second directed her attention outward, toward others and toward salvation.

The projects that would eventually come to be following these events were in both cases initially expressed to her by others: one of Teresa's companions in the case of founding Saint Joseph and the father general of the Carmelites in the case of founding the other monasteries. This reality is emblematic both of the quality of Teresa as an instrument, acting through the guidance of others, but also of the apostolic nature of the projects she would carry out.

While the divine origin of each intervention was initially hidden, Teresa soon received clear divine confirmation that let her know that the Lord was indeed at the heart of the work.

The course of action necessary in each case was fraught with powerful obstacles. The overcoming of such strong oppositions signaled that the project was indeed God's. The presence and activity of the Holy Spirit was clear in the power of melting the opposition of some people to the work, the power of hiding certain difficulties and obstacles from view, and the power of persistence needed to continue on in the midst of all of this. We can recognize the power of Gift also at work, since Teresa recognizing her own powerlessness, received everything: the desires, the projects, but also the capacities, both spiritual and material, to carry them out.

In both cases as well, final attacks by interior doubts or explicitly by the devil confirmed the degree of combat in which she had been engaged. These attacks struck a personal chord for Teresa, calling into question her personal integrity (obedience, pride, unworthiness) and the consequences for others (the happiness or unhappiness of her sisters, the possible need to return to their monastery).

Finally, both instances concluded with the accomplishment of success in all respects. The parallelism between the two "calls" and the continuity of their apostolic aspects confirms them as two moments with the same inspiration. The story of the founding of Medina del Campo enhances features of the more arduous experience of the gestation of Saint Joseph by amplifying the harmonics. All of this allows us to sketch more confidently the role of the Spirit in the work of salvation.

CONCLUSION: THE SPIRIT, INCARNATOR OF SALVATION? AN INITIAL SUMMARY

In Teresa's account, salvation is an incarnate reality. And Teresa brings to light the place this incarnation happens. The theme of salvation's space, its place, is ubiquitous in her writing. From her description of the vision of hell, the place of nonsalvation par excellence, a place without space, without air, suffocating, narrow. Completely different is the place of salvation, a place where one can breathe and live. From the start, Teresa's grief for the loss of so many souls became the desire to found a monastery, a house, a place of salvation.

This place of salvation, in her story, will lead to the foundation of monasteries, but they will always be a place of relationship—a household. In her vision, Saint Joseph, Our Lady, and Christ appeared together, creating the space in which the monastery will be inscribed. In her own relationship to God, Teresa was constantly accompanied by third parties (Guiomar, future nuns, and so on), ensuring that the space created was not a place for an exclusive, one-to-one relationship, but an open space with room for others from the start. The dimension of dispossession that we have emphasized has an obvious role here.

The strong gospel flavor of the story of the founding of Saint Joseph monastery alerts us to the presence of the Spirit as the source of movement and power behind events. This emergence of the Spirit as agent of incarnation is also illustrated in Teresa's account of her encounter with Father Salazar and in her evocation of the "divine language in which it seems the Holy Spirit was speaking."

The incarnation of salvation can be recognized in Teresa herself. First, her body is involved in many ways in her experience of God. Above all, however, she is called to greater openness to the action of God in and through it. Salvation is not encountered independently of it. On one hand, she loses the fear she harbored about her own salvation. In addition, she learns to receive the gift of God, the capacities God offered so that she could accomplish her mission. This reception was lived in humility and in an ever-greater correspondence between her life and desires and the desire of God, as we saw in the comparison between the Teresian dynamic during the process of establishing Saint Joseph monastery with that of the monastery of Medina.

This Teresian movement of growing openness to the will of God that tends toward incarnation echoes the movement that we can recognize in the Trinity between the inspiration of the Spirit and the Incarnation of the Son, the face of God. It is always Christ who is seen, but the Spirit is movement. Through the movement of incarnation in which she participates, Teresa identifies herself with Christ—sometimes even explicitly. But it is the Spirit of God that sets in motion and keeps in motion the incarnation of God's salvation.

Chapter 2

A Divine Movement of Salvation

Chapter 38 of the Life

Unlike chapters 32 to 36 of Teresa's *Life*, which recount the series of events that resulted in the establishment of the monastery of Saint Joseph in Avila, chapter 38 is a sort of extension of the book in which Teresa offers a series of various kinds of favors, visions, events, reflections, and commentary on her prayer.[1] This chapter generally covers events that took place between the founding of Saint Joseph (1562) and the time of the final redaction of the book (1565). Writing at the request of both the Lord and church authorities, Teresa's approach here is more introspective, less narrative.[2]

Despite a heading that suggests it presents a variety of subjects,[3] chapter 38 is in fact quite coherent. Several important visions are described here, along with other less consequential ones. Teresa draws rich, new connections between the themes of salvation, heaven, indwelling, life and death, the Spirit, Christ and the Father, the Eucharist, and glorification. These connections further unfold the themes developed narratively in the previous chapter. The story that emerges in these pages is not primarily about a great event, nor is it strictly chronological. The chapter's unity lies elsewhere, discreetly, in the movement that takes shape.

In addition to the "topology" developed in the previous chapter, what emerges here is an "odology" that offers a deeper understanding of salvation and the Spirit.

A great deal of honesty is revealed in these pages of the *Life*; Teresa reveals uncertainties, doubts, and things unsaid. If Teresa sometimes indicates that it would be useless to write more here or to write in a more detailed way there,[4] demonstrating her mastery as a writer of narrative, she does not hesitate to acknowledge that her words are an imperfect attempt to describe an experience. Teresa, a seeker of God—as her lively cries to the Lord remind us[5]—is in a relationship with the Lord of which she is a recipient. She is not the master of her experience; it is not her possession. This nonreification of experience leaves its contours open. Sometimes the nature of an event is so baffling or sublime that it becomes ineffable, and Teresa says that she is unable to say anything about it,[6] not because she wants to hide the gift that was given to her, but out of a simple recognition of the impossibility of saying anything that could convey adequately what she experienced. What is unspoken is therefore made clear. On the other hand, she is more capable of recognizing and expressing the traces of God's activity in herself and in events. Teresa does not hesitate at times to express her doubts—confirmed or not—about a vision or at other times to affirm with certainty the authenticity of what she experiences.[7] She is particularly sensitive to the weight that each type of spiritual phenomenon carries.[8] This candor helps the reader to navigate the various moments of the story with confidence and to welcome even her uncertainty.

Through the course of this composite chapter, a movement in five stages emerges. First, a vision of heaven introduces the subject and leads Teresa into a reflection on true life. Second, a vision of the Holy Spirit—a rare occurrence for Teresa—highlights the place of the Spirit in divine visitation. Third, at the heart of this chapter is a vision of the humanity of Christ in the bosom of the Father, an eminently trinitarian vision. Fourth, she recounts a vision of Christ related to the Blessed Sacrament and offers a touching reflection on the Eucharist. Finally, she recounts further visions concerning salvation or its forfeiture by specific individuals.

ON HEAVEN AND (TRUE) LIFE (*LIFE* 38:1–7)

The Vision of Heaven: An Echo of the Vision of Hell

The vision with which Teresa opens this chapter should be read in counterpoint to the vision of hell she describes in chapter 32 (which had provided the initial impetus toward the foundation of Saint Joseph), both because of its structure and its content. Whereas in the first case Teresa experienced herself "put in" (*metida*) hell, this time, she experienced herself "brought into" (*metida*) heaven.[9] Each vision inaugurated a journey for Teresa, though of very different sorts. But as with her vision of hell, the vision of heaven Teresa describes clearly places this journey in the orbit of salvation. This is how she describes it:

> One night, being so ill that I wanted to excuse myself from mental prayer, I took my rosary in order to occupy myself in vocal prayer. I tried not to recollect my intellect, even though externally I was recollected in the oratory. When the Lord desires [something], these devices are of little avail. I was doing this for only a short while when a spiritual rapture came upon me so forcefully that I had no power to resist it. It seemed to me I was brought into heaven, and the first persons I saw there were my father and mother. I saw things so marvelous in as short a time as it takes to recite a Hail Mary—that I indeed remained outside myself; the experience seemed to me too great a favor. (*Life* 38:1)

Teresa clearly indicates a specific context of time and place for this account, though not in relation to the other events described in this chapter. Its placement within the context of the entire chapter is also important.

The context and location of the experience (at prayer, in the oratory) were oriented toward encountering God, but Teresa approached them somewhat half-heartedly; she was ill and expected to pray only vocally. She was in the right setting and circumstances, the right time and place, for encountering God, but she was not very disposed to it. Despite this, God took the initiative to go to meet her. The fact that something happened in such circumstances highlights the gratuitousness of this initiative and the gift of God.

Suddenly and vividly, and for a short time (*breve espacio*), Teresa experienced a powerful spiritual rapture (*un arrebatamiento de espíritu…con tanto ímpetu*). According to the traditional terminology, *arrebatamiento* has a sharper, more vibrant character than *arrobamiento*,[10] although they are both often translated as "rapture,"[11] and the *con…ímpetu* further emphasizes the strength of the experience. The sudden and vibrant character of the experience is characteristic, in Teresian teaching, of a divine intervention, while temptation or spiritual desolation[12] is usually seen as more languid.[13] Furthermore, *arrebatamiento* is often closely associated with one's spirit (*espíritu*), as is the case here with *arrebatamiento de espíritu*.[14]

The brevity of the vision of heaven compared with the greatness of the things seen, although ineffable, gives it a paradoxical nature that is typical of mystical experience. This powerful initial shock would continue to unfold later for Teresa: "As time went on, it happened—and continues to happen sometimes—that the Lord showed me greater secrets."[15] It is characteristic of an inaugural vision to be completed only later, just as the vision of hell was also subsequently enriched by further, complementary visions (*Life* 32:3).

Teresa measures the length of the vision by the time it takes to pray a Hail Mary.[16] At first glance this might seem like a quaint, anecdotal reference. But a richer understanding of the comment can be drawn from a consideration of the background of this traditional prayer. The Hail Mary, after all, is rooted in the infancy narratives of the Gospel of Luke, specifically of the accounts of the annunciation and the visitation (see Luke 1:28, 42). Both of these events are marked by the presence of the Holy Spirit and both by the typical effect of the Spirit on those who encounter the Spirit: joy. We have already seen in the previous chapter how the Lukan drama informed Teresa's narrative. Her reference to the Hail Mary in her description of the vision of heaven—which, significantly, is followed immediately by her description of a vision of the Holy Spirit—acts as a discreet reminder of both the Incarnation and the visitation, each of which bear in themselves, in a sense, the seed of salvation.

Teresa notes only three elements of the content of this vision.

First, it seemed to her that she was "brought into" (*metida*) heaven. That is, she experienced her whole being engaged in the vision; she was inserted inside of the place God wished her to contemplate. She includes a note of uncertainly about what she experienced (*parecíame,* "it seemed to me") that also appears at the beginning of the vision of hell ("I had seemingly been put...," *Life* 32:1). But unlike the vision of hell, of which Teresa offers us detailed descriptions, she provides no description of heaven.

Second, the only concrete element of the vision Teresa offers is that she immediately saw her father and mother there. Thus, while she saw no one in hell, she experienced heaven as an inhabited place, and even inhabited by specific people whom she recognizes. This is the only internal characteristic of heaven that Teresa reveals: heaven is a place of personal encounter. The text leaves open the possibility of encountering other people, but Teresa's mention of her parents is not trivial. In effect, the image of Teresa, her father, and her mother together means that heaven, the place of salvation accomplished, is presented as a household space. This household is not just any; it is the one through which Teresa came into the world. The initial presence of Teresa's parents suggests heaven as a new iteration of birth, entering into a new life and a new place.

Third, Teresa notes that she saw "things so marvelous," but offers no specifics at all. We simply learn that she "remained outside [her]self" as a result of this vision and that it was for her a great favor (*muy demasiada merced*). For Teresa, what she saw in heaven was in the order of the ineffable. This discretion is amplified by other considerations, among others a comparison with Saint Paul and Saint Jerome,[17] although this is in the form of interior tension.

Teresa insists then on the ineffable character of this vision of heaven. She comments that she would have liked to explain what she learned through this vision, but knew it was impossible (*Life* 38:2). She offers an analogy, comparing "the light we see" to the light that she saw in this vision, where everything is light, saying "there is no comparison," since even the light of the sun itself seems "blurred" by comparison (*Life* 38:2). And so Teresa clearly indicates here that there is a limit to the human capacity to express the divine: "The imagination, however keen it may be, cannot paint or sketch what this light is like, or any of the things the Lord gave me knowledge of" (*Life* 38:2). The only thing Teresa is able to express is the sensory and spiritual traces in her of this vision. This ineffability forces Teresa to relinquish reliance on the spoken word and to speak from beyond it. But for Teresa, the nature of the word is intimately linked to the person of Christ. Her vision of heaven therefore pushes this mode of presence by the word to its limit and opens the way to an awareness of other forms of God's action.

Lastly, beyond its content, the vision of heaven entails for Teresa a departure from herself, a displacement carried out by God who brings her to another place. As she did in describing her vision of hell, Teresa clearly emphasizes the origin of this displacement: "When the Lord desires...."[18] In her vision of hell, this departure from herself had meant being locked in the narrow confines of hell. But in this case, being pulled from herself meant being brought to a place of "a delight so sublime" (*deleite tan soberano*), a place where "all the senses rejoice to such a high degree and in such sweetness that the delight cannot be exaggerated" (*Life* 38:2). Teresa notes that she "remained outside myself" (*Life* 38:1)—in another place—even after this brief vision ended. This penetrating interior awareness of the passage of God by the trace left in the human being is an essential moment for understanding God's action.

The divine displacement that happened in Teresa can also be read on another level. The vision of the place of hell initiated a long process that had led to the creation of a new place, the monastery of Saint Joseph. The vision of the place of heaven is a sort of echo of the earlier one, and it confirms the path upon which Teresa had embarked; it offers a glimpse of a new call, to establishing more places where God will dwell.[19]

Seeing in Order to Tell: An Apostolic Posture

Teresa's vision of heaven and the related ones that follow offer an opportunity to understand more clearly the proclamatory nature of the mission that Teresa would pursue for the rest of her life. She wrote that on one occasion, after showing her "admirable things" for more than an hour, the Lord told her, "See, daughter, what those who are against me lose; don't neglect to tell them" (*Life* 38:3). With the vision—seeing wonderful things—comes the injunction: Look! But God does not intend this contemplation of heaven, the endpoint of salvation, to be only a moment of personal joy for Teresa or to serve only for the advancement of her own spiritual life. A second injunction comes: Tell others what you see; speak.

Seeing in order to tell—this is a fundamentally apostolic posture, a turning toward others, that Teresa is invited to take up. Already, the apostolic dimension of this posture is clear; it reflects the motto so dear to the Order of Preachers: *contemplata aliis tradere* ("to hand on to others the fruits of contemplation"). At the end of chapter 35 of the *Life*, Teresa had already expressed a similar stance. She wrote of her desire to cry out "to everyone" about her past blindness in order to help open the eyes of her contemporaries, while asking the Lord to open their eyes (*Life* 35:15).

Significant too is the fact that the invitation was to see what those who are against God "lose." This is closely related to the pain felt by Teresa for all those who are lost. The previous chapter showed how this pain fueled Teresa's apostolic desire. But the loss also shows salvation's proximity and its character as gift. One can only lose what one has or, at the very least, what one who is willing has access to. The loss is made all the more tragic by the fact that the gift is at hand. Indeed, the gift Teresa refers to is one that is offered and can be accepted, but that is instead actively lost.

Faced with divine injunction, Teresa exclaims, "Ah, my Lord, if Your Majesty doesn't give them light, what little benefit will what I say bring to those whose deeds blind them!" (*Life* 38:3). Then she protests her fundamental incapacity, since no one will want to listen to anything said by "someone as dreadful and wretched as myself" (*Life* 38:3). Teresa realizes that her words alone are not enough to open the eyes of those who cannot see, even if she recognizes in herself the benefits that her experience and understanding have brought her (*Life* 38:3). In this, Teresa was consistent with what she said earlier about the nature of this divine "light," which would make even the light of the sun seem dim, but whose description, unfortunately, is out of her reach. Only God can offer it; it is a gift.

The movement thus sketched out is one of "seeing in order to tell," on the part of the apostle, and then of "hearing in order to see," on the part of the listener in a process completed, or else "remaining blind" in order to miss what there is to see. Sight not only reveals an object at a distance, it also reveals a dynamic object, extended by God toward the human being, offered and shared. Through this movement of seeing in order to tell, Teresa's apostolic orientation is clear. Guided by God, she will no longer be the quiet contemplative, but rather the founder in action. Equipped with this apostolic impulse, all other concerns are eclipsed.[20]

On Life

One of the major consequences of the vision of heaven was to shed new light on "everything earthly." The great secrets and revelations of this vision were such that "the least part of it would have been sufficient to leave me marveling [*espantada*] and very proficient in considering and judging all the things of life as little" (*Life* 38:2). A few lines later, Teresa exclaims that having contemplated such admirable things, "afterward I wanted to remain in this state always and not return to everyday living, for the contempt [*desprecio*] that was left in me for everything earthly was great; these things all seemed to me like dung, and I see how basely we are occupied, those of us who are detained by earthly things" (*Life* 38:3).

At this point in her account, Teresa relates an episode from her stay in Toledo. During a period when she was sick, her hostess gave orders that Teresa be shown some of her precious jewelry because "she thought they would make me happy" (*Life* 38:4). On the contrary, Teresa felt pity at this demonstration of what was so important to some people. In contrast, she concludes that a great inner freedom of the soul, which she calls *señorío*,[21] is essentially a gift from God (*Life* 38:4), a characteristic that is brought out even more when the gift is given in a short period of time.

This freedom from the things of this life would be accompanied by the loss of the fear of death.[22] On the contrary, death seemed to Teresa to be a very easy thing for one who serves God, "for in a moment the soul finds it is freed from this prison and brought to rest" (*Life* 38:5). The vision of heaven was similar to passing through death to go to a new place: "I think these raptures in which God carried away the spirit and reveals to it such excellent things are like the departure of the soul from the body, for in an instant these good things are seen all together."[23]

This passage through death, which Teresa no longer feared, clearly became the entry into a new life that God had already shown her in this life, causing her to lose all attachment to earthly things. Seeing the destination, "our true country…where we shall live" (*Life* 38:6), seemed to Teresa to be of great help to we who are "pilgrims here below" (*Life* 38:6). Having seen the end of the road makes the difficulties of the journey—"a heavy cross" (*Life* 38:7)—easier to bear.

In the end, the vision of heaven leads to a complete reversal of perspective by Teresa: "Everything I see with my bodily eyes seems to be a dream and a mockery. What I have already seen with the eyes of my soul is what I desire; and since it is seen as something far away, this life is a death" (*Life* 38:7). This life on earth is death, while the place beyond death is where real life is lived. Teresa pushes this way of thinking farther when she speaks of those who live on earth or in heaven:

> It happens to me sometimes that those who I know live there [in heaven] are my companions and the ones in whom I find comfort; it seems to me that they are the ones who are truly alive and that those who live here on earth are so dead that not even the whole world, I think, affords me company, especially when I experience those impulses [*ímpetus*]. (*Life* 38:6)

The "real" living ones are therefore those who live in heaven! Teresa feels so strongly drawn to these heights that she thinks it might not be possible for her to live if the Lord did not allow her memories of this vision to fade from her mind at times (*Life* 38:7).

This dichotomy between life and death, between artificial life and true life, does not strictly follow a temporal divide. Teresa says that the Lord "desired that I understand something of so many great blessings and in some way begin to enjoy them" (*Life* 38:7). It was therefore God's desire that Teresa in some way enjoy, here below, the gifts of above, the gifts of heaven. It was more than just seeing them in order to give her a clearer and more vibrant focus on the end of the journey; there was an interpenetration between the place of the endpoint of salvation—heaven—and the earthly world, in which the gifts of heaven can already be enjoyed, in a certain way, by one who serves God. The human fragility in the reception of this gift from God is illustrated in the prayer that Teresa then addresses to the Lord, in which she asks that her fate not be that of Lucifer, who through his own fault lost everything.[24]

Excursus: Life and Death in Paul

Following her account of her vision of heaven, Teresa describes her fear of telling her confessor about it, and in doing so refers to Saint Paul (*Life* 38:1). Notably, Paul's account of his vision of being caught up in heaven (2 Cor 12:2–4) is similar to Teresa's in several ways. But beyond this direct connection, the reflection by Teresa on life and death that unfolds in this chapter bears a remarkable affinity with Pauline thought. A brief consideration of how this is so will offer new insights into Teresa's teaching.

One of Paul's striking statements about life and death is found in his letter to the Galatians, where he writes, "I have been crucified with Christ; and it is no longer I who live, but it is Christ who lives in me" (Gal 2:19–20). Since this verse is part of a reflection by Paul on Christ and the Law, its context is quite far from that of Teresa in this chapter.

Moreover, in 2 Corinthians 5, Paul speaks of our earthly lives as an "earthly tent" that will one day be destroyed (v. 1), and of his desire to take up a heavenly dwelling (v. 2), "so that what is mortal may be swallowed up by life" (v. 4); it is God who made us for this and who gave us the Spirit "as a guarantee" (v. 5). Our mortal life means living "away from the Lord" (v. 6), so much so that Paul says he would prefer to leave his body to be "at home with the Lord" (v. 8). Above all, he invites us to aspire only to please God, whether we are living in our bodies or not (v. 9). Thus, while distancing himself from earthly life, Paul's ultimate emphasis is on an orientation toward God and God's will, while personally maintaining an interior freedom with regard to life or death.[25]

Another Pauline passage that is especially important to our investigation is Philippians 1:20–26. Paul loved the Christian community at Philippi dearly, and that love was at the heart of the antagonism he experienced between life and death. On one hand, Paul says Christ is "exalted...in my body, whether by life and by death" (v. 20). For him, "living is Christ, and dying is gain" (v. 21). But Paul is an apostle, so his relationship with Christ is not exclusive or individualistic; those to whom he is sent are part of the equation. The opportunity to do fruitful apostolic work makes him reluctant to leave this life (v. 22). Despite the fact that being with Christ would be much better, for the sake of his dear Philippians, for their spiritual progress and joy in the faith, he prefers to continue his journey here (vv. 23–25). However, this choice is not a resignation to an existence without life in Christ; the life he lives is already radically transformed, since it is oriented to Christ and offered in the service of his brothers and sisters. It is a new life.

Teresian thought is similar. It includes a dichotomy as strong as the one we find in the Letter to the Galatians. Teresa, however, dwells more on the negative aspects of life here and the disgust it can inspire in one who has tasted celestial joys. Oriented toward the heavenly place that she visited, she feels a very strong desire for life beyond. As in 2 Corinthians, one can discern in Teresa her strong aspiration to go resolutely toward God. At the same time, Philippians helps us recognize the fundamentally apostolic orientation that is present in germ in Teresa's thought. In summary, the overall movement could be formulated as one of great interior freedom with regard to death—death to a life oriented toward oneself and earthly things—opening to birth to a different life oriented toward God—by already tasting the fruits of the future life—and toward others—being called by the Lord to proclaim what one has seen.

THE "VISION" OF THE HOLY SPIRIT

Teresa's Account of the "Vision"

Teresa continues this chapter by describing an incomparable favor, even greater than those she has just briefly described (*Life* 38:8). The greatness of this favor can be measured by the great goods that flow from it and by the strength it left in her soul. Here is how she describes this vision:

> One day on the vigil of Pentecost I went to a secluded spot after Mass where I often prayed, and I began to read about this feast in a volume by the Carthusian.[26] Reading of the signs beginners, proficients, and the perfect must have in order to recognize whether the Holy Spirit is with them, it seemed to me that by the goodness of God and insofar as I could make out He was not failing to be with me. I praised Him and remembered that once before when I read the passage I really lacked everything; I had realized this very clearly, just as now I understood the opposite about myself. So I knew that what the Lord had granted me was a great favor. Thus I began to consider the place I had merited in hell on account of my sins, and I gave much praise to God because it didn't seem I recognized my soul by the change I saw. While I was reflecting on this, a great impulse came upon me without my understanding the reason. It seemed my soul wanted to leave my body because it didn't fit there nor could it wait for so great a good. The impulse was so extreme I couldn't help myself, and it was, in my opinion, different from previous impulses; nor did my soul know what had happened, nor what it wanted, so stirred up was it. Although I was seated, I tried to lean against the wall because my natural power was completely gone (*Life* 38:9).

Teresa continues by describing the heart of this vision:

> While in this state I saw a dove over my head. It was very different from doves on earth since it didn't have

> earthly feathers, but the wings had little shells that gave off great brilliance. It was larger than a dove. It seems to me I heard the noise it made with its wings. It fluttered about for the space of a Hail Mary. My soul was already in such a condition that in losing itself it lost sight of the dove. The spirit was quieted by so good a guest; for, in my opinion, a marvelous favor like this should have frightened and disturbed it. And when it began to enjoy the guest, the fear was taken away and the joyous quietude began while the soul continued in rapture. (*Life* 38:10)

Finally, Teresa comments on the importance and the effects of this vision:

> The glory of this rapture was extraordinary. I remained for the rest of Pentecost so stupefied and stunned I didn't know what to do with myself, or how I had the capacity for so great a favor and gift. I neither heard nor saw, so to speak, but experienced wonderful interior joy [*gozo*]. I noted from that day the greatest improvement in myself brought about by a more sublime love of God and much stronger virtues. May He be blessed and praised forever, amen. (*Life* 38:11)

An Initial Reflection

The prayerful context of this experience is quite clear. It is the vigil of the Feast of Pentecost, the feast of the Holy Spirit. After Mass, Teresa steps away to one of the hermitages at Saint Joseph monastery and reads a text relating to the feast. As with the vision of heaven, the time, place, and activity are right for an encounter with God, but on this occasion Teresa is also more interiorly disposed. With regard to the different modes of the presence of the Holy Spirit, she notes with joy that the Sprit "was not failing to be with me." Teresa is therefore able to discern a habitual presence of the Spirit in her, which she recognizes as a great gift.

It was at that moment, in an atmosphere of praise, that she recalled the place in hell that she had seen prepared for her. The usual presence of the Spirit in her is therefore contrasted starkly with the place of nonsalvation from which she has been saved. Thus, the presence of the Spirit—the Spirit's indwelling—discerned in meditation, is by a mirror effect related to salvation.

A Sudden Transport

It is then that a sudden "impulse" (*ímpetu*) begins Teresa's rapture. She emphasizes the "extreme" force that seemed to push her soul from her body and disorient it. Taken out of itself, her soul was led by another, to another place.

This impulse was so violent that Teresa indicates that all her natural strength vanished. She felt so weak that she could not even sit up straight. Such loss of power and control was a kind of death; Teresa's soul was outside of herself and her vital forces failed her so that she couldn't remain upright, even when seated.

This unexpected event recalls many of the beginnings of encounters with the Lord in Teresa's writings, including her vision of heaven. The Holy Spirit is usually not mentioned, and this occurrence is no exception. Teresa was meditating upon a text about the presence of the Spirit and giving thanks to God; thus the central object of this encounter with God in the form of a "vision" would also be the Holy Spirit. By drawing a link between the initial context and the content of the vision—both centered on the Holy Spirit—it is possible to identify the source of this departure of the soul from itself in order to lead it to God. The relative discretion of the agent is consonant with the "personality" of the Spirit and will moreover be maintained in the very heart of the vision.

Vision and Audition

At the heart of Teresa's encounter with God, in the short time of a Hail Mary—not the first time she has offered this as a measurement of time—an image was seen and heard. It was a dove, though one unlike earthly doves. Teresa could hear its wings flapping. This vision was both clear and distant. Clear, because through the image of the dove, it was the Holy Spirit that Teresa "saw." It was so clear, both in context and in traditional imagery, that she does not say so explicitly. The fact remains that it was through a form of mediation that she saw the Holy Spirit, who remained essentially faceless.

Moreover, Teresa heard the sound of the flapping of the dove's wings. A noise is not a word; in this sense, it was an audition unlike those in her visions of Christ. But the same sensory channel was used, though in this case without a message; it was simply a sound that conveyed a presence and a movement. The description is precise; we could draw the dove accurately and imagine the noise of the wings. But the main thing is not there. Contrary to the vision of heaven, where the fundamentally ineffable character is underlined while the message is clear, here the description is precise, but there is no obvious message. Teresa saw without seeing and heard without hearing. Or rather, she saw the invisible and heard the inaudible. The image of the dove and this noise have the analogical function of making sensibly present what is always invisibly and inaudibly present, exposing the mechanics of a movement that is here led as its culmination to an empty place. This is the illustration of the language in which the Holy Spirit speaks.[27]

In this sense, a "vision" of the Holy Spirit is fundamentally different from a vision or audition of Christ, who is both the Word and the face of God. This "vision" engages the same senses as in Teresa's encounters with Christ, but the content is not Christic. All attention is upon the Spirit, despite the discretion that is part of the Spirit's very nature. Teresa reports that in the period following the vision, "stupefied and stunned," she "neither heard nor saw" (*Life* 38:11). This emptiness of the senses directed all attention interiorly, to the place where the heart of the encounter happened. The whole space is open to the exercise of the spiritual senses; it is therefore in this place that the Spirit is to be discovered.

Presence and Impression

After seeing and hearing the dove, Teresa's soul was "in such a condition that in losing itself it lost sight of the dove" (*Life* 38:10). The vision of the dove therefore constitutes a stage in an ascent that led Teresa first out of herself then to the reception of an interior guest. The expression *perdiéndose a sí de sí* ("in losing itself"), which clearly suggests moving out of oneself, is traditional in mystical terminology to speak of entering into ecstasy.[28] This register of loss and gain, of the loss of self in order to gain an Other, was also very present in the mystical experience surrounding the "divine language in which it seems the Holy Spirit was speaking,"[29] highlighting a strong correlation between Spirit and ecstasy. This coming out of oneself in two stages, with an astonishing visual component, is the heart of ecstasy.

Then a transition occurs, from the operation of *seeing* to a simple mode of *presence*. Teresa confides that her spirit "was quieted by so good a guest," signaling an indwelling of one whose presence had previously been mediated. What remains then is at the affective level of impressions: she refers to peace (*sosegarse, quietud*), joy (*gozo*, twice[30]), loss of fear, and rapture (*Life* 38:10). She also notes the "wonderful interior joy" (*Life* 38:11) that remained with her throughout the day of Pentecost. Again, the center of attention is somewhat surprising; she says nothing about what happened to the dove, nor about the identity of this "guest" (*huésped*) in her. Attention is focused instead on the affective traces left by the passage of the one whose image was seen. And these marks are characterized first of all by peacefulness and joy. In the biblical tradition, peace and joy are both closely associated with the Holy Spirit, as its fruits (e.g., Gal 5:22). On the other hand, the vision of heaven, a vision of the endpoint of salvation, had also brought out similar characteristics, which underlines the relationship between the action of the Spirit and salvation (represented by heaven).

There is a firm correlation between joy and the Holy Spirit. In this vision, for example, the dimension of joy is most prominent, more even than the glory that, because of its vivid character, predominates in more "visual" visions, like those of Christ.[31] These associations of glory with Christ in a visual dynamic, and of joy with the Holy Spirit in a more interior and affective relationship, are not strict and exclusive, but they are strong enough to serve as hints in which the effect points to the cause. Joy, as a feeling and an interior state, is the indicator par excellence of the action-presence of the Holy Spirit and the sign of an incomplete, but already begun, enjoyment of its fruits.

Regarding peace, in connection with the Feast of Pentecost, it can be considered in the light of the consequences of the resurrection of Christ. Glorified, filled with the Holy Spirit that he would subsequently impart, the risen Christ is presented as the one who confers peace.[32] Peace, then, is the sign of the presence of God through the Son and the Spirit within the apostles; it is presented as prolonged in them by the gift of the Holy Spirit.[33]

Even in this vision in which the Spirit takes a central place, we see the Spirit only obliquely, through a traditional representation. Teresa does not even say explicitly that the object of her encounter is the Holy Spirit. But the liturgical context, the text she was reading, the fact that she was at prayer, the absence of words and a face, as well as the reality and the strength of the encounter are all clear and consonant with the traditional characterization of the Spirit. Moreover, recognizing the effects of its action—among other things, by the deep impression left behind—makes it possible to discern this action in any extraordinary encounter with God, or even at the heart of Teresa's daily life.

As the vision begins, after reading from Ludolph of Saxony's *Vita Christi*, Teresa is thinking about the transformation of her soul over the years, and she offers thanksgiving. Likewise, at the end of the vision, she is aware that she has been transformed, with a greater love of God and a strengthening of the virtues in her (*Life* 38:11). In the case of both transformations, the first over a long period of time and the other quite sudden, a decisive action can be clearly recognized through its consequences. Teresa sees them as gifts of God, and she gives thanks for them.

A Teresian Pentecost?

Teresa's vision of the Holy Spirit unfolds in the context of the liturgical celebration of Pentecost. Teresa specifies this, and she also reveals that the text she was reading was Ludolph of Saxony's *Vita Christi*,[34] specifically a text based very much on the narrative of the Acts of the Apostles (chapter 2). The connections of Teresa's experience with the account of Pentecost found in Acts are clear.

The apostles were together, occupying a place of fraternity and prayer proper to their vocation (Acts 2:1; cf. Acts 1:14); Teresa, too, was in a place (both in terms of location and frame of mind) of prayer. At Pentecost, the Holy Spirit came suddenly and filled, like a strong wind, the entire house the apostles occupied; in Teresa's case, the unpredictable nature of divine interventions in general, but also in this vision in particular, is clear—the impetuousness of the Spirit of Pentecost is thus the agent of the Teresian impulses, which is made obvious in this vision.

Then the apostles see tongues of fire, they are filled with the Holy Spirit, and they speak in other languages. They see, they are filled, and then they are pushed toward others; this is the movement at work in them. They do not "see" the Holy Spirit, but rather something that was to later become one of its symbols: tongues, like fire. This "vision" is accompanied by a new state: beyond the initial, impersonal presence of the Spirit (as wind) in the place—the house—where they are, they are each personally filled with the Spirit. This interior presence prompted them immediately to apostolic action, proclaiming "God's deeds of power" (Acts 2:11). We can recognize this same triple movement of vision, indwelling, and apostolic impulse in Teresa's experience of her vision. She sees the dove, then she senses the divine guest in her. The apostolic dimension will not develop in as immediate a manner as in the Acts of the Apostles, but already in the posture previously indicated by the Lord—seeing in order to tell—this apostolic dimension is sketched. In Teresa's description of a subsequent vision, which we will consider later, of a dove flying over a Dominican father, this apostolic dimension that marks the culmination of the movement will be reinforced.

Both for the apostles and for Teresa, we can note the confidence that springs from this visit of the Holy Spirit, which translates into peace and joy. The discourse of Peter speaks of this fruit of joy (and demonstrates it in his actions) brought about by the Holy Spirit, citing the words of the Psalmist (Acts 2:26, 28, quoting Ps 16). The whole experience of Pentecost is finally directed toward proclamation, toward a shared word that says Jesus Christ and invites those who hear it to salvation, as evidenced by the conversions recounted following Peter's speech (Acts 2:37–41), signs of a word received. For Teresa, too, beyond her work of founding monasteries, an essential aspect of her ministry was words, most often written, inspired by the Spirit. This is illustrated by the very text that is the subject of this analysis.

The text of the *Vita Christi* on Pentecost, the one Teresa mentions she was reading, also brings out other aspects that resonate deeply with her story.

Commenting on the ways the gift of the Holy Spirit was made apparent to the apostles, Ludolph first considers the two modes under which the Holy Spirit descended upon Christ: as a dove at his baptism and as a cloud at his transfiguration.[35] The dove, Ludolph writes, "a very proud bird," symbolizes the "spiritual generation of grace" in souls through the sacraments. For this reason, the Spirit's appearance in the form of a dove in Teresa's Pentecost vision identifies her with the person of Jesus Christ, and it identifies her founding activity with the baptism of Jesus, the first theophanic moment revealing his identity, prior to any work on his part. For Teresa, then, the most immediate meaning of the vision of the Holy Spirit may not be about being sent, like the apostles, but rather about identity, being configured to the person of Christ.

Another striking echo of this text of the *Vita Christi* can be seen in the levels of progress in the spiritual life that Ludolph identifies—"beginners," "proficients," and "the perfect"—which Teresa referred to in her account of the vision. These levels are particularly important because, as Saint Bernard (quoted by Ludolph) indicates, the Spirit has neither color nor sound, is not air or material: "How are his ways found? How does one know his presence? How can I feel that he is with me? To this I answer that it is by the new movement of my heart that I have known his good and salutary presence."

This differentiated action and presence of the Spirit can be recognized "by some effects and signs." This is what serves as the starting point for Ludolph's presentation of the signs marking the various stages of spiritual life. One, in particular, is significant in connection with the Teresian narrative; it is the third sign of those who are perfect in prayer: the desire to leave (*salir*) this life and the "prison of the body" in order to be with Christ. This, which reflects Saint Paul's words, is the highest level of an active and dynamic presence of the Holy Spirit in a soul. However, although Teresa does not mention in her account of the vision of the Holy

Spirit what signs led her to say that the Spirit was always with her (*Life* 38:9), in this chapter of her *Life*, she accurately describes the interior movements and reflections that accompany, according to Ludolph, the desire to be already with God in true life. Teresa's reading of Ludolph may have helped to crystallize in her this interior freedom vis-à-vis life itself that opened unsuspected spaces of gift of an apostolic nature. But above all, Ludolph's text reveals the link between the strong desire for life in God—tempered by apostolic desire—and the work of the Holy Spirit, since the desire for life in God, and therefore to depart from this world, is a sign of the action of the Holy Spirit in the "perfect."

At the end of this Pentecost journey, both in the biblical account and in the commentary of the *Vita Christi*, one can see the links between the active presence of the Holy Spirit, the desire for life in God, and apostolic momentum.

Personalized Visions

In the course of her account of the visions of heaven and of the Holy Spirit, Teresa briefly refers to other visions whose content is related, but she doesn't provide a chronological context, simply anchoring them in an indefinite *otra vez* ("another time"; *Life* 38:12, 13). Teresa is not a stranger to digressions in the context of her writing, acknowledging them herself,[36] but here her account of these personalized visions is not unrelated to what precedes it. Each provides a particular light that illuminates the path already traveled or the one that will be followed subsequently. Their unity is found as much in their "visual" dimension as it is in their personal character.

The first of these personalized visions concerns a Dominican priest, Father Pedro Ibáñez,[37] over whose head Teresa had previously seen the dove appear, except that it seemed to her that "the rays and splendor of the same wings extended much farther" (*Life* 38:12). She concludes, "It was made known to me that he would draw souls to God" (*Life* 38:12). With her words, Teresa establishes a link between an increased presence of the Spirit—by the resplendent figure of the dove—and a greater salvific impact. While Teresa's meditation on the place of nonsalvation at the beginning of her vision of the Holy Spirit subtly emphasizes the theme of salvation in this experience, this is the first time Teresa makes a clear correlation between presence of the Spirit and the direct impact on the salvation of others, suggesting strong connections between the Spirit and salvation.

A second vision concerning a Dominican, possibly the same person,[38] offers rich harmonics. First, Teresa relates that Our Lady gave the priest a mantle in thanks for his services in the establishment of the monastery of Saint Joseph (*Life* 38:13). This mantle signaled that Mary would guard his soul and keep him from falling into mortal sin—the concern for salvation is never far away. Tying this account with Teresa's previous concerns even more is the dialectic between life and death and beyond. This religious later "died with great joy and desire to leave this exile" (*Life* 38:13), Teresa writes. Such joy has already been identified as a sign of the Spirit, and the movement out of oneself, here expressed by the desire to "leave this exile," is also strongly associated with this ascent to the place of heaven. This overlapping for the believer of heaven and earth is strongly emphasized by two other features. First, a witness to this priest's death told Teresa that, before he died, he had said that Saint Thomas was with him (*Life* 38:13). Second, the priest experienced such intense rapture in his prayer, especially after celebrating the Eucharist, that the weakness of his body made it difficult for him to handle it, and he was tempted to avoid prayer for that reason. He even sought advice from Teresa on the subject before his death. These two traits show that for the believer, earth and heaven are not two separate domains, but that even on earth, one is already a citizen of heaven. Teresa further notes that after his death this Dominican appeared to her on several occasions in great glory, telling her different things (*Life* 38:13); this illustrates further the same compenetration of heaven and earth, but this time in reverse. It is easy to recognize here a real continuity between the two.

This brief account of the Dominican father existentially ties together various elements of our investigation: the interpenetration of life and death, the foretaste of God, and the enjoyment of God's gifts and presence in this life—in one instance, against one's will—the divine presence in opposition to sin, the presence of joy as a sign of the Spirit at the time of going through death, and finally visitation by one in glory. It is worth noting that Teresa relates that this priest, from his heavenly glory, spoke to her. That is, having passed through death, he is depicted in a Christic context: he is visible, he is glorified, and he speaks.

The following vision draws out another theme that will be deepened later by Teresa. This time it concerns a Jesuit priest. Teresa comments that she saw some "wonderful favors"[39] granted by the Lord to this man but adds that she will not describe them. She simply relates an episode that happened during a time when this priest was experiencing a severe trial. While attending Mass, Teresa saw Christ on the cross at the time of the elevation. Christ spoke to her, giving her words of comfort that she was supposed to pass along to the priest, reminding him that Christ had suffered for him and inviting him to prepare himself for suffering of his own. This vision of Christ on the cross at the heart of the celebration of Mass foreshadows a more developed vision that comes later in this chapter of the *Life*. On the other hand, while it is not very present in these pages, the theme of suffering emerges here, a sign that the cross is looming on the horizon.[40]

In summary, these few personalized visions subtly underline several aspects of Teresa's visions. They also demonstrate that the significance of her visions is quite concrete and goes well beyond Teresa herself and her own spiritual life.

THE VISION OF THE MOST SACRED HUMANITY, VISION OF THE TRINITY PAR EXCELLENCE (*LIFE* 38:16–19A)

Preparation for the Favor

Once again in the context of prayer ("one night while I was in prayer"; *Life* 38:16), the Lord "began to speak some words" that reminded Teresa "how bad my life had been," which caused her sorrow and pain (*Life* 38:16–17). This was a memory of a past state rather than her present one—Teresa says, "I hadn't done anything" (*Life* 38:17)—but faced with this situation of alienation from God, she experienced her usual response: sorrow. She writes that this sorrow was "consuming" (*que deshacen*) and that her consideration of her smallness, instilled by God, "reduce[d] [her] to nothing" (*me deshago*); it undoes her.[41] As this reality was brought back to her memory by divine will, it became as an "engraved" truth that could not be evaded (*Life* 38:16).

Even as this was taking place, Teresa sensed there was a reason that the Lord was having her experience it:

> I wondered, in the midst of tears, if He [the Lord] desired to grant me some favor. It ordinarily happens when I receive some favor from the Lord that I am first humbled [*deshecho*] within myself so that I might see more clearly how far I am from deserving favors; I think the Lord must do this. (*Life* 38:17)

At the level of the personal dynamics of divine grace, a movement of undoing, of humbling (*deshacer*) often precedes the reception of a divine favor; a space is created, a void, that makes room for the divine gift.

This movement of *deshacer* can also be understood in light of what Teresa was experiencing at that point in time—the opposition that threatened the fragile existence of the monastery of Saint Joseph.[42] Faced with this potential suppression and the pain it engendered, it was the assurance of the omnipotence of God that swept away her sorrows (*Life* 36:16). Thus, the palpable threat of suppression caused her pain, but reminded her that the initiative was the Lord's, that God was the builder, both of the monastery and of Teresa's own soul as a dwelling place for God. It was a gift that abides through trials and ultimately builds a transfigured place, inhabited by God's presence.

A Vision of the Most Sacred Humanity

The vision of the most sacred humanity, the climax of this whole chapter, begins in the same abrupt way that we have seen previously with the striking manifestations of God in the Spirit:

> After a short while my spirit was so enraptured it seemed to me to be almost entirely out of the body—at least the spirit isn't aware that it is living in the body. I saw the

> most sacred humanity with more extraordinary glory than I had ever seen. It [the Son of God] was made manifest to me through a knowledge admirable and clear that the humanity was taken into [*metido en*] the bosom of the Father. I wouldn't know how to describe the nature of this, because, without my seeing anything, it seemed to me I was in the presence of the Divinity. My amazement was such that I think for several days I couldn't return to myself; and it always seemed to me that I went about in the presence of that majesty of the Son of God, although the experience wasn't the same as when it first happened. This I understood clearly, but the vision is so strongly engraved on the imagination [*imaginacíon*] that no matter how short a while it lasts the impression left cannot be removed for some time; and the impression is very consoling and beneficial.
>
> I saw this same vision three other times. It is in my opinion the most sublime vision the Lord granted me the favor of seeing, and it bears along with it marvelous benefits. It seems it purifies the soul in an extraordinary way and removes almost entirely the strength of this sensitive part of our nature. It is a great flame that seems to burn away and annihilate all of life's desires. For even though, glory to God, I didn't have any desires for vain things, it was made clear to me in this experience how everything was vanity. How vain, how truly vain[43] are the lordships [*señoríos*] of earth! It is a powerful lesson for raising one's desires to pure truth. There is impressed upon one a reverence I wouldn't know how to speak of; for it is very different from the kind we can acquire here on earth. Great fear is caused in the soul when it sees how it dared, or how anyone can dare, to offend so extraordinary a majesty. (*Life* 38:17–18)

Teresa calls this the most sublime vision she ever experienced. What she saw was indeed striking: the Son in the bosom (*metido en los pechos*) of the Father. The word *metido* is the same one Teresa uses in describing the vision of hell,[44] and then also in that of heaven, at the beginning of this chapter (*Life* 38:1), and finally in a vision described at the beginning of the last chapter of the *Life* (*Life* 40:1), but in each of these cases, it is Teresa herself who is *metida* (put in, brought into, taken into) some place or a state. But here, it is Christ who is "put" someplace, in this case, the Father's own bosom or heart.[45]

Christ is no longer presented simply as the visible endpoint *of* relationship, but as the endpoint-*in*-relationship—that is, with the Father. Moreover, Teresa herself is present in this divine relational place—a striking assertion expressed in cautious words. Teresa declares that she "wouldn't know how to describe" what she saw, while at the same time saying that the vision happened "without my seeing anything." Nevertheless, she saw herself clearly "in the presence of the Divinity," and what she saw was the Son in the bosom of the Father. Teresa was, then, an exterior witness to the indwelling of the Son in the Father, the very trinitarian compenetration. Her awareness of the divine presence stayed with her this time, she wrote, for several days, though she now clearly associated it with the person of the Son,[46] who serves as the doorway to this relationship to God through the vision.

The most sacred humanity appears in great glory. This glory emanates from Christ, the face of God, expressing his divine origin. The prominence of glory in this account underlines the importance of the vision. It is important to note the emphasis on humanity in this vision of divinity. It is the Son of God's *humanidad sacratísima*, his "glorified humanity," that is contemplated, even as he is seen in his relationship with the Father—indeed, within the Father. This human element at the heart of the divine evokes the possibility of the transformation of humanity and its conjunction with the divine. This glory of the most sacred humanity of Christ will also be reflected in other human persons, but its source is already crystal clear.

We can recognize a very schematic movement in this vision. First, around the verb *deshacer*, Teresa is "undone," brought to an attitude of great humility, in tears. Second, when the vision suddenly happens, Teresa feels as though she has left her own body, no longer living in it. This is the moment of being taken up by God, who leads her where he wants. Where he leads her, in a third moment, is into the presence of the very divinity of God, the Son within the bosom of the Father.

At both the beginning and the end of this movement, its meaning is crystallized in her through something she experiences to be "engraved"[47] upon her. At the beginning, commenting on her awareness of her own wretchedness, she writes that such an awareness "engraves on us an undeniable truth" (*Life* 38:16). Then at the end of the vision, she comments that the vision of the majesty of the Son is "strongly engraved" in her mind (*Life* 38:17). Finally, in describing the consequences of this vision, she speaks of an indescribable reverence that is "impressed upon" one who experiences what she did.[48] Through such strongly etched impressions, Teresa takes account of the deep and lasting traces of God's action in her. But they have a paradoxical character—though engraved images, they are engravings of a place marked by emptiness, first the emptiness of Teresa's personal wretchedness, illustrated by the *deshacer* initiated by God, and second the emptiness at the heart of this vision, Teresa's seeing a presence without seeing at all. But these "engraved" absences become markers and crucibles—markers of a path from one to the other, crucibles of a new life that needs space to be born and grow.

The Vision of the Most Sacred Humanity: A Vision of the Trinity

Teresa plainly identifies the object of her vision as being the most sacred humanity of the Son of God. What she sees is Christ in his humanity, in great glory, in the bosom of the Father. The Father is not described at all, and the Holy Spirit is not even mentioned. Yet is this not an authentic vision of the Trinity? Certainly, it is.

The fact that everything that Teresa describes of the vision is Christic in nature is not surprising. Christ is the face of God, and therefore even the face of the Father. The Father is "seen" in this vision only through the reference to his bosom where the Son rests. It is through the Son that something of the Father is seen.

Even in Teresa's "vision" of the Holy Spirit, the Holy Spirit does not appear, except through the mediated image of the dove. It is therefore not surprising that the Spirit is not seen at all in this one. The sequence of the two visions—first, the vision of the Holy Spirit, followed closely by this vision of the most sacred humanity—suggests a certain continuity and therefore a presence of the Holy Spirit. In a paradoxical statement, Teresa also asserts that "without my seeing anything, it seemed to me I was in the presence of the Divinity"; seeing without seeing and feeling the presence—this is how she spoke of the experience of the Spirit made first under the guise of presence, rather than vision or audition. Furthermore, Teresa's characterization of the entire vision as "a great flame" calls to mind the traditional representation of the Spirit as fire, which is based on the coming of the tongues of fire upon the apostles in Acts 2:3 and found, notably, in Ludolph of Saxony's commentary on Pentecost in the *Vita Christi*. In reverse, with this identification of the "great flame," with the Spirit Teresa imputes to the Spirit the acts she associates with it: purification of the soul, the burning away of "life's desires," realization of the vanity of seeking greatness.[49]

In summary, through the visual doorway to the Trinity, that is, Christ in his humanity, Teresa was given a fully trinitarian "vision." This vision did not reduce the trinitarian Persons to a single mode of presentation, preserving instead the specificity of each. The Father was seen as the place of dwelling of the Son, while the Spirit was perceived by its presence and the effects of its action. This brings us closer to articulating the role of the Spirit in the work of salvation in a trinitarian framework.

THE VISION OF THE LORD IN THE BLESSED SACRAMENT (*LIFE* 38:19B–23)

Following the vision of divine majesty, of which she notes the great benefits, Teresa describes two further visions interspersed with lively reflection—most often in the form of a prayerful appeal—that continues the movement of the first vision. The first vision is one of the majesty of the Lord in the Blessed Sacrament (*Santísimo Sacramento*; *Life* 38:19), while the second, a few paragraphs later, is one of the Lord present in the host (*forma*), confronted with the demons surrounding an impure priest (*Life* 38:23). A triple movement emerges in this section: a movement of incarnation; a state of contrast, even paradox; and finally, a movement of (non)reception.

The movement of incarnation is visible in the transition from the vision of the majesty of the Son in the bosom of the Father to the vision of the Lord in the Blessed Sacrament. After having presented himself in his most sacred humanity in great glory, the Lord is now a "most glorious body"[50] present in the host, foreshadowing other glorified bodies that will be evoked later, those of people who have entered the glory of heaven. This transition from the Father's bosom to the host brings the Son closer to humans.

This movement of incarnation is also a movement of abasement, since the God who is contemplated in his majesty also makes himself visible and accessible.[51] There is a great contrast between the majesty of God and the humble way God is present in the Blessed Sacrament, as Teresa notes: "majesty as extraordinary as this concealed in something as small as the host" (*Life* 38:21). Such a vision, which Teresa does not describe in detail since it occurred "often" (*Life* 38:19), made Teresa's hair stand on end and "seemed to annihilate me" (*parecía me aniquilaba*).[52] But Teresa was also struck by the contrast between herself, in her smallness, and the God of majesty who gives himself. Although she felt "annihilated" before the greatness of the gift of God, she also enjoyed, despite her weakness, magnificent favors (*Life* 38:19). The God of incredible majesty chooses to become present in a small way that does not frighten people, but allows them to enjoy the gift.[53] This contrast reaches its height in Teresa's experience of seeing a priest at Mass, holding the sacred host but flanked by demons because, she understood, he was in a state of mortal sin (*Life* 38:23). In this case, God himself was in the presence of the threat of nonsalvation.

This movement of abasement by God therefore finds an echo in Teresa's movement of response; before such a divine gift, she puts herself in a position of humility, until she is nothing, recognizing herself, at the very heart of her smallness, simply as "the debtor" and the Lord as the one to whom the debt is owed (*Life* 38:22). Teresa continues this movement of abasement by noting the great affliction her soul feels in the service of the Lord (*Life* 38:22). However, everything brings her back continuously to acts of thanksgiving, which are present throughout these few paragraphs (*Life* 38:19b–22). Every word gives witness to the power of the Eucharist or its transforming role. Emphasis is entirely on the paradox of greatness in smallness and on the impact of such awareness in the existential reception of such a gift in Teresa and beyond.

We also see the dynamic of reception—in this case in a negative form, one of refusal—in the unworthy priest. He was in a state of mortal sin, and his hands holding the host offended the Lord (*Life* 38:23). Teresa understood that it was very wrong to receive this holy sacrament in an unworthy manner, and how much more than others priests are obliged to be good (*Life* 38:23). At the moment of coming forward to receive Communion, Teresa saw, at the same time, the demons taking the poor priest by the throat and the Lord in majesty in the host, held in his hands. The Lord then addressed her asking her to pray for this priest and wanting her to see "His great goodness since He places Himself in those hands of His enemy, and all out of love for me and for everyone" (*Life* 38:23). Thus, the Lord demonstrated the depth of his self-giving, going so far as to expose himself to the enemy in supreme abasement. Salvation no longer appears simply as an established place, but as what is at stake in a true battle. Furthermore, the first words of the Lord after the vision were a request, that Teresa would pray for this priest and so contribute, in her own way, to the work of God, as a response to what she had contemplated. From seeing to praying.

GOD IN (OR NOT IN) OTHERS: FROM THE DAMNED TO THE SAVED (*LIFE* 38:24–32)

The vision of demons in *Life* 38:23 serves as a transition to introduce a new vision in which demons also have a role. In the last paragraphs of chapter 38, Teresa relates several visions pertaining to the deaths of various people. In each of these stories, the place of the person's salvation—or damnation—will be paramount.

Hell Realized

The first vision in this section constitutes in some way an incarnation of the illustration of hell that Teresa described in chapter 32 of her *Life*.[54] Before the funeral of a man who had lived a bad life and died without confession, Teresa saw demons toying with his body (*Life* 38:24). During the funeral, Teresa saw no further demons, but then, as the body was being lowered into its grave, she saw "a multitude of them inside ready to take it" (*Life* 38:25). "Frantic" at the sight, Teresa had to make great efforts to remain composed (*Life* 38:25). She concludes her account:

> May it please the Lord that what I have seen—a thing so frightful!—will be seen by all those who are in such an evil state; I think it would prove a powerful help toward their living a good life. All of this gives me greater knowledge of what I owe God and of what He freed me from.[55]

In her previous vision of hell, where Teresa had seen the place prepared for her by the demons, she gave thanks for what she had been saved from (*Life* 32:4). But here, hell is no longer a hypothetical place; the life of this anonymous man had come to an end and he received his reward. Having lived "a wicked life," he had become God's "enemy" (*Life* 38:24). The industrious activity of the demons that Teresa had discovered in hell was now happening before her eyes with the unfortunate man's body. Seeing it, Teresa was frightened at the thought of what those same demons were doing with his soul (*Life* 38:25). The Lord, in his kindness, did not allow others to see the true state of this soul (*Life* 38:24). Through her experience with this man, Teresa is able to reflect on the fate of the wicked, of one who is in a state of nonsalvation.

From Hell to the Salvation of a Priest

After the description of nonsalvation of one who has died, Teresa turns to other visions—happier ones—that also concern the dead (*Life* 38:26–32). These stories, which Teresa notes from the outset as brief, relate to five religious men and women.

The first, which is the most developed, merits special attention. Teresa recounts learning of the death of her former provincial. She "feared for his salvation" (*Life* 38:26), because he had been in charge of many souls for twenty years. Disturbed, she went to an oratory to pray for him, that his soul might be freed from purgatory (*Life* 38:26). In response, the Lord offered this vision:

> While beseeching the Lord for this as best I could, it seemed to me that person came out from the depths of the earth at my right side and that I saw him ascend to heaven with the greatest happiness. He had been well advanced in years, but I saw him as only about thirty, or even less I think, and his countenance was resplendent. This vision passed very quickly; but I was so extremely consoled that his death could never cause me any more sorrow.[56]

It is noteworthy that chapter 38, which opens with a vision of heaven, presents in its last paragraphs the image of the ascent to heaven of someone who had died whom Teresa knew. Three elements are striking here. First, a clear movement of "[coming] out from the depths of the earth." The verb used here, *salir*, is the one Teresa uses when she mentions her own experiences of being outside her body, in the context of her visions, under divine power. But rather than a metaphorical exit from the body, which is temporary, the exit from the earth here is definitive and permanent.

The second striking feature is the ascent, a going up to heaven marked by a great happiness. This ascent is part of the continuation of the previous movement, that of exit, but is accompanied by a sign of the divine presence associated with the Holy Spirit: happiness (*alegría*). This strengthens the link between the earthly place and the divine place that is heaven.

A final surprising element is essential: the dead man's face. Rather than seeing him as he was at the time of his death, Teresa sees him at the age of thirty, with a "resplendent" face. This resplendence of a thirty-year-old introduces a Christic dimension: a radiant face like the face of the risen Christ.[57] Although Christ is not mentioned in this passage, this description of the man's face is a clear reference to him. The man goes up to heaven like Christ; he is configured to Christ even in the appearance of his face.

Other Personalized Visions of Nuns and Religious

Teresa then relates two visions of the souls of two sisters leaving the earth and going to heaven (*Life* 38:28–29). Since no nun had yet died at the monastery of Saint Joseph,[58] we can conclude that these were nuns from Incarnation monastery, which implies that the story presented here is organized more thematically than chronologically. Teresa says that these were not "imaginative"[59] visions, unlike the previous one (that is, the vision of the soul of the former provincial ascending to heaven).[60] The entry into heaven of these two good nuns was prompt: a day and a half in one case and four hours in the other, and in both cases in the context of Teresa participating in community prayer in the chapel.

Two other visions of this kind follow, one concerning a Jesuit brother and the other a Carmelite friar.[61] In both cases, Teresa was attending Mass when a "deep recollection" (*gran recogimiento*) occurred. In the case of the Jesuit, this meditation took place even though Teresa was experiencing difficulty in prayer but was praying for the dying man. She saw him ascend to heaven "in great glory, and the Lord along with him" (*Life* 38:30). She understood that it was a particular favor for the brother to be accompanied by Christ in this way (*Life* 38:30). Christ is therefore not the usual agent of ascension to heaven.

In the case of the Carmelite, Teresa's vision happened at the time of his death, while the dying person was in another place. Exceptionally, this priest did not spend a single moment in purgatory but went straight to heaven (*Life* 38:31). Teresa notes that it is one of the only three times she saw this happen in the visions she had.[62]

The presence of these visions of various people at the end of this chapter opens new perspectives. First, salvation is presented in a more incarnate way. Beyond the theoretical consideration of heaven or hell of other visions we have considered, salvation—or its absence—is found in its concrete outcome in a given person. Second, beyond the individual dimension of salvation, there is a collective dimension; there is a saved "people," who are not unrelated to the living.[63] Would these people not be the incarnate and extended counterpart of the place of the monastery, the place that has so guided the Teresian quest?

Teresa concludes this short excursus with an interesting comment on heaven and its different "places": "In the case of some, the Lord was pleased that I behold the degrees of glory they possess, and he showed me the places [*lugares*] assigned to them. Great is the difference that lies between the glory of some and that of others" (*Life* 38:32).

Thus, in heaven—the very endpoint of salvation as life with God—there is a kind of differentiation. Salvation is not purely disjunctive—heaven or hell. It is qualitative. Various degrees of glory are possible for those who are saved. This differentiated glory translates into different "places," although all of them are in heaven. Here Teresa's thought reflects the Gospel of John, in which Jesus told the disciples that there are many "dwelling places" (*monai*) in his Father's house (John 14:2).[64] The "places" in heaven may not correspond directly to the mansions (*moradas*) of *The Interior Castle*, but they take up the idea of progression and differentiation in proximity with God. Thus, the very endpoint of salvation is not an undifferentiated state; it occurs in places representing a degree of one's glory.[65]

CONCLUSION

The Movement of the Chapter: Ascent

Beyond a sequential analysis of the various important points of chapter 38 of the *Life*, it is interesting to consider the overall movement that carries them through the five stages we have identified. What emerges is a profound ascent followed by the unfolding of incarnation.

The first stage is the vision of heaven, the endpoint par excellence of salvation, the place of God, an inhabited place in which Teresa sees herself put. This experience produced in her an existential reconfiguration of the relationship between life and death, with her ascent to heaven marking a tearing away from the earth. The dichotomy that could have resulted is softened by the already begun enjoyment of the goods promised to an eschatological fullness.

The second stage sheds light on the agent at work in this movement: the Holy Spirit. The Spirit is revealed beyond images and words as a sensible presence inhabiting Teresa, marking her affectively with joy. She recognizes that her soul has been transformed.

The third stage is the climax of this movement. It carries Teresa to the heart of it, to the very place of the Trinity: she is carried by the Spirit to the Son in his most sacred humanity within the bosom of the Father. The Son "inhabits" (or dwells within) the Father, and Teresa is brought into this place. Teresa is inserted into the horizon of God, and she speaks vividly of the extraordinary impact of the experience both on her inner life and on her perception of the world around her.

Having reached this summit, an unfolding begins in the life of the world. The fourth stage of the journey is the vision of Christ in the Eucharist, as a presence tirelessly offered to the world, discreetly but powerfully. This presence flows from the previous vision of the most sacred humanity in majesty. Faced with the paradox of the presence of such a majesty in such a small and sometimes ignored form, Teresa erupts with praise and prayers to the Lord.

The last stage is the reception of salvation in the glorified bodies of men and women, or, alternatively, their refusal of that salvation and the results of that in their bodies. These visions represent an incarnate counterpoint to the vision of heaven. She even saw that for one individual in particular, the hell that she had previously experienced in a vision became a sad reality. Both here and in the vision of the Eucharist, the action of the Spirit in the imparting of salvation is clear. From Teresa's vision of heaven to her vision of some of her contemporaries ascending into heaven, the journey is complete. What began as a separation from the earth by an ascent to heaven ends in the image of the incarnation of salvation in others—in differentiated ways. In short, there is a trajectory from the human being raised up to the place of God to God dwelling in the human being, passing by way of God himself.

Divine Places

These stages span the various *places* that punctuate chapter 38 of the *Life*.

The first is heaven, an undifferentiated and inhabited place—as illustrated by the presence of Teresa's parents. It is a place lacking description because it is ineffable. It is a place where Teresa is brought as an individual.

The second place is the indwelling (or inhabitation) of the Son in the Father, with the presence of the Spirit also clear, and the presence of Teresa herself to the divinity. What Teresa sees reveals it as a place of fullness, but also at a distance, since she sees without seeing. The focus of this whole chapter is found here, in this place of indwelling that is first of all a dwelling of God in God, but which Teresa sees and to which she is present.

The last place is the fullness of place, with heaven mirrored in the glorified people that Teresa sees ascending there. The singular route begun with the vision of heaven thus finds its culmination in a differentiated place inhabited by others, others whose bodies have been glorified. Dispossession and fullness go hand in hand here, since this place is inhabited, but by others. Yet it is Teresa who sees and tells.

These three places reflect the journey of the Spirit described by Ludolph of Saxony in the section of the *Vita Christi* that Teresa was reading on the eve of the Feast of Pentecost. Ludolph writes that the Spirit "breathes for beginners, dwells in the proficient as in a temple, and provides the perfect with his fullness and abundance."[66] Here we see the Spirit presented as one who has the property of breathing (*espirar*), dwelling in (*morar*), or filling (*henchir*). The simple movement of the Spirit's breathing, which displaces people, is illustrated in this chapter by the vision of the Holy Spirit, a vision that sheds light on the movement the Spirit prompts, movement that had been seen at work in the vision of heaven. Then, dwelling within people "as in a temple" is reflected in the vision of the humanity of Christ in the Father's bosom, into which Teresa was drawn; indeed, she saw herself present at the very heart of the trinitarian relationship that animates the entire temple. Finally, the gift in fullness and abundance, which characterizes the perfect, manifests itself strongly in Teresa's visions of glorified bodies, reflecting the divine presence until they are configured in their very appearance to the face of God.

Between these three places we find three distinct aspects of relation to the body.

First, we must note the movement of *deshacer*, a prolongation of which is seen in Teresa's experience of her soul leaving the body (e.g., *Life* 38:9). In this experience that is both mystical and bodily, we see a certain distance in relation to the body, with the Holy Spirit revealed as the engine of what happens. The (difficult) movement of *deshacer*—being undone—creates an open space within Teresa that prepares her to receive the gift of the presence of God. This *deshacer* was previously seen when the threat of suppression (expressed with the same word in Spanish: *deshacer*) of the nascent monastery was looming (*Life* 36:16). Teresa was troubled, but the monastery was saved by God's intervention. Here, in contrast, *deshacer* takes the form of interior preparation for the vision of the most sacred humanity of Christ (*Life* 38:16). Something melts in her, comes undone, in order to make room for something new. Teresa herself comments that this is a common way the Lord proceeds before granting a great favor (*Life* 38:17). But this dislocation acquires particular strength here from the fact that it is inscribed on the threshold of a vision of the humanity of Christ. The space created by *deshacer* comes to be taken up by another humanity, that of Christ, which guides the ordering of her own through the exposure of the "full" place of Christ in the Trinity.

Second, Teresa's vision of the eucharistic body, which comes between that of the Trinity and that of glorified bodies, features a body that reveals a presence greater than itself. This presence is not intended only to be contemplated; the eucharistic body is to be shared and eaten, and thereby to offer the presence that it bears. For this reason, Teresa's contemplation of the majestic presence of Christ in the eucharistic body is linked to her vision of the Holy Spirit. In the latter, the instrument of the elevation of the human soul toward God is revealed, whereas here, what is revealed is the visible means of the transformation of the human being into the glorified body, a means that passes through its reception to reach its end. This end will be illustrated by the various glorified bodies that Teresa sees at the end of the chapter.

Finally, Teresa sees the bodies of several persons that reveal the presence they bear. Some of these bodies are resplendent, glorified, youthful, or accompanied by Christ; others are surrounded by demons. They demonstrate and reveal what inhabits them. In the case of a person who is an enemy of God, their dead body will be the subject of toying and torture by demons. Teresa doesn't describe this body's own state—ultimate annihilation—but what is done to it by the demons, diminishing it to its sole quality as object. Meanwhile, she sees the bodies of people close to God transfigured in death. Already filled with the Spirit, the passage through death configures them to Christ by the glory that is revealed through them, by the resplendence of their faces or even by accompaniment by Christ himself in their ascent to heaven. The inaugural vision of this chapter, of Teresa experiencing herself an ascent to and visit of heaven, therefore finds a complete fulfillment in others, in these men and women who died in Christ.

Insights and Directions

Let us conclude this chapter by noting some of the fresh insights and orientations that have emerged: Teresa's trinitarian orientation; her configuration to the Trinity; the link between the Spirit and salvation; and finally the purification of Teresa's desire and her apostolic vocation.

In the first place, Teresa's trinitarian orientation emerges strongly in the vision of the sacred humanity of Christ in the Father's bosom. This reveals the intimate home that animates the real life that Teresa sees and desires. Seeing herself present at the heart of the Trinity in this vision helped Teresa understand this God who wishes to dwell in the human being. This trinitarian inhabitation is also expressed in the link between earthly life and eternal life through the visions of men and women who have allowed themselves to be inhabited and transfigured during their lives by God. At the time of their death, this transformation becomes manifest through the ascension of their glorified bodies to the place that is heaven.

Second, at the level of the trinitarian configuration, while the figure of the Father appears in these visions on a single occasion—through reference to his bosom—the Son and the Spirit are depicted with more clarity. For example, the internal and external references of the vision of the Holy Spirit bring to light, through their resonances, acts that say something about the Spirit's action: suddenness of approach, movement of displacement, simple presence as a way of being, joy as a sign of that presence. As for Christ, he is remarkable for his visual presence and his word, but also in the configuration of his sacred humanity, which he makes present both in the Eucharist and in the glorified bodies. In this, the Spirit and the Son, while acting together, allow themselves to be grasped in their distinction.

Third, the bonds between the Spirit and salvation have been drawn tighter. The role of the Spirit in Teresa's mystical experiences and in orienting Teresa through them toward the salvation of others has become clearer.

Fourth, in the preceding chapter of this research, the place of Teresian desire and its progressive purification in the order of a purely apostolic orientation, toward the good of others, was noted, but here this purified desire has grown even greater, as if the decentering were accomplished. A kind of dispossession by emptiness has emerged, both in *deshacer* and in the particular dispossession of visions—seeing without seeing—and even of the narrative in itself, marked by an impossibility of adequately translating the experiences into words. The dispossession of the taste for life here below, understood in a Pauline light, reinforces the apostolic orientation of a life lived for the benefit of others. This fundamental orientation can also be discerned in the personal visions of glorified bodies of the dead that close the chapter; Teresa sees them saved, but she has nothing to do with the salvation of these people. However, she will be called upon to play a role for the salvation of other souls, like this Dominican over whom the dove of the Holy Spirit shone brightly.

Finally, Teresa's posture of proclamation is revealed by the very words of Christ and will extend not only to her way of living, but also, very concretely, to her writing. "See...[and]...tell" (*Life* 38:3). See in order to tell. And Teresa does this. Visions abound, large and small, striking and familiar. Then she speaks, she writes. She writes what she sees, to the best of her ability, with great care for precision. While Teresa is at the heart of this process—she is the one who sees and who writes—she sees and writes what another shows her in order that others—those who are "against" God (*Life* 38:3)—be able to see and turn to God to be saved. Teresa, in her actions, received from an *other,* from God, in order to transmit it by telling what she saw to others. Teresa's role is then situated at the intersection of Christ and the Spirit. Her posture makes appeal to sight and speech; she thereby touches on two modes by which Christ makes himself present to her. As for the Spirit, it is through her work of disinterested transmission of God to others that Teresa becomes, in the Spirit's image, the language God speaks.

Chapter 3

The Dynamics of the Spirit

Having analyzed two particular narratives from Teresa's *Life*, we now take a step back to take a broader look at what we have learned and to put it in relation to the rest of the Teresian corpus. The texts we will consider here were generally written after the *Life*, giving us an opportunity to recognize the further development of the question of salvation and the role of the Spirit within her thought, the main components of which have already been identified.

Because it is more theological in nature than the *Life* and because of its maturity (it was completed twelve years later), *The Interior Castle*, or *The Mansions*, is particularly important to our analysis. Although Teresa's intention for this book was to continue the narrative she had offered in the *Life*, she was unable as she wrote to refer to a copy of the latter, forcing her to retell much of the story.[1] Though she was presenting similar material about her personal experience, this time she inserted it into a new theological framework, with the images of the mansions and the spiritual betrothal and marriage.[2] And so while *The Interior Castle* bears a strong kinship with the *Life*, it includes a more theological interpretation of events that bears a greater potential for more general application.

Another set of texts that will be helpful for our consideration here is the *Spiritual Testimonies*, a collection of around sixty spiritual writings. Many are short, ranging from a few lines to a few pages, and they are sometimes addressed to an ecclesiastical authority, often a confessor (hence the title "Accounts of Conscience" that is sometimes given to them). These texts are usually about some gift or audition experienced by Teresa. In this way, *Spiritual Testimonies* is more similar to the *Life*, which Teresa at times referred to as "On the Mercies [or Favors] of God," than *The Interior Castle*. The generally lively and narrative character of its texts is also similar to the *Life*. A majority of the texts of the *Spiritual Testimonies* were written in the 1570s, thus covering the period that falls between her composition of the *Life* and *The Interior Castle*. The last known text of the *Testimonies* was written in May of 1581, a little more than a year before Teresa's death; we will treat this one separately, at the end of chapter 4, as Teresa's "last testament."

In addition to *The Interior Castle* and *Spiritual Testimonies*, we will call upon other Teresian writings when they are able to shed new light on various questions we consider below.

In this chapter and the next, we will seek to look again at the vital elements previously considered, this time in light of the whole of the Teresian corpus, to deepen our understanding of the role of the Spirit for salvation. In musical terms, one could say that it is not so much a question of finding a new melody but of adding enriching new harmonics to the melody already sketched and inserting it into a symphonic setting. To do this, rather than the synchronic approach used in our previous chapters, following the course of a given text, we will now engage a diachronic approach, considering texts from various times in order to construct a thematic framework. We will first consider the role of the Holy Spirit (chapter 3) and then the subject of trinitarian indwelling as the heart of salvation (chapter 4).

The role of the Spirit, even its "language,"[3] cannot be understood only with words, even those of Teresa herself; the Spirit is understood by its activity. It is this pneumatological activity that we will define in four stages.

First, we will consider the ways the Holy Spirit is represented in the Teresian corpus. Then we will analyze the nature of the soul's spirit in Teresian anthropology, which will in turn help us understand the correspondences between the (human) spirit and the (Holy) Spirit and how they shape Teresa's pneumatology.

In a second step, we will explore the most significant activity of the Spirit—first the dynamic of displacement and decentering, then the dynamic of *deshacer*, and finally that of inspiration. These three dynamics represent an overall momentum that takes the person outside of herself, opens up a space within her, and finally carries her forward.

In a third step, we propose a hermeneutic key that allows us to synthesize the dynamic of incarnation experienced and professed by Teresa under the movement of the Spirit. This key emerges from our study of Teresian texts and can be presented in the form of a triptych: *See—Incarnate—Tell.*

Finally, our reflection will take place in a resolutely trinitarian context in order to explore the relationships between the Son and the Spirit, between the Incarnation and glorification—both of Christ and of others—before concluding with an analysis of the role of the Spirit as "introducer" of the Trinity.

FROM SPIRIT TO SPIRIT: REPRESENTATIONS OF THE SPIRIT AND TERESIAN ANTHROPOLOGY

Teresian Representations of the Spirit

Writing one day to her brother Lorenzo, who questioned her about a mystical experience, Teresa quoted Saint Augustine saying that "the spirit of God passes without leaving a trace just as an arrow passes through the air without leaving one."[4] But while the Holy Spirit passes discreetly, Teresa is aware of the passage and its very real effects. The Spirit's presence is expressed in her writings with an abundance of representations and metaphors that attempt to identify and describe the Spirit's work. Jesús Castellano emphasizes that "in addition to the explicit mentions [of the Holy Spirit in the Teresian corpus], there is a vast field of biblical allusions, symbols, and operations through which a whole theology of the Holy Spirit is present; prayer, gifts, virtues, and many mystical graces have a marked pneumatological character."[5]

If Christ is the unique image of God,[6] Teresa's representations of the Holy Spirit seek to express something about One who is not an image. In this section, the range of ways Teresa represents the Spirit will be considered. These representations are grouped under four distinct types, without being absolutely watertight: the pictorial, the visual, the affective (relating to the emotions), and the liturgical. These representations often constitute the doorway to expressing something about the action of the Spirit in Teresa's writing. An analysis of these various representations makes it possible to identify certain features of Teresian discourse on the Spirit. We reserve for a later analysis, in this chapter, the more implicit forms of representation.

Pictorial Representations

By pictorial representations we mean images of the Spirit, in the sense that they literally depict the Spirit—for example, in a painting. There are two images to consider. The first tells us something about the way others understand Teresa; the second about the way Teresa herself understood the Spirit.

A first pictorial reference, which is a primary expression of the reception of Teresa and her teaching, is the dove. In the iconography that became common after Teresa's death, she was often depicted in the act of writing, with a dove hovering beside or over her.[7] This was intended to symbolize the inspired nature of her writing.[8] The specific connection between the dove and inspiration is not found in Teresa herself, although she relates visions of the Spirit in the form of a dove above an individual, including, on one occasion, herself (*Life* 38:10, 12). In this pictorial representation of the Spirit in the form of a dove over a writing, Teresa expresses the positive reception that was given to her work and the recognition by her contemporaries of its inspired character.[9] This symbol thus expresses a validation located not in the text itself, but in its subsequent reception.

Second, testimony has come down to us about a pictorial representation of the Spirit designed according to the instructions of Teresa herself. It seems that Teresa once ordered an image of the Holy Spirit to be produced that she could slip into her breviary.

She chose to have the Spirit represented as "a handsome young man, surrounded by flames or flaming volcanoes."[10] Leaving aside the visual elements of the flames in order to consider its central figure, it is notable that Teresa did not choose to have the Holy Spirit represented by a symbol (such as a dove) but by the image of a young man. For Christian iconography, the "young man" who personifies God par excellence is Jesus Christ, God made human. That is, rather than being intended as a partial representation, the Spirit is literally depicted in this image as a Divine Person of whom the Son is the only face.[11] The Son, the sole image of God, is the only proper image of the Spirit, although the latter can be represented, symbolically or otherwise, in various ways. Thus, we begin our consideration of the various representations Teresa used to express the Spirit by noting the privileged bond of the Spirit with the Son. As there is for Teresa no shortage of pneumatological representations (as we will see), her choice in this case reveals a strong trinitarian sensibility.

Visual Representations

The visual representations of the Spirit in Teresa's writing can be grouped into two main kinds: birds and fire.[12] Both express a dynamism of action.

The first figure used by Teresa to visually represent the Holy Spirit is the dove. The occurrences are not numerous, but they occur at strategic moments. The dove is depicted in action: it flies—she sometimes even describes the sound of the rustling of the wings—and positions itself in relation to a particular individual—emphasizing the role of this person for the salvation of others[13]—or to the Blessed Sacrament.[14] The figure of the dove represents the actantial role of the Spirit from a relational perspective. The dove is a common symbol of the Spirit, based on its appearance in the New Testament at the baptism of Jesus (Matt 3:16; Mark 1:10; Luke 3:22; John 1:32). In the gospel account, it is a visual sign[15] of a supernatural presence that accompanies a divine word—though it does not speak itself—and points in the direction of a specific human person, Jesus. The structure is analogous in the Teresian use, first because the dove points in the direction of a tangible reality—an individual or the Blessed Sacrament—and second because it is a figure accompanied by a message, not that it offers itself—it does not speak—but by means of a spoken word or an interior understanding.[16] Teresa, then, reflects the biblical approach of a relational representation of the Spirit as a marker of mediation between God and humanity.

The second major visual figure that Teresa used is fire, which is a traditional way of representing the Spirit.[17] Calling the Spirit "a mediator between the soul and God," Teresa writes that "He enkindles it [the soul] in a supreme fire."[18] In another place, in one of the *Soliloquies*, after having noted the great delight (*deleite*) and the great love (*amor*) in the relationship between the Father and the Son, Teresa emphasizes "the enkindling love" (*inflammacíon*) of the Holy Spirit.[19] The Holy Spirit is presented, then, as oriented toward others and toward an increase, in the manner of a catalyst. Taking up an image similar to fire, Teresa also makes appeal to light.[20] Light is transparent and allows one to see. She does not present light as the Spirit itself, but as a gift from the Spirit.[21] This image provides a good grasp of Teresa's understanding of the Spirit; light permits visibility—and is indeed essential for that—while not itself becoming what is seen. It also "illuminates," both in the spiritual[22] sense and in the sense of allowing understanding.[23] Along with the element of mediation between the human person and God already expressed in the symbol of the dove, this second image adds the dimension of growth and of the involvement of the subject on which divine action is exerted by the Spirit. These two visual representations therefore demonstrate an understanding that goes beyond the conventional and that contributes to revealing Teresa's own unique conception of the Spirit.

Affective Representations

Other discursive representations point to the effects in the human person of the Holy Spirit's presence, resulting not in visual images, but in emotional experience.

Connected to the avian imagery mentioned above, but this time without specific visual support, we find the image of the "flight of the spirit"[24] (*vuelo de espíritu*), which refers to a mystical experience like rapture. This image places less emphasis on the Spirit as an agent than on the person who is the object of the Spirit's action. This rapture, sometimes also called ecstasy, is a mystical phenomenon of moving out of one's own body in such a way that the human faculties, led by God, are as if suspended while the person simply enjoys an object.[25] "Flight of the spirit" is more a discursive image than a visual one. The phrase "of the spirit" refers to the spirit of the human person who experiences the flight, but it also subtly suggests the cause of the experience, the Holy Spirit. We will return to this later. The image of flight, which occupies us here, attempts to capture the experience of rapture into a language image. Like the movement of a bird, aerial and free, the Spirit in its flight is detached from any spatial or temporal mooring. That being said, the metaphorical use is limited to the word *flight* alone, so that the point of this representation relates more to the expression of a felt effect—leaving oneself, suspension—than to the actual deployment of the metaphor. This image of flight, however, supports the visual representations of the Spirit as a dove.

A second set of affective representations of the Spirit in Teresian teaching is the feelings of joy (*gozo*) and enjoyment (*gozar*) following the visitation of the human person by the Holy Spirit. Called a "fruit of the Spirit" by Saint Paul (Gal 5:22), joy is for Teresa the sign par excellence of the presence, and even of the indwelling, of God, and especially of the Holy Spirit. We have previously noted this positive correlation between joy and the Holy Spirit. This does not imply an exclusive correlation of this gift with the Spirit—Miguel Ángel Díez notes its application to each of the Persons of the Trinity[26]—but rather a privileged link that says something about the One who is its bearer. This joy, sometimes exuberant, is marked above all by the fact that it is akin to a state rather than a feeling, that indicates a presence. Joy is distinguished from peace (although it is closely related) in that the latter will be more associated with the person of Christ. Nor does it have the shining character of glory, which both dazzles and is the sign of God par excellence. Joy, unlike glory, is not essentially a visual representation, but is properly affective, although it can be seen indirectly in the one who experiences it. The affective representations of the Spirit, as the effects of its action, express an action that comes to join the human person in the concreteness of life in a way that is both powerful and lasting.

Liturgical and Prayerful Representations

Another way the Spirit is present discursively in Teresa's writing is in liturgical occurrences. While the Holy Spirit is not the Divine Person who most often appears liturgically, the Spirit does emerge in this way at key moments in the Teresian journey. This liturgical presence of the Spirit is more than anecdotal, marking in passing a particular day or season; when Teresa relates various events linked to such a feast or a prayer, she asserts a causal link between the liturgical occasion and a spiritual event. In this way, the liturgical representation of the Spirit is not trivial; it indicates an anchoring and a concrete effect of the Spirit in the believer's life. Thus, one of the richest visions on the Holy Spirit took place on the vigil of Pentecost[27] (or as Teresa sometimes called it, *Pascua del Espíritu Santo,* "the Holy Spirit's Easter"[28]). Then, on that same liturgical feast a few years later, Teresa offered the Holy Spirit a special vow of obedience to her confessor to commemorate the favor formerly granted.[29] In this sense, the liturgical element is not a mere context for a story she happens to be telling; rather, it bursts into Teresa's existence, both in welcoming the action of the Spirit and in confidence in the pneumatological inspiration of her confessor. The liturgical representation of the Spirit is thus correlated to its action.

To this significant presence of the liturgical feasts is added a simply prayerful presence. Teresa invokes the Holy Spirit frequently, especially in her letters. She also prays to the Spirit; notably, it is her praying of the *Veni Creator* hymn (upon the suggestion of a Jesuit spiritual director, Father Juan de Prádanos) that brings about Teresa's first experience of rapture (*arrebatamiento*).[30] An existential effect so suddenly brought about by prayer to the Holy Spirit thus confirms that representation of the Spirit that the prayer itself makes. The work of the Spirit that the very words of the traditional hymn asks for was quickly experienced by Teresa in a concrete and incarnate way.

Ultimately, the liturgical and prayerful representations of the Spirit indicate the Spirit's proximity and dynamism.

Conclusion

This brief cartography of the representations of the Holy Spirit in the Teresian corpus offers a glimpse of their many occurrences in her writing. The variety of figures used and the significant role they play demonstrate a constant awareness of the Spirit, even if the references are not overabundant.

Many of these images are of biblical origin and may seem fairly conventional. Even by not identifying the Spirit with a single image, Teresa demonstrated her proximity to biblical sources. While taking up these conventional representations, Teresa at the same time makes use of them in her writing in original ways.

The coherence of all of these pneumatological representations can be recognized in particular by the dynamic character that emerges from it: the Spirit is depicted in relationship, as a mediator, acting at the heart of human life. Taken together, what emerges is a sense of strong awareness of the breath of the Spirit's action. While the originality of the Teresian approach is not immediately obvious to the casual reader, a closer look at the variances, the peculiarities, and their intersections allow us to perceive that the representations that one might have thought to be "static" betray an unexpected dynamism.

The Soul's Spirit in Teresian Anthropology

Teresa's anthropological terminology is not absolutely consistent. Teresa uses the concepts of soul and spirit quite liberally. Sometimes she uses the two words in analogous senses; at other times, she clearly distinguishes the spirit (*espíritu*) as a component of soul (*alma*) with its own function.[31]

In Teresa's writings, the spirit is most often understood as a place in the soul. Teresa spoke of the spirit as the "superior part" of the soul,[32] above the usual functions of the soul, such as understanding, memory, will, and imagination. The (indirect) influence of Rhine-Flemish mysticism on Teresian anthropology is notable, in particular for the way it assigns to the spirit, among the various components of the soul, the higher place, beyond the rational faculties.[33] The spirit is a place in the soul, not subject in the same way to the influence of the senses, even of other faculties of the soul. It is the *sanctum sanctorum* where the encounter with God happens. The person encounters God, communicates with God, and unites with God more easily there.[34]

For Teresa, the spirit is the leading edge of the soul in the human person, while the soul is at times in movement outside of itself, echoing the movement of "going out" that Teresa identifies as a characteristic of the action of the Holy Spirit. Teresa sometimes calls this rapture (*arrobamiento*) a "flight of the spirit,"[35] signifying thereby its capacity to be extracted in some way beyond its own boundaries.[36]

By taking as an example Augustine's effort to identify an *analogon* of the Trinity in the human person,[37] one could say that for Teresian anthropology the spirit in the soul is an *analogon* of the Holy Spirit in the Trinity. The point of this analogy rests on the similarities noted between the spirit in the soul and the Holy Spirit in Teresian thought: the capacity for movement, the plurality of images that express it, and an openness in activity that leaves room for novelty.

Beyond the analogy between the spirit in the soul and the Holy Spirit in the Trinity, Teresa sees a real relationship between the spirit and the Spirit. This proximity becomes clear in moments where her prose reflects a recognition that they are intertwined.[38] It is often through their contact that a union can take place between the human being and God. Indeed, for Teresa the spirit and the Spirit work together to advance the human person toward a close union with God: "One can say no more—insofar as can be understood—than that the soul, I mean the spirit [*el alma, digo el espíritu de esta alma*], is made one with God. For since His Majesty is also spirit, He has wished to show his love for us...."[39]

The place of this mysterious union is the center of the soul, the dwelling that God enters without going through the door.[40] But even more, this union of the soul, which has become "pure spirit"[41] (*puro espíritu*), with God is realized, according to Teresa, through the uncreated Spirit; she writes of the soul's "heavenly union with the uncreated Spirit."[42] The meeting of the spirit and the Spirit thus constitutes the place of intimate contact, even of union, between the human being and God.

The analogy between the highest part of the soul and the Spirit is also found in the fifth mansions of *The Interior Castle,* expressed as a metaphor, when Teresa uses the image of a butterfly to represent the soul.[43] This butterfly is intended to fly, as the spirit and the Holy Spirit do metaphorically. If initially the analogy focuses on the common element of flight, it will be reinforced when Teresa calls the butterfly a *palomica*,[44] a possible variant of "little butterfly," but which can also mean "little dove." Between Spirit being a dove and the soul being a little dove, the analogy is obvious. With this avian metaphor, Teresa reinforces the correspondence already mentioned above between the spirit and the Spirit and also reinforces its place in her teaching by reiterating it metaphorically.

The spirit in the soul is thus presented as this place that allows the Spirit of God to reach the heart of the person in a concomitant movement where the person reaches a place clear of herself and engaged in God. Having noted the place of this meeting, it remains to identify the dynamism at work in it, both on the side of the Spirit and of the human person. This will be the subject of the next two sections of this chapter.

THE MOVEMENTS OF THE SPIRIT

In Teresa's writings, the Spirit is understood in the mode of action and movement. Among all her works, those which suggest this sense of movement most strikingly are her letters.[45] Here the Spirit's role is prominent and also surprising. Indeed, Teresa's letters typically include an incipit with the name of Jesus, followed very often by a wish for the presence of the Holy Spirit to the person to whom she writes.[46] One could dismiss this as an insignificant literary convention.[47] But this intentional invocation of the Holy Spirit at the beginning of so many of her letters, which represent interpersonal encounters, the sharing of daily concerns, and the exchange of news about mutual friends, associates, and loved ones, introduces at the center of these quotidian interpersonal relations the active figure of the Spirit alongside that of Christ, the face of God. In the context of the fragility of human relationships, Teresa's appeal to the presence of the Spirit can be seen as a call for the Spirit to guide the flow of these relationships by touching minds and hearts. By this marked insistence on the presence of the Spirit in daily life, Teresa gives the Spirit a central role there. Secundino Castro sees the same thing in this opening appeal to the Spirit: "[It is] a paschal greeting; like Christ, she [Teresa] wishes to communicate the Spirit. This fact, in our judgment, is very significant, since it indicates that in this gift, she sees concentrated all the goods that one can desire for her relatives and friends."[48]

Indeed, with this common epistolary greeting, Teresa adopts the posture of the risen Christ, both inhabited by the Spirit and giver of the Spirit.

The representations of the Spirit in Teresa's writings suggest the importance of movement in characterizing the Spirit's work. The "language of the Holy Spirit," which is more than words, suggests that the Spirit acts discreetly, unlike the more visible character of God's action through the person of the Son.

The Spirit's vitality and salvific activity in the world can be systematized into a pneumatological dynamic of three moments. This structure, drawn from a close analysis of the Teresian texts, is what we will develop in the following pages. These "moments" of the Spirit's movement are presented here in a sequence that may be understood chronologically, but not solely or strictly so, since the sequence in which we describe them is primarily logical and systematic. First, the Spirit prompts a movement of *displacement,* a movement of decentering, marked by leaving oneself. Second, and more striking, the Holy Spirit prompts a movement of—to adopt Teresa's effective Spanish verb—*deshacer,* an unmaking of the self that opens a space where God can move and create something new. Third is a movement of *inspiration,* in which the Spirit imparts a word oriented toward action. This set makes up the triptych of fundamental movements explicitly associated with the Holy Spirit. This does not exclude, of course, that the Holy Spirit acts in a multitude of ways. But we find here a clear range of the Spirit's action, as well as a pneumatological and salvific dynamic.

A Movement of Displacement and Decentering

Teresa's spiritual life, in its most mature phase, was strongly marked by mystical phenomena.[49] Several types of these experiences involve "leaving the self" in some way: the nouns "rapture," "suspension," "transport" (*arrobamientos, suspensión, arrebatamiento*), "flight of the spirit" (*vuelo de espíritu*), "impulse" (*ímpetus*), or the verbs "to be carried out of oneself" (*sacarse*[50]) or "to lose oneself" (*perderse*). It was on the threshold of entering a "new life"[51] that Teresa experienced these phenomena for the first time (*Life* 24:5). The context of these favors is important, since it reveals their author, namely, the Holy Spirit; they "raised Teresa's awareness of the mystery and action of the Spirit and led her to understand her presence in the Trinity."[52]

Beginning this new life with God, Teresa still lacked some foundation in virtue. The favors she recounts were so exceptional that some feared they actually came from the devil.[53] A Jesuit priest encouraged her, however, assuring her that what she experienced was clearly "from God's Spirit."[54] Another priest, Father Juan de Prádanos, set Teresa on the road to "greater perfection" (*Life* 24:5). To help her discern the possible abandonment of disordered friendships, he advised her to consider this matter in prayer and to pray the *Veni Creator Spiritus*, asking the Lord to show her the best way forward. Teresa described this time of prayer like this:

> One day, having spent a long time in prayer and begging the Lord to help me please Him in all things, I began the hymn [*Veni Creator Spiritus*]; while saying it, a rapture came upon me so suddenly that it almost carried me out of myself. It was something I could not doubt, because it was very obvious. It was the first time the Lord granted me this favor of rapture. I heard these words: "No longer do I want you to converse with men but with angels." This experience terrified me because the movement of the soul was powerful and these words were spoken to me deep within the spirit; so it frightened me—although on the other hand I felt great consolation when the fear that, I think, was caused by the novelty of the experience left me. (*Life* 24:5)

This account is fascinating. Teresa was at prayer, in a posture of supplication. Her supplication was redoubled by the very words of the hymn that she reads: "Come, Creator Spirit...." These words, taken from a prayer of the church, are addressed to God by her invocation.

It is at this very moment that she was praying that a response occurred in three stages. The first was an interior event—rapture, the leaving of herself. Teresa was thus pulled out of herself, her vocal supplication being answered by an internal movement. In a second step, Teresa heard; she received words. She writes very clearly that she "heard these words"—not simply heard something, but "these words," which she reports confidently and with precision. And the message she heard itself concerned words, the exchange of words, conversation. Her words were no longer to be exchanged with people, but with angels. Teresa, we can say, heard a word telling her to speak differently. This message provided the answer to the question that she had sought in prayer, but the answer was characterized by excess—Teresa received (or heard) more than she could have expected. Finally, these "spoken words" were accompanied by affective responses: confusion, fear, an experience of power and depth, but above all a great consolation that remained. The word came full circle—words addressed by Teresa to the Holy Spirit, at the request of her confessor; words offered and answered by spoken words that call for a new way of communicating; a word that initially disturbs and troubles before leaving in the flesh a great consolation as an indelible sign of its passage.

Teresa's account leaves no room for doubt about the identity of the one who brought about this rapture. She prayed to the Holy Spirit with a Pentecost hymn, and it was at the very moment that she prayed that she experienced leaving her own body. It is moreover in the divine place in her par excellence, "deep within the spirit" (*espíritu*), that the word of God is addressed to her and responds to her questioning of the moment. A first experience of this sort—it was her first rapture—suggests strongly an eminently pneumatological reading of the most extraordinary mystical experiences, even when at the heart of them God is revealed as Word—as it is in this audition—or as face. The Spirit moves Teresa. The Spirit leads her to God.

In a literary vein, one can recognize the dynamic of movement that we are attributing here to the Holy Spirit in the invocations that Teresa addresses to the Spirit throughout *The Interior*

Castle. At no time does Teresa say specifically that it is the Spirit who advances the soul from one mansion to another; on the contrary, she even indicates that it is "the Lord of the castle" (*Señor del castillo*) who does this.[55] But it is the Spirit whom she invokes at important junctions of this path, when passing from one mansion to another and especially when she arrives at the higher mansions.[56] A complementarity is established in this sense with the figure of Christ. Thus, at one point in *The Interior Castle,* Teresa invokes the Spirit's help after saying that she would speak of the manner in which the Lord takes care of his betrothed ones;[57] in other words, in order to speak well of Christ, she calls upon the Spirit for help. More broadly, the literary practice of appealing to the Holy Spirit at key turning points suggests, by a mirror effect between writing and life, that the Spirit is at work in the passages that the soul experiences through the mansions.[58]

In *The Interior Castle,* this experience of displacement in the journey from mansion to mansion is accompanied by an experience of decentering.[59] The latter culminates in the metaphor of a sponge, absorbing and becoming saturated with water as the soul does with God.[60] The movement of decentering may eventually lead to a form of disappropriation, even kenosis, as we will see below.

Decentering can also be experienced as orientation toward God—sometimes even specifically toward the Holy Spirit—through human mediators. Teresa relates an episode when, wishing to thank the Holy Spirit for a favor (*merced*) that occurred on the vigil of Pentecost, she debated and then decided to make a vow not to hide anything from her confessor and to do whatever he tells her to do.[61] The confessor in question was the young Carmelite priest Jerónimo Gracían, then apostolic visitor and commissioner. Teresa could see nothing else that she could do in gratitude to the Spirit beyond what she was already doing, other than some service (*servicio*) she might carry out. The decentering that took place then consisted in going through the mediation of another (her confessor) to receive the fruits of divine light, which she believed would follow. Surrender to God was found in a reciprocal relationship of trust in another person. In doing so, even the Spirit was decentered, since the Spirit's action must happen through the mediation of another person.

This Teresian decentering was also expressed on an existential level by Teresa's multiple protestations of nonpower and nonknowledge:[62] she was a simpleton, she was only a woman, she was unimpressive (*ruin*[63]). These are hardly rhetorical conventions of her prose,[64] although one cannot exclude the reality of a certain standard rhetoric in such protestations. However, all of this was ignored by the competent authorities, who asked her to recount the favors she received from the Lord so that they could in turn help others,[65] despite Teresa's personal discomfort in doing so. The favors given by God were therefore shared with others, against her will, at the request of a third party. They were no longer completely her own. God who visited and inspired her, as witnessed by religious authorities, worked through her to touch others without her really being in possession of this movement—neither its origin nor its development, its destination nor its fruits. This decentering, a certain form of leaving of oneself, thus leads to a recentering on God.

This movement of decentering did not just affect Teresa as an object; it led her to embrace the entire way of being proper to the Spirit, who exists as a continual decentering in the relationship that the Spirit establishes eternally in the Trinity between the Father and Son, and in time between God and humanity. This decentering already announces the radical diminishment that is characteristic of the movement of *deshacer*.

A Movement of *Deshacer*

The movement of *deshacer*[66] opens up the space for something new to happen.[67] Teresa sometimes uses this term in the sense of destruction, like the threat that hung over the very young monastery of Saint Joseph.[68] More often, it is a sort of unwinding, a decluttering of oneself, where everything that fills it seems to melt. This dimension also appeared early in the context of an audition of the Lord that invited Teresa to this *deshacer* so that he could enter into her.[69] A kind of kenosis, or annihilation, however partial, is then experienced. This leads to a lack, a simplicity that opens up a welcome. We even come to a dynamic of dispossession, of disappropriation of the self. A space must be created to transform, to live in a new way.

This *deshacer* is at work in the economy of salvation. It is the kenosis of the Son of God (e.g., Phil 2:5–11). It is the openness of Mary in the annunciation. It is the poverty of Bethlehem and Nazareth. It is the Son's obedience to the Father's will on the cross. It is also, in a Teresian register, the way in which God becomes small in order to be accessible to the human being, for example, through gradual visions or through the Eucharist, where the greatness of God is manifest in a discreet form.[70]

In the Trinity, the figure of *deshacer* is the Spirit, who acts behind the face of Christ. In Teresa, through the Spirit, one perceives this effacement of her own face in *deshacer*, an effacement that allows her to take on a likeness to Christ, while at the same time assimilating Teresa to the Spirit's way of being. *Conformed to Christ, she is configured to the Spirit.*

In *The Interior Castle*, the allegory of the silkworm and the butterfly,[71] which culminates in the death of the butterfly, is a good illustration of this movement. Before arriving at the latter, from the first mansions, Teresa insists on the importance of persevering in "this nakedness and detachment [*esta desnudez y dejamiento de todo*]"[72] that keeps our eyes focused on the true love of God. Still further, she talks about the importance of making oneself humble and detached (*se humillare y desasiere*).[73] Having become a butterfly, the soul has not reached an apotheosis. "It sees within itself a desire to praise the Lord; it would want to dissolve and die a thousand deaths for Him."[74] The butterfly dies so that Christ may live in it.[75] The "first effect" of this death of the butterfly—the ultimate form of *deshacer*—is forgetfulness of self (*olvido de sí*), "for truly the soul, seemingly, no longer is....Everything is such that this soul doesn't know or recall that there will be heaven or life or honor for it, because it employs all it has in procuring the honor of God."[76]

The movement of *deshacer* thus brings about a subsumption of one's place by the annihilation of what encumbered it. Teresa, entirely configured to God, becomes other, in the conformation of her will to God's, whose will is salvation,[77] even choosing the latter beyond the enjoyment of God.[78] Like Saint Paul, this *deshacer* culminates in the very loss of the desire to die to see God, in the hope of being able to serve him here below.[79]

In a striking—and famous—example, the movement of *deshacer* can be recognized at the heart of the grace of transverberation.[80]

Although the Spirit is not explicitly mentioned as its principal agent, many specialists believe that by going through John of the Cross, one can consider that "there is no doubt that it is a grace very particular to the three Persons of the Holy Trinity attributed to the Holy Spirit, who is the *sweet burning* and the *pleasant wound*."[81] Castellano considers it to be an "extraordinary infusion of love, a *baptism of fire in the Holy Spirit*."[82] An angel with a flaming (*encendido*) face approaches Teresa holding a large golden dart with a tip of fire. He plunges it several times into her heart, and deeper, so that when he pulls it out, she feels as though her entrails are pulled out with it. She is left ablaze (*abrasada*) with love for God.[83]

Such a fire, such a burning, such a love effectively points in the direction of the Spirit. This favor brings to light the divine initiative of this movement and the gift. On a symbolic level, it also reveals that the withdrawal that is part of the *deshacer* is not an annihilation or a simple loss; the entrails that seem to leave Teresa in the piercing give way, in the midst of their absence, to an unimaginable love offered by God. Such a loss has its gain.

A foray into semiotic theory offers interesting insights here, since it focuses on the concept of *doing* in the context of the relationship between the subject of being, a receiver (in this case, Teresa, or more broadly the believer) and a sender (here, God or the Spirit).[84] *Deshacer* happens on the same level of "doing" (*hacer* in Spanish) through a deconstruction, an undoing, that leads to a new doing, through a moment of inspiration, which we will deal with shortly. In the narrative schema of semiotic analysis, three modalities are in play: the power-to-do, the will-to-do, and knowing-how-to-do. In the moment of *deshacer*, Teresa recognizes her non-power-to-do, but also her non-knowing-how-to-do, and even her non-willing-to-do (because of her internal resistances). These Teresian nonmodalities constitute the soil in which the modalities (power-to-do, will-to-do, and knowing-how-to-do) can be planted, and which will be accepted as gifts. In doing so, the Teresian "doing" of *deshacer* serves to loosen, to clear away, to excavate a space for the reception of the gift made by the sender, both as modalities and as the narrative program—on the one hand, the creation of the monastery of Saint Joseph, but on the other, as an open finality, the Trinitarian indwelling.

A Movement of Inspiration

The Spirit's role as introducer, guarantor, and guide in *The Interior Castle,* as well as the Spirit's emblematic presence in the opening lines of so many of Teresa's letters, have already been noted. A third important movement, illustrated first in a literary way, is that of inspiration. It is the movement that most directly drives action, a creative movement.

In the prologue to the *Meditations on the Song of Songs,* Teresa presents herself as a writer inspired by the Holy Spirit:

> If this writing is such that you may see it, accept this poor little gift from one who desires for you as well as for herself all the gifts of the Holy Spirit, in whose name I begin. If I succeed in saying something worthwhile, the success will not be from me.[85]

Teresa recognizes and welcomes this work of the Spirit who guides her, by his gifts, but who is also both the guarantor and the source of any success of the work. She therefore recognizes herself to be dependent on this inspiration that comes to her from God. In this literary context, the assignment of this role to the Spirit is unequivocal.

One can therefore legitimately look for this same movement in other places and recognize it as a sign of the Spirit there as well. This is how this movement of inspiration, even of conversion—when the subject initially is resistant to this divine inspiration—was noted at work in the story of the foundation of the monastery of Saint Joseph, both as an initiating impulse and also as a continuing impulse.[86] This inspiration, which also passes through others, underlines the collective dimension of God's action and especially of God's work of salvation. The inspiration of others by the Spirit was essential to the success of Teresa's project.

Teresa rarely goes as far as to say clearly that "the Holy Spirit was speaking through" someone,[87] but that is what she did when speaking of Father Diego de Cetina, a twenty-three-year-old Jesuit whom she consulted to find out whether the extraordinary graces that were given to her came from God. She wrote, "As to someone who well knew this language, he [Cetina] explained to me what I was experiencing and greatly encouraged me. He said it was very recognizably from God's Spirit, but that it was necessary to return again to prayer."[88]

Teresa notes that she emerged from this encounter transformed.[89] She therefore recognizes in this man the word of the Holy Spirit because he knew how to understand the Spirit's language that is revealed through the supernatural favors of which Teresa was not necessarily worthy. The comments made by Cetina to Teresa, inspired by the Spirit, allowed her to move forward confidently in her encounter with God.[90]

Along with the movement of displacement, which orients one's attention outside of oneself, and that of *deshacer*, which proceeds by undoing, the movement of inspiration is a positive movement that is oriented from the outset *ad extra*, by pushing to action—or to writing—and guaranteeing its fruitfulness. Subsequent analyses will extend and refine the positive movement exemplified by inspiration. As for the important movement of incarnation discerned in chapters 32 to 36 of the *Life*—where the Holy Spirit plays a fundamental role—it will be treated in the section that follows.

AN OPEN, SALVIFIC, AND APOSTOLIC DYNAMIC OF INCARNATION

In the previous chapter, we noted the proclamatory nature of Teresa's mission, starting from the Lord's words: "See, daughter, what those who are against me lose; don't neglect to tell them."[91] We see here a connection between "seeing" (which can be compared to hearing) and "telling." Between the two, what is seen, for the purpose of being told, is what is lost by those who oppose God. What is lost, the existence of which is not suspected by some, and what is seen by Teresa are "the things of heaven";[92] these "things" are not objects to be possessed by Teresa, but rather, they mark out the horizon of the space of a place to be inhabited. What emerges, then, is a progression from seeing to telling that happens by way of the inhabitation of incarnation. The proclamatory nature becomes an existential one because it provides a hermeneutic key that allows us to consider from another angle the pneumatological movement of salvation in Teresa's thought. This key can be summarized in a triple movement of *seeing—incarnating—telling*. We can visualize it as such:

This is an anthropological movement—in the sense that it is experienced in the human being—that corresponds with the movement of the Spirit we have just considered above. This correspondence is not imposed artificially; it can be recognized in the natures of each of the two movements independent of one another. A gap persists between them, which we do not want to try to bridge arbitrarily.

It is, however, very much the same momentum that we have seen in the movement systematized above, from the perspective of the Spirit acting in the human person under the triple mode of *displacement—deshacer—inspiration.* Now we consider this from the perspective of the human being who welcomes the action of the Spirit, which is intrinsically salvific action. Between these two movements a correspondence emerges that is not artificially imposed. Fundamentally, we find an anthropological process that is in tune with the action of God in the Spirit.

This anthropological process is also pneumatological because the Spirit guides it. If this is not immediately obvious, another consideration of the narrative of the Incarnation in the Gospel of Luke will make it clear. We have already noted, in chapter 1, that Teresa understands the foundation of the monastery of Saint Joseph within the biblical structure of the annunciation, Incarnation, and visitation. Although she does not explicitly express a self-identification with the pregnant Mary in her *Life,* she does in the *Meditations on the Song of Songs.* Here the work of Incarnation acts as a referent to express the union between God and the soul, expressed in the image of bride and groom.[93] As in Luke's account, the role of the Holy Spirit is clearly expressed.[94] Indeed, just before speaking of the Spirit's role as mediator between the soul and God,[95] in order to express the riches received from the Holy Spirit by those who practice prayer,[96] Teresa quotes part of the verse from the story of the Incarnation when the angel tells Mary, "The power of the Most High will overshadow you" (Luke 1:35).[97] This tells us that an assimilation to the figure of Mary welcoming the God who is incarnated in her by the work of the Holy Spirit is familiar in the Teresian universe, but even more, that Teresa herself traces the link between the historical experience of the Incarnation and the welcoming of God in the human soul.

The existential posture inspired by an audition from the Lord can easily be recognized in condensed form in Luke's narrative. First, Mary is addressed by the angel and hears his words (Luke 1:28–29).[98] Then, she accepts what is given to her from God and consents to God's dwelling and taking flesh in her (Luke 1:38); it is the inauguration of a movement of incarnation. Finally, when she meets Elizabeth, Mary's words burst forth, putting what has happened in the context of the history of salvation and also looking to the future in thanksgiving (Luke 1:46–55). *Mary "sees," consents to the incarnation of God, and speaks/tells,* unfolding the very tripartite movement we are considering.

Seen from Teresa's point of view, the "see—incarnate—tell" movement reaches its endpoint: seeing God, letting God become incarnate within her, and speaking of God to others, so that others may in turn see God, let God become incarnate in them, and speak of God. From God's point of view, in regard to Teresa, the point is to be seen, to dwell within, and to be told of. Finally, we can also duplicate the movement centered on Teresa by shifting it to others, who would see God (directly or through God's action in Teresa), let God become incarnate in them, and speak of God to others. In this sense, the place of "others" opens up infinitely toward other people.

A basic movement is sketched out here that unfolds as "seeing—incarnating—telling," starting from God, passing through Teresa, and going beyond to others. There are three personal "places" crossed by this movement: God, Teresa (self), other people (others).

Three actions are at work here: vision, incarnation, and speech. If Teresa participates in and acts in these three actions—

she acts, even if in the sense that she lets it be done—it is as neither the instigator nor the master. This movement is initiated outside herself, both on a human and supernatural level. On the other hand, the visible matrix of the movement is found in God himself. In fact, even in God, through the Son, we find seeing, incarnation, and speech, since the Son is the (incarnate) face and Word of God. The very impulse that leads to the duplication of this pattern in Teresa and in others, is the Holy Spirit, as highlighted by the Lukan narrative where we see it play out. Considered from the perspective of the Holy Spirit, the movement therefore is a making-to-see, making-incarnate, and making-to-say, of which the Spirit is the agent without being the face.

The discreet—one might say invisible—action of the Holy Spirit is consonant with the character proper to the Spirit's presence in the Trinity itself, according to Teresa's thought. Thus, in the vision of the most sacred humanity within the Father,[99] the Spirit is not made visible, yet is making it visible and is thereby made eminently present. Beyond the visibility of the Son, the action of the Spirit should not be overlooked.

Considering the centrality of this unfolding of a movement in seeing, incarnating, and telling for a reading at human level of the experience of the action of the Holy Spirit in the work of salvation, we will now explore each moment of this triple movement in the light of the Teresian corpus and echoing the triple movement of the Spirit analyzed above.

Seeing

The first element of the movement under study is "seeing," which sometimes takes the related form of "hearing."[100] In the Teresian spiritual dynamic leading to the mystical marriage, even before the betrothal (*desposorio*),[101] the first moment—modeled on the customs of the time—was that of "meeting together" (*venir a vistas*),[102] visiting in person, allowing the future spouses to get to know each other. Sight, more broadly than mystical vision specifically, constitutes this point of entry into the relationship. But for Teresa, this gaze, as a *habitus,* was experienced primarily in the paradigmatic experience of the mystical vision. This was for her always an interior experience; she saw "with the eyes of the soul," an "intellectual" vision or an "imaginative" vision. "Exterior" visions were never part of her experience.[103]

Vision implies that something is seen. In Teresa's experience, what was seen was often in the order of a place, a location, such as heaven or hell. But even as a space, the place is defined by its habitation. Teresa experienced hell as a place she had been saved from, marking her nonhabitation. In heaven, on the other hand, she saw her father and mother, drawing the space of a household.

However, the most frequent object of Teresa's visions was Christ in his sacred humanity.[104] In the sequence of chapter 38 of her *Life*, we read of visions of the Son alone, speaking to her; the Lord in majesty, seen in the host; and finally the Son in the bosom of the Father. He is the focus of Teresa's experience of visions. The most elevated vision reported by Teresa in this chapter is that of the Trinity, which is essentially a vision of relationship. In it, the Holy Spirit is not visible, and the Father is only visible through the Son. But within this framework, beyond the figure of Christ—though without leaving him behind[105]—it is an *indwelling* that she witnesses, an indwelling to which she is present, without being at the center of this stage.

Christ is also the face of the Word. The words Teresa hears in her auditions are usually spoken by Christ. But there are also instances when she experiences the Father and the Spirit speaking.[106] Thus Teresa mentions in the sixth mansions that "the very spirit that speaks puts a stop to all other thoughts and makes the soul attend to what is said."[107] But the language the Spirit speaks is without words.

Sight is the way to salvation. On the human level, nonsalvation is presented as a refusal to see or hear. Indeed, hardened sinners are those who do not see, who refuse to see the salvation offered, and who do not hear, whose eyes are obscured or obstructed with a blindfold or mud.[108] This is the state of the soul in the first mansions: it is "blind and deaf."[109] Teresa had even complained to the Lord about her inability to be of any help to people who were blind in this way[110]; their sight obstructed, they were cut off from a possible saving relationship with God that begins with seeing.[111] The story of Teresa's own personal conversion began when she was already religious, although lukewarm, in 1554, in response to the sight of a statue of the scourged Christ.[112] This sight shook her interiorly. It is by receptivity to an initial divine call—heard or seen—that begins a process of drawing closer to the Lord. Thus, Teresa writes of the Lord making his voice heard even by those who do not hear well.[113] The pedagogy of this listening moves the person from an indistinct feeling,[114] short of speech, to a clear and distinct hearing of the voice of the Spouse.[115] In *The Interior Castle*, this progressive process of attention and reception of God by sight and hearing culminates in a vision that Teresa places under the aegis of Saint Paul by her reference to the scales that finally fall from the eyes.[116] The object of this important vision is not trivial: it is about the Trinity revealing itself to the soul:

> When the soul is brought into that dwelling place, the Most Blessed Trinity, all three Persons, through an intellectual vision, is revealed to it through a certain representation of the truth. First there comes an enkindling in the spirit in the manner of a cloud of magnificent splendor; and these Persons are distinct, and through an admirable knowledge the soul understands as a most profound truth that all three Persons are one substance and one power and one knowledge and one God alone. It knows in such a way that what we hold by faith, it understands, we can say, through sight—although the sight is not with the bodily eyes nor with the eyes of the soul, because we are not dealing with an imaginative vision. Here all three Persons communicate themselves to it, so to speak, and explain those words of the Lord in the Gospel: that He and the Father and the Holy Spirit will come to dwell with the soul that loves Him and keeps His commandments.[117]

The accomplishment of "seeing" is thus lived, according to Teresa, in an intimate grasp of a knowledge of the triune God, in the relationship that the soul experiences with each of the persons of the Trinity, and finally in the trinitarian indwelling in the soul. The entirely interior way in which this vision is realized underlines its character of presence already achieved in itself. A world separates this vision from that of Christ with wrathful eyes[118] that initially set Teresa on her journey, a vision that marked the distance, both by its mode and its object.

In this movement of "seeing," although the emphasis is on the one who sees, the one who makes himself seen is active. God speaks himself, through the Spirit, in order to be shared. Full reception of the vision will occur when what is seen becomes fully incarnate in the one who sees and then shares it.

Incarnating/Inhabiting

"Becoming incarnate," or "inhabiting," is the second and central part of the movement under study. What is seen is not intended only to be contemplated; it is called to take flesh at the very heart of the one who sees. Seeing brings the one who sees in contact with what is seen and is intended finally to call the former into conformity with the latter—to make incarnate what she has seen.

This movement of incarnation takes place at the intersection of various "places"—from the Trinity to the Incarnation in Jesus Christ, from the plan of God for his incarnation in Teresa herself, then in the foundation of the monastery of Saint Joseph and beyond, in others or in other monasteries. After God and Teresa, other places, open to infinity, constitute this "other" toward which Teresa will speak and act.[119]

The movement of incarnation, which allows the reception of what comes from another—from God—gathers the fruits of the movement of *deshacer* analyzed earlier. This movement opens a space to transform, to inhabit in a new way. This translates into radical availability. The metaphor of the sponge, used by Teresa in this regard, is a good illustration of this acceptance of God in the soul that is transformed.[120] This image suggests the nonreification of what is at the heart of the movement here under study; it is not so much an "object" that is sought or attained, but a space where incarnation can occur.

Indeed, the new contours of the place of incarnation are those of a home, a household, a space fundamentally marked by relationship. This is true as much for Teresa herself and for the Trinity, as it is for heaven, the inhabited place and eschatological horizon of salvation—unlike hell, which is presented as a non-space, a suffocating and impersonal space.

By the radical disposition of welcoming, a *habitus* of fruitful reception is inscribed in the heart of this movement. One does not incarnate oneself; what must take flesh in oneself is received from another. This other may be God—and it is in a paradigmatic way—but others also contribute to this project. Thus, the Teresian project is teeming with examples where important roles are played by various agents, including providing the very idea of the establishment of a new monastery.

Continuous reception involves allowing *deshacer*—which untangles internal or external resistances that can block the path to the arrival of something new and unexpected—to happen. In chapter 1, we saw how these resistances threatened the creation and then the survival of the monastery of Saint Joseph. Teresa sometimes explicitly sensed the hand of God behind their being overcome.

The personal role of the Holy Spirit in this process of incarnation is approached head-on in *The Interior Castle,* where Teresa uses the metaphor of the silkworm weaving its cocoon and then becoming a butterfly. This silkworm begins to come to life when, "by the heat of the Holy Spirit,"[121] it receives the help offered by God through the sacraments, sermons, and so on. The Holy Spirit, in other words, is a sine qua non condition for the development of this silkworm—and by analogy of the soul called to be reborn in Christ.

The gifts represent already a presence of God and bear the mark of the Giver. But the presence and the action of God are not limited only to God's gifts and benefits, although they are many, but extend to the communication of God's very self. This graduality of the gift, progressing from simple things like reading books and hearing sermons before finally reaching its dazzling fullness in the gift of God's own self, rather than reflecting a divine desire to be given only sparingly, is more a pedagogical concession to the human difficulty of welcoming such majesty from the outset.[122]

Such seeing leads to incarnation; seeing brings one closer to what is seen, the distance decreases. God gradually takes shape in the human person who receives him; God lives in her, becomes incarnate in her. This is one meaning of the succession of mansions of *The Interior Castle,* all oriented toward the one at the center, that of God. At the summit of the vision of the Trinity of chapter 38 of the *Life,* Teresa finds herself before the very Trinity; she is before God and God is in her. There is a compenetration and juxtaposition of these two places, fruits of this "divine company" in the soul.[123] But the union, as deeply intimate and compenetrating as it is, is surprisingly not the end result of this process.

Telling

The movement begun by seeing could have ended with incarnation. We could speak of a completeness, a wholeness, between the starting point of the seeing and ending point of incarnating this vision (ultimately, God) in an individual. A simple back and forth between these two poles would ensure development and growth.

However, there is a third essential point—that of "telling." In *The Interior Castle,* the movement of the soul leads it from its initial blindness, not only to seeing, but to speech, and speech that is effective. This third moment does not come unilaterally in succession from the others, but is added to it, providing an apostolic dynamic to the concurrent deepening of all the dimensions of this triple movement. Orientation toward others is, then, a constitutive and essential moment of the movement of salvation. Without the "telling," salvation does not reach the generous fruitfulness that decenters it, moves it from being a relationship between God and the individual, and pushes the movements of seeing and incarnating (responding respectively to the Spirit's displacement and *deshacer*) to their climax.

The last moment of the movement, this telling expresses an orientation toward others, toward a larger body, toward a new incarnation. It is the movement out of oneself, not for one's own sake, but in order that others can hear or see. It is the movement that animates the Trinity when it reveals itself, expresses itself, especially in the historical Incarnation of the Son. This thrust is brought about by the Holy Spirit, both in Christ, who spoke and acted under the inspiration of the Spirit, and in Teresa, who was guided by the Spirit along her path.

In intimate contact with God, Teresa responded in a double movement of sorrow for others—upon seeing those who are lost—and a desire for their salvation, an apostolic desire.[124] In the emblematic case of Saint Joseph monastery, this desire for salvation was apostolic because Teresa saw herself acting upon the inspiration of God, in contact with whom this desire was born, and by whom it would later be supported. Decentered from herself through seeing and incarnation, Teresa could all the more easily turn resolutely toward others, adopting for this purpose the Christic position of the Word. Decentered from herself, she could speak vigorously and humbly so that others could hear and see what she had seen, heard, and welcomed in herself. Teresa's desire over time became increasingly pure and oriented toward others, a sign that she had adopted the very posture of the God who lived in her.[125]

This telling represents an essential component of the Teresian apostolic character. Like Saint Paul, she wanted to be an apostle of the word—a word that she wrote in order to allow a wider dissemination than the mere conversations with fellow nuns would allow; a word that was often written in response to the commands or communications of others; a word, finally, that took shape as her spiritual life crystallized, her career as a writer developing at the same time as her vocation as founder and reformer, often against her own will, in obedience to God and to her superiors.

Teresa also complained bitterly about the obstacles that her public speech faced because she was a woman.[126] She expressed envy for priests who could exercise this ministry freely, which has led some Teresiologists to conclude that she felt, in a certain way, a priestly vocation.[127] Her ministry of the word allowed her to unfold for others what she had seen, so that others too could be taken up in the same movement.[128]

This telling carries within itself a doing, a desire for new incarnation; it is not an empty word. The transformation of some people around Teresa made her path easier, but it was above all the establishment of a place of incarnation for others that represents Teresa's moment of telling: a monastery, followed by still others. The telling, then, does not simply follow from being incarnate/inhabited; rather, it concretizes the new, apostolic purpose that this moment has as its vocation to develop.

Thus, this moment of telling underlines the essential place of others in Teresa's soteriology. The relationship that comes to be through indwelling is not limited to a one-on-one relationship with God alone, however transparent it may become; the space of the relationship bears the vocation of being widened and not to be closed up in a narrow I-Thou. The push toward others—one who hears Teresa, the new community she forms, the reader of her various writings in her own time or far into the future—widens this space of encounter and provides it with a third point that opens out infinitely. As this happens, the central space of the indwelling is constantly enlarged.

Conclusion

The anthropological structure described here, a clear and systematized reading of the Teresian corpus, can be put into dialogue with other structural ways of understanding the constitution of the human subject. The structuring that we propose here of the dynamics of salvation for the human being gives rise to the architectonics of the full development of the human person in a Teresian, even a Christian, sense. The threefold movement deployed in a "seeing—incarnating/inhabiting—telling" joins other theories of anthropological structure from horizons as diverse as psychoanalysis or semiotics. A dialogue with them could help to further refine the model whose highlights we have outlined.

THE SPIRIT WHO GLORIFIES, THE SPIRIT AND THE SON, TRINITARIAN SPIRIT

As we conclude this chapter in which we have explored the role of the Holy Spirit, it is appropriate to consider finally the Spirit in relation to the other Divine Persons of the Trinity. Congar insisted in his time on the importance of a christological criterion for a sound pneumatology,[129] and the examination of Teresa's thought clearly shows that one cannot isolate the figure and the action of the Spirit from that of the Son, because of the Son's function as Word and face of God. Let us now consider the connection between the Spirit and the glorified Christ, as well as the role of the Spirit as a movement of entry into the Trinity.

The Spirit and the Glorified Christ

The dynamic of God's taking on a body through the Spirit, as seen in the Incarnation, is renewed in glorification,[130] by which a body is marked by the excellence of the divine presence that is glory. While the Incarnation is the initial moment of inhabitation by the divine, glorification is another, this time directed outward.

This movement of glorification seems to be about Christ, but it also links Christ with the Spirit since the glorified Christ is from the outset filled with the Holy Spirit. For Teresa, the Eucharist, too, links the glorious body of the Lord to the action of the Spirit, presenting another instance of glorification. Finally, this movement does not stop solely with the person of Christ and is not limited to the *eschaton*; glorified bodies of eminent persons witness also to the work of incarnation by the Spirit modeled on the image of Christ.

Teresa's Christ, Risen Christ

Teresa's Christ is the risen One[131]—the glorified Christ, manifestly full of the Spirit of God; the post-paschal Christ, although marked by the wounds of his crucifixion. This essential pneumatological component of the Teresian Christ is revealed in particular by the importance and the recurrence of the evocation of the gift of peace by the risen One.

In the post-paschal appearances of Jesus, his first words to his disciples are often a greeting of peace (Luke 24:36; John 20:19, 21, 26). These appearances demonstrate that the person who presents himself to them is the same as the one they had known previously, though different. The peace he invokes is meant to be a sign of presence, the presence of God that he makes transparent, a presence that dispels fear. The Gospels insist that the risen One can sometimes surprise, appearing suddenly among the disciples, passing through walls, yet not being merely an illusion. It is a very concrete, bodily Jesus Christ who presents himself as risen (Luke 24:39–43; John 20:20, 27; 21:13).

This figure of the post-paschal Christ imparting peace is very important in Teresa's body of work[132] because she uses it as an image of God entering the soul to be present and to dwell there.[133] Teresa compares this peace of God to the peace of the king who is secure in his castle; even if wars rage outside, he is untroubled.[134]

This peace-imparting Christ is both fully inhabited by the Holy Spirit and also ready to hand the Spirit over to the apostles. It is this figure of Christ-in-the-Spirit that Teresa privileges above all others, emphasizing the close link between Christ and the Holy Spirit.

The Spirit and the Sacramental Christ: The Eucharist

Another moment when the Spirit and Christ are closely intertwined in Teresa's work is the Eucharist. The incarnational function of the Spirit, here in the incarnation of Christ in the host at Mass, is emphasized by Teresa to be *in relationship.*[135] After describing a vision of the Trinity, she relates that one day,

> when I was about to receive Communion, and the host was still in the ciborium[136]—for it hadn't been given to me yet—I saw a kind of dove that was noisily fluttering its wings. It so alarmed me and caused suspension of my faculties that much effort was required to receive the host.[137]

As we have seen, the dove reveals concretely the presence of the acting Spirit. Teresa clarifies this obliquely when she writes immediately afterward, "This all happened at St. Joseph's in Avila. Father Francisco de Salcedo gave me the Blessed Sacrament. On another day, while hearing his Mass, I saw the Lord glorified in the host. He told me that Father Francisco's sacrifice was pleasing to him."[138]

Here, Teresa establishes a relationship, through the host,

between the incarnating Spirit and the glorified Lord. Furthermore, in the host, being in essence a gift offered, the communicant is able to receive this glorified Christ, inhabited by the Holy Spirit, and to allow herself to be transformed by this movement. Indeed, the "form"[139] of Christ exposed in the host is not intended only to be contemplated; it is an invitation to configure oneself to the Christ who is present. This configuration finds various instances of expression similar to these dual visions of the Holy Spirit above the host and the Christ glorified in the host, whether it is the flight of the pneumatological dove over a person[140] or the entry of individuals into glory.

From the Glorified Christ to Glorified Bodies

Though glory belongs first of all to God, and the risen Christ is the glorified body par excellence, bodily glorification extends also to the human person. Teresa relates several examples of people appearing in glory shortly after their death, when entering heaven.[141] These glorified bodies are similar in their luster to the glorified Christ.[142] The context in which such visions happen for Teresa is normally prayer, and it is certain individuals, holy people—both lay and religious—who thus appear glorified. In some cases, these visions show individuals a few months or even a few years after their death. The vision of the glorified body goes beyond the simple communication of a state and also includes a message. Thus Peter of Alcántara speaks of his joy and the blessed character of the penance that has now gained him such a reward.[143] In the case of Catalina de Cardona, a socialite who had become a hermit, the vision took place when Teresa had just received Communion in the church built near the cave where Catalina had gone to live.[144] Her glorified body was accompanied by angels. She encouraged Teresa to move forward, which left Teresa comforted and eager to continue her mission.[145]

These visions trace a link between heaven and earth, and they reveal, in these resplendent bodies, the sign of the Spirit who inhabits them and had configured them to Christ, even in the word. The glorified bodies bear witness to the fact that this gift made to Christ is offered also to human beings, although not everyone is receptive to this opportunity. They thus constitute the final evidence of a process of conformation to Christ very incarnate in life and which is revealed in death. The Spirit is not seen directly, but having seen the Spirit at work in the glorified body of Christ, we can recognize the Spirit's active presence in this case, too.

The Spirit: Movement of Entry into the Trinity

We have shed light on the role of the Holy Spirit as the engine of incarnation of the Word in Mary and of God in Teresa—and more broadly, in the soul of the believer and even in the world. We can further discern an analogous role for the Spirit in drawing the soul into the trinitarian relationship.

Christ is the Face and the Word of God, and in these capacities, his role as doorway of entry into union with God, beginning with an individual encounter, is essential. But in addition to that, the Spirit always plays a role. Teresa does not hesitate to call the Spirit "a mediator between the soul and God, the One who moves it [the soul] with such ardent desires."[146] This description appears immediately following comments she made on the annunciation and the experience of Saint Paul.[147] There is, then, a clear awareness in Teresa of this specific role of the Spirit as *introducer* to God.

This role is played from spirit to Spirit,[148] in a union with the uncreated Spirit who brings us into participation in divine unity with the Father and the Son. This is what Teresa explains in this passage on the seventh mansions—the most elevated point—inspired by the Gospel of John:

> Since His words are effected in us as deeds, they must have worked in such a manner in those souls already disposed that everything corporeal in the soul was taken away and it was left in pure spirit. Thus the soul could be joined in this heavenly union with the uncreated Spirit. For it is very certain that in emptying ourselves of all that is creature and detaching ourselves from it for the love of God, the same Lord will fill us with Himself. And thus, while Jesus our Lord was once praying for His apostles—I don't remember where—He said that they were one with the Father and with Him, just as Jesus Christ our Lord is in the Father and the Father is in

> Him. I don't know what greater love there can be than this. All of us are included here, for His Majesty said: 'I ask not only for them but for all those who also will believe in me'; and He says: 'I am in them.'[149]

The Holy Spirit is thus presented as the one who brings the human person into the trinitarian union, not as the door itself, which is Christ, but as a movement. By analogy, one could say that the Holy Spirit is the one who integrates—or even incarnates—the human person in the Trinity.

Conclusion

In the presence and action of a hidden God, the role of the Holy Spirit is not easy to grasp. Some images, such as the dove, suggest an aerial activity marked by movement, or—in the case of light or fire—a certain immateriality. The affective representations—joy, among others—as well as the liturgical and prayerful representations reinforce the idea of a constant presence in Teresa's imagination, active but little theorized. Surprisingly, Teresian anthropology, regarding the "spirit of the soul," suggests a privileged path of access between God and the human being that puts in value the role of the Holy Spirit as a mediator.

Beyond these first, more pictorial elements, the action of the Spirit pierces here and there in a way that allows a broader reading from some explicit elements. The epistolary and literary allusions highlight the role of the Spirit's impulse, just as they disclose Teresa's constant attention to the topic. They also open the way to recognizing the structure of movements such as those we have described: displacement/decentering, *deshacer*, and inspiration that commits one to action. Recognizing these movements helps us to articulate Teresa's coherent and subtle teaching on the Spirit and its action.

The centrality of the movement of incarnation, analyzed from the point of view of Teresa herself in the context of "seeing—incarnating—telling," also unfolds the latter in the light of the action of the Spirit by highlighting the coherence of an action understood this time from the side of its reception. This movement of incarnation impelled by the Spirit reveals the backbone of Teresa's life and mission, animating the christological images so prominent there.

Nor can we ignore the inescapable trinitarian orientation of the action of the Spirit. The glorifying Spirit is positioned in a privileged bond with Christ that goes so far as to suggest that the Spirit plays the role of *introducer* even within the life of the Trinity. The indwelling of this Trinity in the human person is the subject of the next chapter, where we will consider salvation and the specific contribution of the Spirit in this regard.

Chapter 4

The Incarnation as Place of Salvation

At the Heart of the Trinitarian Indwelling

Teresa of Avila does not present her concept of salvation in the form of systematic teaching.[1] However, the theme of salvation is omnipresent for her, both as a question and as a motivation that drives her forward. Teresa understands salvation not as a purely eschatological reality, but as a place, an inhabited place. By a mirror effect, this place will be monastery, soul, and Trinity. Where this inhabitation is accomplished, it is oriented toward being extended, both in space (or number) and in time.

In this chapter, we will first consider Teresa's understanding of her own personal salvation and also how she talks about salvation, its sacrificial dimension, and its relationship to Christ. We will then explore the "places" of salvation and their interconnection, from the monastery to the trinitarian indwelling, within the same movement of incarnation. Trinitarian indwelling, as the endpoint of salvation, will then be analyzed in its relationship to a trinitarian configuration first contemplated. This indwelling is salvation already lived, a place of joy and a place of communion. Finally, taking up an important text from Teresa that has a witness value, we will attempt an existential synthesis.

TERESIAN SALVATION AND CHRIST

"Christ enters Teresa's life as Savior; this is her key experience."[2] This assertion by the great Teresian scholar Jesús Castellano is the fruit of careful theological study to discern the heart of Teresian thought. It is not self-evident.

In fact, Teresa applies only with an extreme parsimony the title of "Savior" or "Redeemer" to the person of Jesus Christ. In all her writings that have come down to us, she refers to Christ as Savior (*Salvador*[3]) only three times, Redeemer (*Redentor*[4]) two times, and in one instance as Redemption (*Redención*[5]). Furthermore, these are the only soteriological titles attributed to Christ in the whole Teresian corpus. When describing or referring to Christ, Teresa typically adopts a more affective vocabulary.[6]

Any description of Teresa's approach to salvation must take account of this discretion in her vocabulary, her conventional repetition of common expressions regarding salvation, and also her tendency to project a soteriological, interpretive framework that is exogenous. This is why it is good to start our investigation by analyzing Teresa's experience of existential anxiety about her personal salvation.

Teresa's Anxiety about Personal Salvation

Teresa's personal history is marked by a certain anxiety about salvation. Even in her spiritual and apostolic maturity, she considered her own salvation to be in question. It would never become a certainty that she possessed as her own; salvation remained pending as a gift from God.

If this nonpossession of salvation had a serene character of abandonment in the latter part of Teresa's life, it was expressed over a long period of time as anguish.[7] This anguish can be read, among other ways, by her understanding of hell as a possible, even probable, eschatological place for her. This is how the fear of having merited hell encouraged her to embrace religious life as a "purgatory."[8] Teresa is also aware that the excessively lax context of the monastery of the Incarnation could have led her to hell without the special graces of the Lord.[9] It was at the heart of this mixed atmosphere that a vision of the angry Christ made her understand that he disapproved of one of her relationships;[10] it was then that she resumed the practice of prayer as "the road leading to heaven."[11] The sight of a statue of the scourged Christ finally constituted the starting point for her final conversion.[12]

To this conviction about deserving hell,[13] which would accompany her until the end of her days, was grafted the security of knowing that God did not want this fate for her and that God was the assurance of going to heaven.[14] This well-rooted and repeated hope was, however, accompanied by a reverential fear about personal salvation,[15] a fear that included a certain detachment.[16] This fear, which no longer included her previous anguish, underlined the fact that as a gift received, salvation was not a certainty based on oneself—just the contrary, in fact, since hell was merited. We can therefore recognize a certain conversion regarding Teresa's apprehension of her personal salvation—acute anguish giving way to confident hope, rooted in proximity with God acquired along the way, but never taken simply for granted.[17]

The Journey of Salvation: From Sacrificial Redemption to Glorification

The Journey of Salvation

It is notable that the rare occurrences of the word "salvation" (*salvación*) in Teresa's writings[18] include a character of travel, of displacement. *Salvación* is often accompanied with words like *carrera* (race), *camino* (path), or *puerto* (port).[19] This element underlines the dynamic dimension of salvation,[20] not enclosing it in a single point of time, but opening rather to an unfolding over time, here represented by spatial metaphors. Salvation is in motion, still in the process of being accomplished.

This viatic dimension of salvation is also found in the dynamism of the Spirit, just as in the idea of a *telos* of salvation, its ultimate place of incarnation, like the image of the place of a pilgrimage's destination that constitutes the endpoint without representing the whole of the pilgrimage.

The Sacrificial Dimension of Redemption

Sacrificial language does not occupy a primary place in Teresian imagery of salvation.[21] This is especially true in her major works.[22] That being said, the sacrificial dimension of salvation is present in her minor works of a freer style, such as the *Soliloquies* or her poetry. Is this because in these works Teresa expressed more freely what she was really thinking? Or perhaps was it because in these writings she habitually made more frequent use of conventional expressions? This relative absence of the sacrificial dimension is even more notable since its presence would emphasize more strongly the redemptive role of Christ, to whom Teresa is so attached.

In the *Soliloquies*, Teresa writes of the blood shed for us by Christ[23] and of the great suffering he endured by dying to save us from sin.[24] In Teresa's poems that have come down to us, which date from different periods of her life, the cross arises as a marker of the sacrificial action of Christ. But it also comes to represent the path to heaven that is following, even imitating, Christ:

Within the cross is life
And consolation.
It alone is the road
Leading to heaven.

The Lord of heaven and earth
Is on the cross.
On it, too, delight in peace.
Though war may rage

[...]

After our Savior
Upon the cross placed Himself,
Now in this cross is
Both glory and honor.
In suffering pain
There is life and comfort,
And the safest road
Leading to heaven.[25]

The cross is therefore not only a place of pain, but also a place of life and of passage with Christ to heaven. In this sense, the cross is already glorious. This is what Teresa writes on the occasion of a religious profession: "In the cross my glory."[26] Place of glory, the cross is also the "Tree of Life," the "verdant tree" that provides shade.[27] Still in this metaphorical register, the cross gives life; it is "an olive tree so dear" that "With its oil anoints us / Giving us light."[28] The cross is therefore very present for Teresa, but it is oriented toward the redemption accomplished rather than toward suffering (without excluding the latter). In the tonality of the *sequela Christi,* the cross is alternately presented as something to take up (*tomar*[29]), to follow (*seguir*[30]), and to embrace (*abrazar*[31]) in the following of Jesus:

To heaven let us walk,
Nuns of Carmel.

Embracing the cross,
Let us follow Jesus,
He is our way and our light
Abounding in consolations,

Nuns of Carmel.[32]

In summary, we can see by these few examples that the sacrificial dimension of salvation is present in the Teresian corpus in a direct way, but it does not constitute its heart. It is the spontaneous character of the *Soliloquies* or the poetry that most often captures the impulses betraying Teresa's sorrow before the suffering of Christ. But even more, it will be through her sharing in the pain of Christ over lost souls that a participation in the intimacy of Christ, even in his passion, will be met. This participation in the pain of Christ will be oriented toward participation in his work of salvation.

Grace and Glory: Divine Proximity and Indwelling

The state of grace (*estar en gracia*) and glory (*gloria*) are two indications of the proximity of the human person with God and signs of salvation accomplished. At the end of the journey of salvation, beyond the trial of the cross, they indicate a state of achievement similar to the trinitarian indwelling.

The word *gracia* (grace) appears frequently in Teresian language, although many of these occurrences are not theological in nature.[33] The expression *estar en gracia*[34] expresses an intimate union of the soul with God. On two occasions, Teresa describes visions related to a soul in a state of grace, in which the relationship with the Trinity suggests a state similar to the trinitarian indwelling.[35] In the first of these passages, the vision of the soul in a state of grace was accompanied by a contrasting vision of the soul in a state of sin.[36] The state of grace is, however, a state in which one cannot simply rest content; concern about salvation, whether one is in a state of grace or not, runs through many pages of the Teresian corpus.[37] This *estar en gracia* represents the concept of salvation as intimacy with God on earth.

Glory is another indicator of closeness with God. Thus, besides the expression *gloria a Dios,* which Teresa is not stingy about using,[38] her use of the notion of *gloria* in the biblical sense of *doxa* [*tou theou*][39] is also quite frequent.[40] Two ideas stand out. *Gloria* can first of all have an eschatological sense, marking the horizon of the divine beyond, the place of the full presence of God, being fully in God.[41] Teresa describes seeing several people who were in their lifetime close to God[42] enter into glory following their deaths[43] or being there.[44] Glory is sometimes also included among a number of attributes of an earthly state marked by a presence of God, along with peace or joy,[45] or it constitutes the sign of a particular presence of God in human beings at prayer.[46]

The adjective *glorioso* (glorious) and the participle *glorificado* (glorified) present two very different ways of taking into account the either connatural or acquired character of the glory shown. On one hand, the adjective *glorioso,*[47] which presents an achieved state, is used almost solely before the names of Saint Joseph,[48] the Virgin Mary, or great saints. The participle *glorificado,* used as an adjective, although of more limited use,[49] has some interesting peculiarities. Half of the occurrences relate only to Christ, either in reference to his glorified flesh (*carne*)[50] or to his presence as glorified Lord in the sacrament of the Eucharist.[51] The other half concerns visions of a glorified body (*cuerpo*), either as a generic vision of heaven,[52] or as a vision of a deceased person depicted as such.[53] A certain analogy is then made between the coming in glory of Jesus Christ by his resurrection and the glorification experienced by the saints, in their flesh and in heaven. Furthermore, this usage indicates the "acquired" dimension of glory, a gift from God that makes one like him. Glorification is then the continuation of the process of incarnation until its culmination; it is the incarnation of glory, a sign of salvation achieved.

We can say, then, that grace and glory are signs of the inhabited presence of the divine in people as well as the space of growth, here below, that such a prospect makes possible.

"Looking After the Honor of Christ": Desire for the Salvation of Others

Teresa's concern for the salvation of others was a source of great pain for her.[54] The contemplation of hell,[55] in particular, left an indelible mark on her. When she speaks in various places of the soul in a state of sin, the descriptions she offers are similar to those of hell.[56] Teresa notes then that "Souls in this condition make me feel such compassion that any burden [*trabajo*] seems light to me if I can free one of them."[57] Indeed, she experiences "great pain…at seeing that God is offended and little esteemed in this world and that many souls are lost."[58] It is from this pain and this love of others that the desire to work for them is born. Teresa writes that she had a heightened awareness of the miserable fate of the sinner—"understanding this condition as I did"[59]—and that people who are advanced in prayer "would give many lives" in order "to draw one soul away from mortal sin."[60] Such a desire grows, she says, in proportion to one's relationship with the Lord:

> Souls brought to this state by the Lord…keep before their minds the benefit of their neighbor, nothing else. So as to please God more, they forget themselves for their neighbor's sake, and they lose their lives in the challenge, as did many martyrs. They are not aware of the words they say while enveloped in so sublime a love of God….These souls do much good.[61]

In fact, it is the love of God and the desire to see God loved that drives the desire for the salvation of others. "It seems to me," Teresa wrote, "that one of the greatest consolations a person can have on earth must be to see other souls helped through his own efforts."[62] But she never forgets the source from which this salvation comes. Thus for Teresa, writes Renault, "procuring the salvation of one's neighbor consisted in communicating to him the 'treasure'[63] that she enjoyed herself, namely, the friendship of Christ."[64] It is therefore the love of God that drives the desire for the salvation of one's neighbor, salvation that happens through the latter's friendship with Christ.

The desire for salvation of others is not that they simply become oriented toward God; it is, rather, that they are made to resemble God's own self. Indeed, Christ made known to Teresa the importance he attaches to the salvation of souls, saying, "My great love and the desire I have that souls be saved are incomparably more important than these sufferings [of the passion]."[65] To seek the salvation of others is to seek what is dearest to God. In so doing, the apostle also carries out the *trabajos* of God on the way to salvation. These *trabajos* include work, effort, trials, and even suffering.[66] Teresa notes the intrinsic relationship between closeness to Christ and such *trabajos* for Mary or the apostles, for example.[67] She wrote, "I doubt very much that those persons who sometimes enjoy so truly the things of heaven will live free of earthly trials [*trabajos*] that come in one way or another."[68] The goal of the union of the soul with God is therefore not so much enjoyment and rest,[69] but rather to share the path of Christ,[70] to bear witness to his love, especially through good works.[71] The Father, moreover, gives greater trials to those he loves more.[72]

The weight of suffering carried along this path is underlined by Teresa's recourse to the figure of the crucified One; it is to participation in his trials that the apostle is called.[73] Teresa strongly encourages her sisters along this way:

> Fix your eyes on the Crucified and everything will become small for you. If His Majesty showed us His love by means of such works and frightful torments, how is it you want to please Him only with words? Do you know what it means to be truly spiritual? It means becoming

> slaves of God. Marked with His brand, which is that of the cross, spiritual persons, because now they have given Him their liberty, can be sold by Him as slaves of everyone, as He was. He doesn't thereby do them any harm or grant them a small favor.[74]

Making oneself a "slave of God," just as the Son obeyed the will of the Father[75]—this path, marked by work and trials on earth, assimilates the human person to Christ, whose earthly life, so important in Teresian thought, began by his incarnation. This assimilation of one's life to that of the beloved Son is the most precious gift that God can give.[76]

To be close to Christ, to be with him, is therefore to share his mission, to work like him for what matters to him.[77] Christ even entrusts Teresa with "looking after [his] honor," the salvation of the world.[78] She relates this experience in two ways. First, in *The Interior Castle*, when speaking of spiritual marriage, she recounts an apparition after Communion of the risen Christ in great splendor, beauty, and majesty, asking her to take care of his affairs (*cosas*).[79] This episode is related to a spiritual writing dated November 18, 1572, that recounts the favor of the spiritual marriage that had occurred two days earlier.[80] In this passage, Teresa describes the vision of Christ and specifies the words he spoke: "From now on not only will you look after My honor as being the honor of your Creator, King, and God, but you will look after it as My true bride."[81]

Teresa is called to a shift from a general consideration of God to a personal stake in God's own honor. This honor[82] is to save humanity. Teresa takes up this task as her own, too.

And in the pursuit of this task entrusted by the Lord, Teresa exclaims, "Oh, my Jesus, how great is the love You bear the children of the earth, for the greatest service one can render You is to leave You for their sake and their benefit—and then You are possessed more completely."[83]

Paradoxically, it is by "leaving" God that we "possess" God. And isn't this the very face of God that is revealed in the Son (Phil 2:5–11)? The adoption of the very posture of God oriented toward humanity as gift thus surpasses the enjoyment that the human person could have of this love of God living within. To look after the honor of Christ in his desire for salvation pushes a person out of herself and to take upon herself this selfless desire for the salvation of others.

PLACES OF SALVATION: FROM THE MONASTERY TO TRINITARIAN INDWELLING

"The Word [*Logos*] became flesh [*sarx*] and lived [*eskènôsen*] among us" (John 1:14). These few words from the Prologue to the Gospel of John express the heart of the experience of the Incarnation of God in its double dynamic of interiorization and exteriorization. It is "interiorization," because the *logos* immerses itself in human flesh in order to animate it, to give it life, to make it radiant. It is "exteriorization," because through that flesh, the *logos* can be seen and touched[84]; it takes its place among the phenomena; it pitches its tent there (*skènè/skênos*), takes a particular form in a particular place.

Our analysis of the last chapters of Teresa's *Life* highlights various figures of salvation, in the form of places. These various places are not just a static series; correspondences and links are woven between them that make it possible to outline a topology of salvation. Set in motion, these places show us the dynamics of salvation. Between the poles of monastery and indwelling, a whole world unfolds.

First, we will develop the theme of places of salvation and their correspondences. Then we will consider the related dimensions of universalization and fruitfulness.

The Places of Salvation

Salvation is often depicted by Teresa as located in a particular place. Collective or individual, each place is marked by a certain permanence and becomes a space of relationship. The traditional, paradigmatic place of salvation is heaven, represented in the Book of Genesis by the Garden of Eden, where God and humanity related easily (Gen 2:8–25).[85] Inspired by the Book of Proverbs, Teresa associated the soul of the just person with heaven itself.[86] Extending the same metaphor, she also writes that the soul, "this brilliantly shining and beautiful castle," is a "tree of life planted in the very living waters of life—that is, in God,"[87] making further reference to the eschatological place in which the Christian hope of salvation crystallizes. God's dwelling place in the soul, the seventh mansion, will moreover be called "another heaven."[88] The soul is clearly the protagonist of this topology of salvation. This topology is not a series of unrelated places lined up one alongside the other; on the contrary, an interpenetration between these polymorphic places reveals a salvation that is both unique and fecund. It is because salvation is a mystery—and therefore elusive—that various images have to be used to express it. As the philosopher and art historian Georges Didi-Huberman has written, mystery, rather than being inexpressible in images, is *only* expressible in images.[89] Writing from a completely different context than ours, the visual arts, Didi-Huberman addresses the reciprocal embedding of various places—through an operation of *collocatio*—that bear witness to the function of the image to present impossible spaces.[90]

The first place in the *Life* that serves as an image of salvation is the new monastery of Saint Joseph.[91] It is a place with surprising origins and a fragile infancy, a place Teresa described in spatial and viatical metaphors: "this little corner so enclosed...a refuge."[92] It is a place inhabited by God, through the promised divine household[93] and through the presence of the Blessed Sacrament.[94] It is a heavenly place not only for Teresa,[95] but also for the other nuns who make up the community of Christ there.[96] Saint Joseph was the exterior space marking in the city the indwelling of God in his servants, the starting point for an even greater enterprise.

However, Saint Joseph monastery was also the first "apostolic" fruit of an incarnation that had begun to take flesh in Teresa, in her soul. It is not incidental that she used the image of a castle with multiple mansions to speak of the soul, at the center of which is the mansion of God. Here, too, there is a double character of internalization and exteriorization. Interiorization through the progressive journey through various mansions, in order to draw continually closer to the mansion of God, who is revealed there as a Trinity living in the heart of the human person in full light. But such a movement of deepening could not be hidden; it also had to be exteriorized, giving a face to what inhabited it. In *The Interior Castle*, Teresa emphasizes forcefully that for the soul that progresses, and especially the soul that reaches the seventh mansions, love for God must be expressed in works (*obras*).[97] Martha and Mary go hand in hand.

In this process of incarnation, in interiorization and in exteriorization, we find a series of analogies drawing together the person inhabited by God, the monastery of Saint Joseph, and the other foundations. In all these instances, we find a place where salvation takes flesh, first and always because each one is inhabited by a deepening presence of God. The push toward God is redoubled in an impulse toward others, extending by stages the space of salvation toward others. Teresa recognizes that true love can only grow; it can never be simply stagnate.[98] This double movement of extension of the exteriorized space, which always has the vocation of being inhabited, and of deepening of the interior space—to the heart of the Trinity—marks out the contours of the way of salvation.

The interior space of the soul inhabited by God—and close to him—is marked by vastness, greatness;[99] a whole world is there. Teresa, speaking of the soul in a state of grace, writes, "We are not reflecting on something restricted to a corner but on an interior world where there is room for so many and such attractive dwelling places, as you have seen."[100] It is through prayer that the soul can enter this castle, since it is only by first entering into oneself that it is possible to enter heaven.[101]

For Teresa, the exterior space is the reflection of the interior space. After the image of the Lord who built a temple in her soul, like the Temple of Solomon,[102] Teresa builds a temple of God, Saint Joseph monastery, in her own time, as an echo. As this interior space grows into trinitarian indwelling, it has a character of infinite development. As it does, the exterior space will also, in a sense, be marked with this character. At the moments when Teresa enjoys a feeling of completeness, of blessedness, something upsets this peace and pushes her even further. First, having passed from mediocrity in religious life to a great union with God in the monastery of the Incarnation, the idea of founding a reformed monastery arose in her, even though she was comfortable where she was.[103] It was a door opened to a first movement of extension—exteriorization—of the interior adventure that was hers and that she already shared with some companions. The founding of a new monastery, more attentive to the original Carmelite vocation, opened up a space where others could more easily enter into the experience of proximity with God that was already Teresa's.

Then, once this first movement of extension was complete, Teresa rested—in God and in the monastery. When she believed her task was complete, a new impulse prompted her to found more monasteries.[104] Her career as foundress ultimately would end only with death. This physical extension of Carmel was not about a quantitative conquest of space;[105] rather, it entailed a conversion of space through inhabitation by establishing other centers of joy, both in the community as a whole and in each nun.[106] Each new monastery was a new place of God inhabited by God himself and by women who were each also a divine place.

In its own way, Teresa's epistolary communications, of which we have traces of an intense activity during this same period of exterior extension, constitutes another space of the salvation that is called to become incarnate. This network—made up of nuns, religious, priests, relatives, friends, benefactors, civil and religious authorities—marked out in dotted lines a space of gigantic dimensions.[107]

The apotheosis and the heart of these places of salvation are hidden in the center of all places, the Trinity itself.[108] She already describes in herself a space for the relationship of the Father, the Son, and the Spirit. As a *telos* of salvation, the trinitarian inhabitation will be discussed in more detail below.

The place of salvation as a space inhabited as a set of mirrors is expressed discursively in the first chapter of the *Life*. When Teresa begins her book with thanksgiving, and even before she praises the God who saves her,[109] she sketches out the contours of a space, a place, of salvation inscribed. She starts with her family—first of all, her father,[110] then her mother,[111] and finally her brothers and sisters.[112] More than the list of relatives, what we see is a space of inhabitation, a household, marked by the personalities of those who live there and who are in relation to the speaker.

Once this space is marked out, Teresa sets in motion a double movement in the order of salvation. First, an *ad extra* push: as a child, Teresa was dazzled by the "forever and ever and ever"[113] (*para siempre, siempre, siempre*) of eternity; she wanted to die a martyr and even decided, in order to do this, to go to the land of the Moors.[114] This impulse was expressed in a child's registry of powerlessness; she realized that the biggest obstacle was "having parents." And so her expedition to the land of the Moors never got beyond the gates of Avila. Then a second movement took shape in her, *ad intra* this time, with the desire to become a hermit; she and her siblings built "hermitages" with small stones—but they soon crumbled.[115] Thus, already we see Teresa's desire to build, to create a (physical) place for God and for her, long before this was actually possible. Under this same inchoate mode, a full Christian life presented itself: prayer, almsgiving, and even the desire to become a nun.[116]

Even as a child, however, Teresa began to expand the bounds of her vision of her family. When Teresa's mother died, when Teresa was twelve, she asked the Virgin Mary to become her new mother.[117] The household as a place of salvation therefore takes on a supernatural component; the Mother of God, mother of Jesus, is invited also to become Teresa's mother.

The final prayer of chapter 1 marks the reversal of the dwelling place between the time she was writing about and the time she was writing. In the account, Teresa writes of her efforts to build a dwelling place for God, both by the construction of hermitages and by the overabundance of devotions. Even her references to the family household suggest it to be a place in which she is inserted. But the final prayer makes clear her understanding at the time she was writing that it was in fact God who was all along preparing a place in her, an "inn" (*posada*), where God would dwell.[118]

Toward a Differentiated Universalization

The movement of exteriorization shows a gradual widening of the horizon of salvation. Out of a concern for her personal salvation, in conversation with a few religious friends, Teresa moves progressively into an expanding concern for others: a few individuals, her order, the church, and the world. Thus, in her first years of religious life,

> [Teresa] practiced a "timeless" apostolate, in the sense that from a start, she limited herself to acting at the level of individual, soul-to-soul relationships, which seemed to her to be self-contained, autonomous, relative to others or the wider world; and at the same time, the only thing she considered worthy of her interest was the blessed life in heaven.[119]

It was through the events leading up to the founding of the monastery of Saint Joseph that the Teresian apostolic vision took a collective turn. The vision of hell radically initiated a desire in her for participation in the saving work of God, even on a large scale. In the midst of this vision, Teresa's grief over the loss of the Lutherans[120]—even though she had had (and would have) no direct contact with any of them during her whole life—indicates that her apostolic horizon extended beyond the confines of a monastery, or even a country,[121] even if the nucleus of this apostolic call was domestic.[122] We have already seen in chapter 1 that the impulse behind the foundation of Saint Joseph and then of the series of other monasteries reveal the same structure, although a new trigger element launched the subsequent foundations. This means that this movement of extension is coextensive with the authentic desire for salvation.

In the historical unfolding of this Teresian commitment to the salvation of others, one can note the awareness—in the judgment of learned men[123]—that Teresa's reform could be useful to the entire Carmelite order.[124] Teresa discovered that this little monastery project could be useful to the church as a whole. And through her encounter of Father Maldonado in 1566, a final widening to the salvation of the world becomes clear. This meeting "would bring about a decisive widening of Teresa's prayer and that of her daughters: it is for the salvation of the world that, henceforth, the Carmelites would converse with Christ."[125] The historical unfolding of this intuition, already present in the foundation of the monastery of Saint Joseph, also accompanied the personal purification of Teresian desire, which became God's own desire.

Teresa adopted the horizon of the God who dwelt within her and whose presence in everything she recognized.[126] By adopting this divine horizon, her personal salvation became inextricably linked to the salvation of others. Salvation happens together.[127]

The universalization of the apostolic horizon of salvation does not mean that salvation is indistinct and impersonal. Taking up the Johannine metaphor of mansions, Teresa echoes that the multitude of mansions of heaven indicates the different degrees of proximity with God reached by people.[128] In the same vein, the variation in the intensity of the glory received, which she saw is not distributed in a binary way, also testifies to the differentiation of experience of heaven.[129] The collective dimension of salvation does not negate its personalized dimension.

Fruitfulness Extended

The movement of exteriorization of an embodied salvation, tending toward universalization, testifies to the intrinsic fruitfulness to which the presence of God calls the soul. The importance accorded by a contemplative nun to apostolic fruitfulness may seem surprising. In Teresa's case, this fruitfulness translated in a very visible way to the people she touched and the monasteries she established. But the fruitfulness of a soul filled with God even goes beyond these exterior considerations.

In her *Meditations on the Song of Songs*, Teresa develops in a succinct and poetic way her reflections on the close relationship between the interior principle that animates action and exterior action in the form of service of God and neighbor:

> I understand by these words that the soul is asking to perform great works in the service of our Lord and of its neighbor. For this purpose it is happy to lose that delight and satisfaction. Although a person's life will become more active than contemplative, and one will seemingly lose if the petition is granted, Martha and Mary never fail to work almost together when the soul is in this state. For in the active—and seemingly exterior—work the soul is working interiorly. And when the active works rise from this interior root, they become lovely

> and very fragrant flowers. For they proceed from this tree of God's love and are done for Him alone, without any self-interest. The fragrance from these flowers spreads to the benefit of many. It is a fragrance that lasts, not passing quickly, but having great effect.[130]

This "lasting fragrance," which "spreads to the benefit of many," evokes the somewhat elusive apostolic consequences of the indwelling of God in a person.[131] In the same book, Teresa indicates that souls led by God to such a high place must not confine themselves within narrow limits: "even if someone who is a religious—especially a woman—cannot help her neighbor, her prayer will be powerful if she has strong determination and ardent desires for souls."[132] She added, "Even, perhaps, the Lord will desire that either in life or in death she will help others."[133] It is therefore from the Lord that this fruitfulness comes, and it is not confined to earthly life. The importance of the apostolic character of prayer in Teresa's monastery was strongly emphasized by François-Régis Wilhélem in his work on Teresa's apostolic mysticism.[134] As an explanation for the importance Teresa gives to apostolic prayer, Emmanuel Renault suggests the fact that it allows one to move beyond any constraint of place and space, thus allowing one to put into practice the universal apostolic aim by which Teresa had been attracted.[135]

In the Teresian corpus, the apostolic fruitfulness of people in whom God dwells is seen, among other things, by supernatural means. For example, Teresa saw a dove hovering, with long rays shining from it, over the head of a Dominican priest, which she interpreted as a sign that he would touch many souls.[136] She also writes that the potential fruitfulness of a soul close to God is such that the devil makes great efforts, sometimes rallying all of hell to his aid, to take such a soul, since then it is not only that soul who would be lost, but also the multitude it would draw to God, as did Saint Ursula, Saint Dominic, Saint Francis, or Father Ignatius.[137] Teresa sees that "one person who is completely perfect would do more good with a true, fervent love of God than many others would with lukewarmness."[138] This expresses an acute awareness in Teresa of the communion of the church and in the church.[139]

Thus, the fruitfulness in the works of others is revealed to be widely coextensive with the deepening of interiorization of the incarnation of God in the human being. The extension of salvation from one place to another—and their coextensiveness—demonstrates fruitfulness to be deeply rooted in the nature of salvation that, even personalized and incarnate, tirelessly opens up to others.

Conclusion: Incarnation as the Engine of Salvation

The compenetration of places of salvation reveals that a movement of incarnation or of inhabitation of these places is at work there, with both an interiorizing orientation—toward the soul, for example—and an exteriorizing orientation—toward the world. This exteriorization aims at a differentiated universalization as well as apostolic fruitfulness.

The dynamic of incarnation—involving inhabitation and deepening—thus constitutes an image of *salvation in act.* Without divine indwelling, the monastery is empty; without exteriorization, the interior habitation is sterile. *The movement of incarnation in its dual dimensions of interiorization and exteriorization can therefore be understood as the engine of salvation.* Incarnation is salvation in progress, because salvation is the endpoint of movement toward God and the incarnation is movement toward God and toward others. Incarnation is salvation. Incarnation is salvation because it entails the indwelling of God, trinitarian indwelling.

TRINITARIAN INDWELLING AS THE ENDPOINT OF SALVATION

For Teresa, salvation unfolds. It unfolds toward a *telos* that is not only eschatological. The very heart of the *telos* of salvation is revealed to be the Trinity. The Trinity is not to be found in some great beyond, but at the center of the human person, in a dwelling place of God in the soul. The trinitarian indwelling therefore constitutes the source and the summit of the dynamics of salvation.[140]

Before considering this affirmation, an exploration of Teresian doctrine of the Trinity is important, in its contemplative dimension and in the invitation to configuration to the Trinity that that dimension offers. After that, various ramifications of the notion of inhabited salvation will be considered, from the *mise en abîme* of the *telos* in inhabitation to praise, before addressing the Johannine influence on the notion of mansions and the character of the Eucharist as a sign of salvific communion.

Toward Configuration to the Trinity

> And should by chance you not know
> Where to find Me,
> Do not go here and there;
> But if you wish to find Me,
> *In yourself seek Me,*
> Soul, since you are My room,
> My house and dwelling.[141]

In her poem "Seeking God," Teresa puts these words in the mouth of God. She expresses God's desire to live within the human person. And since God lives there, this is also where God can be sought. Found and contemplated there, God can then become a model to live and follow.

Considering the unalterable christological orientation of Teresian doctrine, the trinitarian flavor we find here is rooted in the *Life* and affirmed in her later writings. Without replacing Christ with the Trinity, the christological horizon unfolds in a more complete trinitarian teaching. Inhabitation by the Trinity constitutes the summit of Christian life—the *telos* of salvation—and it is situated also as the (universal) source of salvation, not only as an experience, but also as a place of contemplation.[142] In the following pages, before considering what it means to be configured to the Trinity, we will analyze contemplation of the Trinity.

Contemplation of the Trinity

Not a theologian, Teresa does not offer her readers a systematic treatment of the Trinity. However, to fully understand this

God who is situated at the heart of the trinitarian indwelling, it is important to be attentive to those writings in which she speaks about the relationships of the trinitarian God. In chapter 2, we considered Teresa's vision of the most sacred humanity of the Son in the bosom of the Father,[143] presented as a vision of the Trinity. In chapter 3, we looked at the important vision of the Trinity that arises in the soul that has attained the mystical marriage and that, the scales having dropped, finally sees this triune God in the heart of her being.[144]

In the *Spiritual Testimonies,* one can discern a rough outline of Teresa's journey of progressive encounter with the Trinity. We will therefore focus mainly on these texts for this part of our research. Besides this, the last text of her *Testimonies*[145] will be dealt with separately, at the end of this chapter. It should be noted at the outset that Teresa was both subtle and discreet in the *Testimonies.* On one hand, she makes unvarnished notes of events, her perceptions, reflections, and feelings. On the other hand, she expresses herself humbly as a writer, indicating that she cannot account for everything, say everything, or explain everything. In this sense, something of the radical distance between the experience and its narration, and even more between God and the creature, is regularly brought to the mind of the reader by this admission of the impossibility of saying everything, or of saying everything properly.[146]

In many of the *Testimonies,* Teresa notes the presence of the Trinity[147] in her soul, or more generally in the soul in a state of grace.[148] She sees the three Divine Persons "imprinted" (*imprimadas*) in her, a "divine company" that immediately brings her into meditation.[149] Sometimes Teresa notes, however, that it is the soul that is with (*con*) the Trinity.[150] This presence of the Trinity even became a "very habitual" (*muy ordinario*) experience for her,[151] and so clear and dynamic that she spoke of it as that of the "living and true" God.[152]

One special character of Teresa's visions of the Trinity is that they strengthen her faith.[153] Indeed, Teresa notes that it cannot be doubted—and that one can understand this truth—that the Trinity is present in our souls "by presence, power, and essence."[154] This presence makes her see, by consequence, the greatness of the human person: "Since I was amazed to see such majesty in something so lowly as my soul, I heard: 'It is not lowly, daughter, for it is made in My image.'"[155] At the heart of this presence of God in her, Teresa finds that the Trinity communicates itself simultaneously to all of creation: "It seemed to me that from within my soul—where I saw these three Persons present—these persons were communicating themselves to all creation without fail, nor did they fail to be with me."[156]

Mention of this presence of the Trinity in writing, which is common in Teresa's work, normally accompanies the relation of an extraordinary fact, often of the order of speech. These indications reveal the edges of Teresa's experience of the Trinity.

Teresa thus becomes keenly aware of the Tri-Unity of God. The Trinity is one God, but it is made up of three Persons[157] and the three Persons of the Trinity are indeed a single "one thing" (*una cosa*).[158] This knowledge leads to concrete consequences in her way of seeing God:

> As a result I haven't been able to think of any of the three divine Persons without thinking of all three. Thus I was reflecting today upon how, since they are so united, the Son alone could have taken human flesh; and the Lord gave me understanding of how although they are united they are distinct [*divisas*].[159]

Teresa repeats this "distinction" between Divine Persons in another of the *Testimonies.*[160] She further confirms it in her descriptions of the distinct roles and gifts of each of the Persons of the Trinity that she experiences.

On one occasion when Teresa was troubled, the Lord said to her, "Rejoice in the good that has been given you, for it is very great; my Father takes His delight in you [*se deleita contigo*], and the Holy Spirit loves you."[161]

Each Person is thus assigned a separate action, although it should not be concluded that it is exclusive to that Person. She wrote that on another occasion, after a vision of the Virgin Mary, as Teresa sat in the presence of the Trinity, "it seemed to me that the Person of the Father drew me to Himself and spoke very pleasant words. Among them, while showing me what He wanted, He told me: 'I gave you My Son, and the Holy Spirit, and this Blessed Virgin. What can you give me?'"[162] Here see a dynamic of gift and also of exchange emerge, with the Father presenting himself as the Gift-giver.

On one occasion, this theme of gift was expressed in a triple gift offered to Teresa after the image of the divine Tri-Unity:

> It seemed to me that all three Persons were represented distinctly in my soul and that they spoke to me, telling me that from this day I would see an improvement in myself in respect to three things and that each one of these Persons would grant me a favor [*merced*]: one, the favor of charity; another, the favor of being able to suffer gladly; and the third, the favor of experiencing this charity with an enkindling in the soul.[163]

The sequence of gifts seems to correspond to the Father (charity), the Son (joyful suffering), and the Spirit (experiencing this charity with an enkindling of the soul). In a single passage, the specificity of each of their actions in the world is characterized. The Father lavishes the gift par excellence, charity. The Son's gift is in his own image; incarnate, immersed into the life of the world, he experienced suffering (*padecer*) firsthand and welcomed it. His gift is an invitation to live incarnation well. Finally, the gift of the Spirit is the gift of God abiding, in a very sensitive way, in the soul. Both "experiencing" and "enkindling" refer to the way in which charity is received and takes flesh sensibly in the soul of the believer. This movement from the heart of the Trinity to the believing soul confirms the specificity of the intervention of the Holy Spirit in the context of the saving action of the Trinity. As Teresa herself points out, "The truth is—leaving aside our gain in having so good a Father—that the Holy Spirit must be present between such a Son and such a Father, and He will enkindle your will and bind it with a very great love."[164]

The distinction between the Persons and their actions does not, however, affect their union. In a fairly subtle reflection, after recalling that "ignorant people" (and saying "us," she includes herself among them) sometimes picture the Trinity as one Person, much like a three-faced body, Teresa notes that the intellect tends to abandon such reflections.[165] She then goes on to describe a vision she saw:

> What was represented to me were three distinct Persons, for we can behold and speak to each one. Afterward I reflected that only the Son took human flesh, through which this truth[166] of the Trinity was seen. Three Persons love, communicate with, and know each other. Well, if each one is by Himself, how is it that we say all three are one essence, and believe it? And this is a very great truth for which I would die a thousand deaths. In all three Persons there is no more than one will [*querer*], one power [*poder*], and one dominion [*señorío*], in such a way that one cannot do anything without the others. But no matter how many creatures there are, there is only one Creator. Could the Son create an ant without the Father? No, for it is all one power, and the same goes for the Holy Spirit; thus there is only one all-powerful God and all three Persons are one Majesty. Could one love the Father without loving the Son and the Holy Spirit? No, but anyone who pleases one of these three divine Persons, pleases all three, and the same goes for anyone who might offend one. Could the Father exist without the Son or without the Holy Sprit? No, because the essence is one; and where one is, all three are, for they cannot be separated. Well, how do we see that the three Persons are separate, and how did the Son take on human flesh and not the Father or the Holy Spirit? This I haven't understood. The theologians know. I know well that in that work so marvelous all three were present, and I don't get involved in thinking a lot about this.[167]

What we can see here is the delicate intertwining between unity and distinction, on the thin thread of orthodoxy, that Teresa tries to express from her spiritual experience. In short, while recognizing the unity of the action of the Divine Persons in a full communion—there is no division between them—it must not be reduced to a unitarism that would accept no distinction.

One of the controversial points of the Teresian doctrine of the Trinity—and, specifically, of her pneumatological thought—is the identity of the silent Person. The core of the problem can be found in an assertion made by Teresa in one of her *Testimonies*:

> It is true…that I can easily affirm who I think is the Person who always speaks; of the other Persons, I wouldn't be able to affirm that they speak. One of them I know clearly has never done so. I have never understood the reason why.[168]

The Person who always speaks, as is clear from the numerous auditions reported in the Teresian corpus, is certainly Christ. Since Teresa goes on to write in the next paragraph, "The first Person, I think, spoke once,"[169] with "first" likely being a reference to the Father, several interpreters have concluded that the Divine Person who never spoke was the Holy Spirit.[170] But this ignores various allusions to the language of the Holy Spirit, and especially the various instances where Teresa mentions that all the Persons of the Trinity have spoken to her.[171] Moreover, it also calls for an abstraction of what Teresa refers to just a few lines later in the same text: "I don't recall that it seemed to me our Lord spoke unless in His humanity, and as I already said I can affirm that this experience is not the work of imagination."[172]

These details of Teresa's prose prompts Miguel Maury Buendía to argue—taking up a hypothesis initially proposed by García Ordás—that contrary to the commonly accepted interpretation, the Person who never speaks is not the Holy Spirit, but the eternal Son understood outside of his humanity, since Teresa indicates that he speaks only through his humanity.[173] This emphasizes the distinction between the eternal Son and his humanity, risking a dissociation between the two and suggesting a primacy of the incarnate dimension of the second Person of the Trinity.[174] But the other option attributes too much silence to the Holy Spirit, which is contradicted by other passages. Rather, our research suggests that the Spirit speaks in the Spirit's own way. The Spirit does not speak in the manner of Christ, who is the Word of God, and does not speak in the manner of the Father, who is Father of the Word. But the Spirit bears his own language by which he makes himself heard without himself speaking.

Considering the extreme importance of the Person of Christ in his humanity in Teresian doctrine, it is not surprising that Teresa had some difficulty moving back and forth from a face-to-face relationship with Christ to a trinitarian mode of relationships.[175]

Responding to this difficulty, the Lord came to her aid: "And the Lord told me today while I was reflecting upon this that I was mistaken in thinking of things of the soul through comparison with corporeal things, that I should know that these spiritual things are very different and that the soul is capable of great rejoicing."[176] What immediately follows is Teresa's metaphor of the sponge: "There came the thought of how a sponge absorbs and is saturated with water; so, I thought, was my soul which was overflowing with that divinity and in a certain way rejoicing within itself and possessing the three Persons."[177] Teresa simply accepts having the full Trinity within herself, without confusion and without containing it entirely. The movement of *deshacer*, already highlighted in the previous chapter, created a space in Teresa. Thus, from a position vis-à-vis God, in the person of Christ, she could pass to one of welcoming the whole Trinity.

Having said that, Teresa does little to address the issue of intratrinitarian relationships. On one occasion, she declared that the Divine Persons "love, communicate with, and know each other,"[178] without explaining her words further. And Teresa regularly notes in her *Testimonies* when she evokes the Trinity the abundance of things learned or seen,[179] but also the difficulty of expressing them.[180] Teresa reaches the limit of articulating what is ineffable.

The portrait of the Trinity that thus emerges is one of contrasts. First, Teresa demonstrates a great intimacy with the Trinity. This intimacy does not make her fearful of tackling delicate questions related to unity and distinction within the Divine Persons, suggesting the "personality" of the triune God. At the same time, the ineffability of this experience forces the reader to reap the fruits with reserve and humility.

Configuration to the Trinity

The concept of the Trinity living within in the human person becomes a matrix for the configuration of the human person to God.[181] This trinitarian configuration can be understood in terms of each Person of the Trinity.

At first glance, the fundamental character of *configuration to Christ* in Teresian theology can be seen on several levels. It is through the figure of Christ that Teresa's spiritual development progressed, starting from her encounter with his angry face,[182] through the mystical betrothal,[183] leading finally to the mystical marriage.[184] It was Christ who spoke to her and Christ whom she saw. It is Christ's honor that she looks after by participating in his mission of salvation. It is Christ whom she serves and honors through the foundation of monasteries. It is also in Christ's image that she becomes word for others.

Configuration to the Holy Spirit is less visible, but it can nonetheless be discerned in the movement, analyzed in the previous chapter, of displacement/decentering—*deshacer*—inspiration. By the emptying of self, the human person becomes all-relationship, receiving oneself from another. In this configuration to the Trinity, if Christ is the door, the Spirit is the means by which one is configured to the Father and the Son, with configuration to the Spirit revealing itself not in a face, but in a manner of being.

Configuration to the Father is seen, as it is in the Son, by obedience to the Father's will. Union with the Father's will is a more important sign of intimacy with him than the enjoyment of his presence.[185] Just as Christ is one with the Father through the accomplishment of his will, so the union of the soul with God is accomplished by conformity with the Father's will.[186] Speaking of the peace that can be attained in the soul, Teresa indicates that this favor comes through "a union with the will of God; such a union that there is no division between Him and the soul, but one same will. It is a union not based on words or desires alone, but a union proved by deeds."[187] The apostle's full collaboration in the saving work of God through cooperation with God's will is such that Wilhélem recalls that "in fact, friendship with the Lord is then so intimate that Teresa does not hesitate to say that God and the soul take turns being in control."[188] Renault summarizes,

> When the human will has been invested with the divine will to the point of espousing its form, being literally "transformed" in it (without however ceasing to be distinct and free), there are no longer two, but "one same will," not at the ontological level, but at that "of desires and of deeds" (*Meditations* 3:1). In other words, what drives the will, the force that animates it and applies

> it to a determined end is the will of God. It is not difficult to understand that the person who has reached this total conformity or transformation into the divine will cannot but want what constitutes the Good of God, which Scripture calls his Glory.[189]

Because the will of God has the power of action,[190] it is by works that one configures her will to God's. Hence, on one occasion when Teresa thought about her service to God and asked why God wanted her works although God does not need them, the Lord answered her, "In order to see your will, daughter."[191] The configuration to God through one's will is realized more through love and works than by a configuration through suffering, though the latter, too, is part of the life of the apostle.

Along the Teresian spiritual path, one can perceive a certain development from the figure of Christ as the image of God to the divine portrait in the Trinity. We can note, for example, that in the *Life*, Christ is presented as a mirror at the center of the soul,[192] while in *The Interior Castle*, it is the triune God who inhabits the central mansion.[193] But this development does not mean moving beyond Christ in order to gain access to some undefined Divinity. On the contrary, even in the seventh mansions, several christological elements are striking.[194] Moreover, even Teresa's vision of the Trinity is marked by its mode of manifestation in Christ. But it is true that a certain subsumption of the Christic image of God into the trinitarian indwelling takes place, when Teresa and the Trinity inhabit one another, beyond the face-to-face, but without the face of God in Christ fading. The role of the incarnate face of Christ is all the more significant since, as Garrido notes, the texts that express a very strong link between the Trinity and the Incarnation were all written subsequent to the consummation of the spiritual marriage.[195]

Christ retains his central role as doorway to the Trinity both chronologically in Teresa's own life[196] and at the broader level of the church's understanding of the Trinity. One even can say that, in a sense, the Trinity is configured to Christ, in that it is in relation to Christ, in his humanity, that each of the Divine Persons are defined. But even this privileged role cannot be envisaged without the roles of the Father—especially by the adoption of his will—and of the Holy Spirit, who models the structure of relationships making possible a visible, full, and inhabited configuration.

An Already-Inhabited Salvation

The Indwelling of Salvation

Salvation is already present. In Teresa's thought, there is a great fluidity between heaven and earth. She emphasizes frequently that we are called to enjoy great goods here on earth,[197] even goods from heaven itself.[198] Indeed, "in some way, we can enjoy [*gozar*] heaven on earth."[199] This enjoyment is first of all that of the presence of God.[200] It will continue in heaven, but it does not start there; it can already be tasted on earth.[201] Teresa writes, "It seems the Lord, like those Israelites who brought back signs from the promised land, has desired to show it something about its future land so that it may suffer the trials of this laborious path, knowing where it must go to get its final rest."[202]

The place of final rest, at the end of this path, is therefore already shown. The path to salvation is not a sort of wandering; it is strongly teleological.

Teresa, then, sees a continuity between the presence of God in the human being—through God's own self and through God's gifts—and the final reward that takes the form of eschatological fullness. The Lord gives us favors while on earth that help us understand what we will receive in heaven,[203] offering hope for a gift in fullness that cannot be fulfilled perfectly in this world.[204] In this, the dynamic dimension of salvation is displayed. Like love, which is intrinsically called to grow, the indwelling of salvation grows, deepens, toward an infinite eschatological horizon. In a sense, indwelling is less reifiable than would be the concept of possessing salvation. While the indwelling can be stable and permanent, it cannot simply be taken for granted.

Any constancy in salvation is rooted in its source, the presence of God and in God. It is God who ensures the permanence and continuity of the relationship at the heart of a changing world and at the risk of human fragility. It is the human being who could separate herself from God once the union is made;[205] God is faithful by nature.

One can therefore already taste in this world something of heaven, of paradise, of God. The presence of the triune God in the human being is a preview of the fullness of salvation.

The Mise en Abîme *of Trinitarian Indwelling*

Soul, you must seek yourself in Me,
And in yourself seek Me.[206]

The trinitarian indwelling, as a *telos* of salvation, both present and eschatological, is a place of ineffable dimensions. It is a *mise en abîme* about which unequivocal logical assertions are difficult. The master image of *The Interior Castle* makes this state of affairs concrete by presenting the soul as a castle at the center of which God dwells. For this image, Teresa draws inspiration from the Gospel of John, where Jesus, speaking of his and the Father's relationship to the person who welcomes them, says, "We will come to them and make our home with them" (John 14:23). But God is also the creator of the soul, and if the soul reaches the seventh mansions, it finds itself in God. *Between the soul finding itself immersed in God and God living in the heart of the soul, a* mise en abîme *emerges that tells the intimacy of the union achieved and the profound depth it reaches.* A double visitation takes place there—God in the soul and the soul in God[207]—that ensures a compenetration between these two places. The ambiguity of this construction is not lost on Teresa:

> It seems I'm saying that we can build up God and take Him away since I say that He is the dwelling place and we ourselves can build it so as to place ourselves in it. And, indeed, we can! Not that we can take God away or build Him up, but we can take away from ourselves and build up, as do these little silkworms. For we will not have finished doing all that we can in this work when, to the little we do, which is nothing, God will unite Himself, with His greatness, and give it such high value that the Lord Himself will become the reward of this work.[208]

In the same way the silkworm pulls silk out of itself to make the cocoon that is Christ,[209] the soul must do what it can to build this mansion of God's, although God alone can truly build it. Here again we find the movement of *deshacer*, in which the human being is undone in order to be rebuilt by God on a new foundation in a new space.

Christ himself hints at this *mise en abîme* in an audition to Teresa: "Don't try to hold Me within yourself, but try to hold yourself within Me."[210] In a dazzling inversion of perspective, Christ invites Teresa to put her very self in God. A few years later, Teresa described this abyss, this time in a way that suggests it swallows up the world: "While in prayer one day, I felt my soul to be so deep in God that it didn't seem there was a world; but while immersed in Him...."[211]

At the endpoint of this journey into the abyss of trinitarian indwelling, we find a suspended place in an uncertain time. The language of "*mise en abîme*" translates the reality of an atopographical place—called to fullness and universality—and a timeless time.

The Subsumption of Place and the Loss of the Desire to Die

For Teresa, trinitarian indwelling entails a reconfiguration of interior space. This space, marked by breadth and largeness, suddenly seems to shrink, reflecting the characteristics of the vision of hell,[212] but not as a regression. Indeed, just as the desire for life that became a desire to die in order to live fully—enjoying God—is subsumed into a death of the desire for death, the place of encounter between the soul and God narrows according to the measure of the intimacy of the union. The soul then lets go not only what it has, but desire itself.[213]

If hell was characterized by suffocation, the space created by the Spirit in Teresa allowed her to breathe. Yet at the summit of that encounter, that space disappears, a sign of a shared breath:

> The Spouse commands that the doors of the dwelling places be closed and even those of the castle and the outer wall. For in desiring to carry off this soul, He takes away the breath so that, even though the other senses sometimes last a little longer, a person cannot speak at

> all; although at other times everything is taken away at once, and the hands and the body grow cold so that the person doesn't seem to have any life; nor sometimes is it known whether he is breathing. This situation lasts but a short while, I mean in its intensity; for when this extreme suspension lets up a little, it seems that the body returns to itself somewhat and is nourished so as to die again and give more life to the soul. Nevertheless so extreme an ecstasy doesn't last long.[214]

In the theological framework of *The Interior Castle*, this description, which comes in the sixth mansions, does not refer directly to a single event, but offers a theoretical account of rapture. It is God—in the figure of the Spouse—who initiates the process by an act of speech: God "commands." This divine word results in an inability to speak because one's breath is taken away. The divine command interrupts ("closes," "takes away") the regular functioning of the body's activity, particularly that of the senses, which sometimes persist a while, but which at other times (*otras veces*) suddenly stop. The encounter with God takes place through the body. It sometimes results in an experience like death: Teresa's hands and body grow cold, the presence of the principle of life (soul and breath) becoming clearer. Teresa passes over in silence the nature of rapture itself, choosing not to describe what happens beyond a sensory perception; there is a narrative void. She speaks only of what rapture interrupts. Then, after having noted that this lasts "a short while," the narrative resumes, the rapture disappears, and again the body continues forward. Indeed, the description of the subsumption of the place of the body that emerges is paradoxical—the body returns in itself; it revives to die again. This return of the body to itself is only the prelude to a new death, which leads to "giv[ing] more life to the soul." The seeming death of the body therefore constitutes, at the end of the rapture, or even beyond, the path to greater life for the soul. Since the soul was given life by breath, greater life for the soul must therefore be characterized by a greater breath. Teresa's insistence on the brevity of the phenomenon of rapture suggests a characteristic of prefiguring. A beyond is glimpsed, although narratively absent, but it cannot be inhabited in an ongoing way. Yet entering this inaccessible place even briefly transforms the soul by giving it greater life and by reminding it of the initiative and the ongoing presence of God.

This rapture anticipates the spiritual marriage as the soul becomes momentarily blind and mute and loses all its senses due to enjoyment.[215] The dialectic between life and death is inscribed in this fundamental reconfiguration. Thus, at the very heart of a soul animated by a powerful desire to be completely God's—often accompanied by a desire to leave this life in order to be only in God—the loss of the desire to die is the sign that salvation is already present and inhabited, and therefore not only a future reality. Inhabited by God and "procuring the honor of God," which is to give salvation, the soul dies to its desire to die, leaving everything in the hands of the Lord.

At an existential level, Teresa repeatedly affirmed her desire to leave this world where everything is so uncertain in order to go to join God.[216] It was the naive expression of a desire to see God unhindered and to constantly enjoy his presence.[217] In *Soliloquy* 17, for example, she complains about the long exile to which life subjects her, wishing, "May this 'I' die, and may another live in me greater than I and better for me than I, so that I may serve Him. May He live and give me life. May He reign, and may I be captive, for my soul doesn't want any other liberty."[218]

Tempered by the desire for the salvation of others, and therefore to do the will of God, Teresa realizes that this desire for death paradoxically turns into a desire to live in order to be able to serve the Lord.[219]

This negation of the desire for death—a complete reversal—brings new life. This is expressed by *The Interior Castle*'s image of the butterfly that, once dead, carries the living Christ in it.[220] In short, it died to itself, but Christ then lived in it. Here Teresa takes up a Pauline theme of the desire to live in order to be at the service of his community despite the desire to be with Christ (e.g., Phil 1:21–25). The initial desire for life becomes, through this process, purified and transfigured into lively apostolic desire.

An Inseparable Union

While there seems to emerge at the end of the sixth mansions the risk of the soul's distancing from God,[221] in the seventh mansions, at the stage of mystical marriage—unlike betrothal or other types of union—separation between God and the soul is simply no longer possible: "The soul always remains with its God in that center."[222] There follows a series of metaphors that speak of this inseparable union: the water of the sky falling into the water of a river; a stream of water entering the sea; a bright light entering a room from two different windows and becoming one in the room.[223] Teresa becomes truly lyrical in her attempts to express this union that nothing can divide.

She then explores this theme with the help of some Pauline images[224]: "But anyone united to the Lord becomes one spirit [*espiritu*] with him" (1 Cor 6:17) and "For to me, living is Christ and dying is gain" (Phil 1:21).[225] She turns immediately again to the image of the butterfly, which can die in great joy (*grandísimo gozo*) because "its life is now Christ."[226] The union between the soul and God is now irrevocable, inseparable. The closeness of this union is naturally called upon to continue permanently beyond physical death, as already anticipated in the death of the butterfly. The endpoint of salvation is then consummated.

Consummated in Praise

At the endpoint of salvation, considered from the personal and the apostolic point of view, one finds praise. Praise is the ultimate "telling," addressed to the Lord, giving thanks for what has been seen and made incarnate in the life of the one who gives praise. It is a sign of a salvation already inhabited and for which one can—and wants to—give thanks. The salvation of the world is "consummated in a song of praise, immense and unanimous."[227]

The desire to praise becomes a corollary of the desire for the salvation of others. Teresa speaks of the paradoxical desire to be in the desert and to be in the middle of the world to help souls to praise God more.[228] This desire extends even to the whole world, since she declares that the soul wants "to have a thousand lives so as to employ them all for God and that everything here on earth would be a tongue to help it praise Him"[229]—a universal longing to give thanks. In fact, alongside the salvation of souls, praise from them constitutes the nourishment (*manjar*) of Christ.[230]

For Teresa herself, praise of the Lord is the final moment of conversion to God, being turned entirely to God. Thus at the very end of *The Interior Castle*, at the conclusion of the seventh mansions, her wish is that she and all her sisters be united in a place where they will praise God always (*adonde siempre le alabemos*).[231] This is the end of the great cycle of salvation, from creation to the utterance of praise, passing by way of the Incarnation of the Word of God.

At the endpoint of salvation consummated, as at the endpoint of the journey of the seven mansions, one thus finds praise. Praise is a way of "telling," the final moment in the anthropological dynamic of incarnation. This way of telling is not addressed to other people and is not expressed directly in action; it gathers the pray-er (the "incarnating" dimension) and addresses itself to the One who is at the origin of the initial "seeing." In doing so, praise takes up the whole process and orients the transformed subject to God alone in words heavy with incarnation.

The Johannine Place of Salvation

The strong Johannine roots of Teresian thought on the trinitarian indwelling have been explored by a number of scholars.[232] Teresa turns to the Gospel of John to support and articulate her reflection on salvation and the trinitarian indwelling,[233] but more broadly still, the contours of the Teresian place of salvation take shape with Johannine tones, in particular its incarnational accents.

This Johannine influence is reflected in her use of the image of mansions as the eschatological place of salvation. The notion of "dwelling place"[234] and "dwelling in" (*menô*), in a more existential than material sense, is strongly Johannine. Teresa uses this image in *The Interior Castle* to speak of the different stages of the journey of the soul to God, but also as an image of the eschatological place of salvation, which God prepares as "dwelling places" or "home" in heaven (John 14:2–3).

In the Gospel of John, the link between the home as a place of salvation and the trinitarian indwelling is strongly emphasized:

"Those who love me will keep my word, and my Father will love them, and we will come to them and make our home with them" (John 14:23). An "abiding in" or "dwelling in" emerges there that opens up to an infinite depth: "Abide in me as I abide in you" (John 15:4). Teresa takes up this dimension of the indwelling of God in humanity, as we noted when we considered the various images by which she suggests the trinitarian indwelling in the human person or more widely in the world. The "dwelling" or "abiding" spoken of by Christ in John is taken up by Teresa.

The final importance of "abiding" in the Gospel of John is related to the strong incarnational theme deployed in its prologue: "The Word became flesh and lived among us" (John 1:14). Already in this verse we find incarnation and indwelling. The final indwelling will come later, but it represents the endpoint of what was sown by the Incarnation of the Person of the Word of God. This Johannine trait clarifies in turn the link established in Teresa between the reception by the human person of Christ in his humanity under the influence of the Spirit—the incarnation living under the form of a configuration to the figure of Christ—and the trinitarian indwelling that is the presence and action of the triune God in the human person. *Incarnation leads to indwelling.*

The biblical references, explicit or implicit, used by Teresa are not trivial. The Johannine theme of indwelling supplements Teresa's very Pauline understanding of her life and mission and the Lukan interpretation of her vocation as foundress,[235] in order to outline the contours of a self-understanding that is shaped by the Word of God.

The Eucharist as a Sign of Saving Communion

The Eucharist occupies an important place in Teresa's thought. Several visions are linked to the Blessed Sacrament, occurring after she received Communion, a singular moment of prayer and proximity with God.[236] Also, the installation of the Blessed Sacrament marked the foundation of a Carmelite monastery by installing the presence of God within it.

Theologically, this centrality of the Eucharist for Teresa cannot be overlooked. The Eucharist is located at the crossroads of the Incarnation and salvation. On one hand, it traces between heaven and earth, in Jesus Christ, a path analogous to that of the Incarnation, as God takes form as bread and wine. On the other hand, it is a reverse path of union between the human person and God and sign of entry into the heart of the Trinity through communion with and in the body of Christ.

Teresa develops in a unique way the theme of the Eucharist in a few chapters (33 to 35) of *The Way of Perfection* in the context of her commentary on the words of the Our Father, "Give us this day our daily bread."

For Teresa, the Eucharist is understood in the context of the relationship between the Father and the Son, a relationship that is expressed by the perfect union of the will, by the love of the Father, and by the obedience of the Son—who, Teresa writes, sought the permission of the Father to remain with humanity always in the Eucharist, despite the affronts it would entail.[237] There is an exchange of love and gift. Even more, it is the identity of will that characterizes the relationship between the Father and the Son, so that assimilation to God passes through the adoption of his will. The gift of God therefore calls for a possible gift in return, from the human being to God, since God has already come to unite with the human being and shows the way of the response by adhesion to the Father's will. The Son united to the Father gives himself and gives the will of the Father through the eucharistic bread:

> Since by sharing in our nature He has become one with us here below—and as Lord of His own will—He reminds the Father that because He belongs to Him the Father in turn can give Him to us. And so He says, "our bread." He doesn't make any difference between Himself and us, but we make one by not giving ourselves up each day for His Majesty.[238]

The gift of God to the human being is affirmed in the Eucharist. Although this gift is made in a humble form that people are able to grasp and understand,[239] it is not just that God gives a gift, but that the gift is God's own self. Teresa comments that because of Christ's living presence in the Eucharist, he is as present to us as he was to the people he was among when "he walked in the world."[240] This special presence of Christ in the human person—

until the disappearance of the accidents of the host[241]—implies an entry of God into the human being, as a form of proto-inhabitation. In this context, Teresa speaks of the person as a "house" or "home" (*casa* or *posada*)[242] where the eucharistic Christ comes to live, even if briefly. The communicant is thus a figure of the place of God's dwelling, like the soul, in the case of the trinitarian indwelling proper, or the monastery. The Eucharist is therefore both an announcement of the possibility of trinitarian indwelling and a material sign that anticipates and nourishes it. Garrido thus suggests a correspondence between the presence of the glorious body of Christ received in the bosom of the Father and the reception of the Eucharist in each believer as a living temple of the Trinity.[243] Teresa suggests the power of the sacrament when she writes, "One day after having received Communion, I truly thought my soul was made one with the most sacred Body of the Lord."[244]

Teresa insists in her commentary on the Our Father on the redoubling of the contemporaneity of the gift, in the *hoy* (this day) and the *cada día* (daily).[245] This repetition opens the horizon of a "forever" (*para siempre*)[246] that places this gift in an eschatological perspective:

> Reflecting upon why after the word "daily" the Lord said "give us this day, Lord," that is, be ours every day, I've come to think that it is because here on earth we possess Him and also in heaven we will possess Him if we profit well by His company. He, in fact, doesn't remain with us for any other reason than to help, encourage, and sustain us in doing this will that we have prayed might be done in us.[247]

The eucharistic gift anticipates the permanence of the union that the Lord desires with humanity; moreover, it is the food that prepares its way. Like salvation, the eucharistic gift admits a deepening and opens up an eschatological perspective.

Finally, we may note that although Teresa, in these pages, understands eucharistic communion in the relational space between the Father and the Son, then between the human being and God, the Spirit is notably absent. The Father is present because the prayer under consideration here was addressed to him, and the Son is present by the fact that he is the one whose body is eucharistic. However, we have seen in other ways, in the previous chapter, that a clear link is established between the Holy Spirit and the Eucharist, or even, more specifically, between the Spirit and Christ glorified in the host. This latter element allows us to understand the eucharistic event in its full trinitarian capacity, both in divine offering and in saving communion. Eucharistic communion therefore becomes trinitarian communion through the Son, a down payment of salvation. After deploring the failures of the Lutheran reformation[248] and asking God either to remedy these serious evils or bring an end to the world,[249] it is, moreover, on a cry of the heart regarding salvation that Teresa ends her eucharistic reflection:

> What is there for me to do, my Creator, but offer this most blessed bread to You, and even though You have given it to us, return it to You and beg You through the merits of Your Son to grant me this favor since in so many ways He has merited that You do so? Now, Lord, now; make the sea calm! May this ship, which is the Church, not always have to journey in a tempest like this. Save us, Lord, for we are perishing.[250]

The Eucharist therefore emerges as an extension of the trinitarian relationship and brings the communicant into its bosom. This trinitarian communion already inhabits the space of salvation.

TERESA'S "LAST TESTAMENT"

One of the *Spiritual Testimonies,* dating from May 1581,[251] is an interesting document in more ways than one. In the context of the Teresian corpus, it is one of the only documents (apart from several letters) that was composed after *The Interior Castle* and therefore bears witness to the final phase of Teresa's theological and existential development, during the year prior to her death. This text is addressed to Alonso Velázquez, then bishop of Osma, to whom she had already gone to confession. She opens her soul to him in all friendship. This is why we can describe these few pages as Teresa's "last testament."[252]

From the outset, Teresa describes well the spiritual landscape in which she finds herself:

> Oh, who would be able to explain to your Excellency the quiet and calm my soul experiences! It is so certain it will enjoy God that it thinks it already enjoys the possession of Him, although not the fruition. It's as though one had given another, with heavily warranted deeds, the promise of a large revenue that that other will be able to enjoy at a certain time. But until then, this latter person enjoys only the promise that he shall have the fruition of this revenue. Despite the gratitude the soul feels, it would rather not rejoice. For it thinks it hasn't deserved anything other than to serve, even if this service be through much suffering. And sometimes it even seems to it that the period from now until the end of the world would be a short time to serve the one who gave it this possession. Because, to put it truthfully, this soul is no longer in part subject to the miseries of the world as it used to be. For although it suffers more, this is only on the surface. The soul is like a lord in his castle, and so it doesn't lose its peace; although this security doesn't remove a great fear of offending God and of not getting rid of all that would be hindrance to serving Him. The soul rather proceeds more cautiously, but it goes about so forgetful of self that it thinks it has partly lost its being. In this state everything is directed to the honor of God, to the greater fulfillment of His will, and to His glory.[253]

Teresa's soul is marked by peace and joy. Her state is similar to what she experienced in some of her extraordinary mystical experiences. Peace, in particular, evokes the presence of God and especially of the risen and Spirit-filled Christ who imparted that same Spirit to the apostles. This peace denotes an indwelling in the castle of Teresa's soul. This peace also heralds perfect union, spiritual maturity, and fullness.[254] At peace and focused interiorly, earthly miseries remain exteriorly for Teresa, like a simple garment that can be put on or taken off at will. She is inhabited by God and in another place, out of step with the world.

This gap opens up a space of continuity between the earth and heaven. Through an analogy involving anticipated revenue and property purchases, Teresa establishes a link between the already real but imperfect experience of joy and its perfect eschatological fulfillment. What is to come is related to what is already, but the current reality is not lived as a sort of permanent possession, with title deed in hand; there is room for hope and expectation of the fullness of the gift.

This gap continues with the detachment that emerges. It is a detachment that is illustrated by the forgetfulness of self and the disinterest that Teresa displays regarding her own profit. It is the culmination of the process of *deshacer* that sees her being in God. This *deshacer* continues at various levels. For her well-being, she must renounce mortifications.[255] At the level of communications with God, although the interior auditions continue,[256] there is a detachment of the imagination: "The imaginative visions have ceased, but it seems this intellectual vision of these three Persons and of the humanity always continues. This intellectual vision, in my opinion, is something much more sublime."[257]

The image has completely given way to presence alone, in the form of an intellectual vision. Teresa had moreover suggested this detachment by noting the end of raptures (*arrobamientos*) in the seventh mansions.[258] The extraordinary phenomena have ceased,[259] having fulfilled their pedagogical function; they were markers that pointed toward the essential, not essential themselves. In doing so, by their exceptional nature, they drew attention to what is surprisingly offered to all: intimacy with God, friendship with God, peace in God. As she comes to the end of her days, then, Teresa's life is crowned not by extraordinary mystical experiences, but by a simple, quiet indwelling that already opens to her the doors of an eternal home in the divine presence. Her detachment extends to all of creation and even to the very glory of heaven.[260] Teresa is pleased that she can do no more; she does not even want death.[261] The only thing that remains, she believes, is loving God and the desire that everyone would serve him.[262] But even there, these feelings are no longer "so extreme" as they once were, tormenting her, although they remain real and active.[263] These desires simply inhabit her.

Concern for the salvation of others strongly marks this text. Teresa reiterates the intrinsic link between the love of God and the salvation of souls,[264] or even, in a negative register, between the loss of souls and offense against God.[265] This concern for souls particularly regards those who are entrusted to her, and of whom she is aware that some are in heaven and of others she is not.[266]

Teresa concludes this last testament by revealing what inhabits her:

> The interior peace, and the lack of strength that pleasures or displeasures have for taking this peace away in any lasting manner...[267]
>
> The presence of the three Persons is so impossible to doubt that it seems one experiences[268] what St. John says, that they will make their abode in the soul [John 14:25]. God does this not only by grace but also by His presence, because He wants to give the experience of this presence. It brings with it an abundance of indescribable blessings, especially the blessing that there is no need to go in search of reflections in order to know that God is there.
>
> This presence is almost continual, except when a lot of sickness weighs down on one. For it sometimes seems God wants one to suffer without interior consolation; but, never, not even in its first stirrings, does the will turn from its desire that God's will be done in it.
>
> This surrender to the will of God is so powerful that the soul wants neither death nor life, unless for a short time when it longs to die to see God. But soon the presence of the three Persons is represented to it so forcefully that this presence provides a remedy for the pain caused by His absence, and there remains the desire to live, if He wills, in order to serve Him more. And if through my intercession I could play a part in getting a soul to love and praise God more, even if it be

> for just a short time, I think that would matter more to me than being in glory.[269]

At the heart of this peace she reveals a habitual presence of the Trinity that inhabits her. It is there that the will of Teresa is rooted, a will that, detached, becomes desire to do the will of God alone. Everything is then oriented toward God, even in the desire of life or death, and thereby toward the salvation of others, so that another soul may turn to God in love and praise. And this is better, today, than to be already in heaven.

CONCLUSION

The dynamic of incarnation already present in germ at the heart of Teresa's efforts to found the monastery of Saint Joseph can be read as a paradigm of the very process of salvation. Salvation as incarnation unfolds as—at the same time—lived, inhabited, present, and eschatological. It is *place*, but in a sense that is not primarily material and opens up to a set of corresponding realities. Some of these are well established, such as between the monastery and the soul, others are hoped for, in heaven, without being known.

Salvation as incarnation underlines the existential dimension of the former. It is in configuration to the trinitarian God by the trinitarian God that salvation is inaugurated and consummated. But this work of configuration already offers a glimpse at the specificity of the being and acting of the Divine Persons. Christ, the face of God, is the figure to whom one is configured. The Holy Spirit provides the form and the impetus. The Father, by the configuration of the obedience of Christ to his will, is revealed as the source of the Trinity.

The Eucharist also has a role here as an ecclesial place. A sign of the presence of Christ in this world, body stripped and given up, it indicates that the way to God passes through the body of each, all united in the common body. The link between Christ present in the Eucharist and the Spirit present in Christ indicates that it is this same Spirit who has the function of glorifying the body by making it similar to the glorious Body par excellence.

Through the movement of the expansion of indwelling, salvation, even individual salvation, cannot be separated from its collective dimension.

Finally, at the heart of this consideration of salvation as trinitarian indwelling, a portrait of the Trinity and its action emerges that reveals both its interdependence, but also its specificity. The Spirit, as the *incarnator of salvation,* brings the human person who receives the Spirit along the path of trinitarian indwelling.

Chapter 5

Synthesis

A Salvation that Becomes Incarnate through the Spirit in the Human Person

What is salvation? What role does the Holy Spirit play in it? These were the questions with which we began this study and that we have sought to answer by consideration of the work of an important spiritual author who is also a Doctor of the Church. Both the Spirit and salvation are topics difficult to pin down, the first because of its discretion, the second because of its seeming obviousness.

Our research began with a consideration of certain Teresian texts, with an eye toward interpreting a set of images of salvation, in particular related to (in)dwelling—the places of the monastery and the soul, among others.

We then sought to understand these images within an interpretative structure drawing on the whole of the Teresian corpus. This analysis made it possible to refine and reframe in a systematic way the strong theological insights offered by Teresa's work. There we outlined the nature of salvation, as well as the Spirit's role in bringing it about.

Through exegesis of Teresa's teaching, we carried out a dialectical journey between the places of salvation and a salvific dynamic. The question of salvation has an organic character in Teresa's thought that the linearity necessary for detailed exposition does not always make clear. This organic character conceals the various interrelated components that can be unfolded as follows. First, there is the historical moment of the Incarnation, when the Word took flesh, inscribing the presence of God in a place. For Teresa, the paradigmatic place of the presence of God is Christ in his sacred humanity. But, for her, other places would also be marked by the presence of God: the monastery, the soul, epistolary exchanges, so that the inscription of the presence of God in a place is not only a unique event *of* God *in* God, but is presented as a dynamic, an incarnational movement that also unfolds elsewhere. This incarnational movement at work in Christ, under the movement of the Spirit, is echoed in the human being, as a movement that is soteriological (a movement *of* salvation), pneumatological (*by* the Spirit), and anthropological (*in* the human being). Finally, the final image of God's saving action is an "indwelling," already visible in the person of Christ and present at the heart of salvation, thereby ensuring the link and the continuity between its current dimension and its eschatological dimension.

In this chapter, we will attempt a synthesis of this soteriological and pneumatological journey that will unfold in three stages. First, we will explore the incarnational dimension of salvation, revealing salvation to be the indwelling of God. We will also draw some broader theological implications of such a conception of salvation. Second, we will develop, in a trinitarian context, the role of the Spirit as the incarnator of salvation, through whom the very movement of self-emptying by the Son in reception of the Father's will is taken up by the believer. Third, we will consider how the pneumatological movement of salvation in the human being characterizes a way of being for the Christian and even for all people, opening a new perspective to the consideration of God's salvific action "beyond borders."

Furthermore, on a methodological note, we noted above that Teresa offers her accounts in a thoroughly biblical structure and language, with even Christ addressing her in her auditions in language that echoes that of the Scriptures. We also noted the ways Teresa reflects Paul's existential apostolic understanding of the relationship between life and death; the Gospel of John's grasp of the trinitarian indwelling; and the perception of the incarnation of salvation of the infancy narratives of Luke. For this final synthesis, we will pay further attention to this Teresian methodological rootedness in a biblical soil in two ways: first by taking note of Teresa's biblical allusions or direct biblical quotations, but also, in some cases, by reflecting Teresa's own biblical harmonics in our analysis of it.

SALVATION AS INCARNATION

A Salvation That Is Incarnate

The birth of Saint Joseph monastery marked for Teresa an important milestone in her relationship with God, as well as the starting point of her career as a founder and, at the same time, as a writer. Rooted in her vision of hell, the place of nonsalvation, this first project was inscribed with a concern for the salvation of others. In her account of its establishment, Teresa adopts a posture like that of Mary at the annunciation—the coming into the world of a place of salvation happens by way of an incarnation, the "taking flesh" of a divine presence.

This founding, followed by others, illustrates that salvation is not a static reality; even in Teresa herself, salvation grew through her ongoing conversion. This growth can be recognized, among other things, in the way she moved beyond anxiety for her own salvation and entered more deeply into a peace that came from God and became more and more inscribed in her, inhabiting her. This growth also took the form of an expansion, as other places were formed and grew.

The adoption by Teresa of an incarnational posture of welcome, like Mary, offers a conception of *salvation as incarnation.* This implies that salvation involves encounter, coming by way of another and needing otherness; that it takes place in living "flesh," constituting it as a new and inhabited place; that it is inscribed in time and is subject to growth; and that it can be understood as an ongoing reception that does not involve possession.

We will consider three aspects of the concept of salvation as incarnation: first, the dimensions of place and time it implies; next, salvation as welcoming the indwelling of God; and finally, some conclusions about Teresian thought on incarnational salvation and the relationship between the Incarnation and Christ's passion.

Salvation: Place and Time

Teresa rarely uses theoretical nouns in speaking of salvation;[1] rather, she understands salvation in action. This characteristic of her use of language on the subject underlines the fundamental orientation of salvation as dynamic. If Teresa says little in a conceptual way about salvation, it can be seen through her accomplishments, places touched by her action, and the presence of God they reveal. These places are very diverse—the soul, the monastery, the Blessed Sacrament, or heaven—but the first of these places is Teresa herself. Her journey reveals the presence of a God who saves, a salvation that is written in the flesh and in time. The incarnate place thus constitutes the anchor that makes it possible to see and grasp salvation; space—*a* space—is needed for salvation to take place.

The inscription of salvation in a living place unfolds in time. It does so first through development, gestation—Jesus's, as well as that of the monastery of Saint Joseph. It also unfolds in time as a reality that is present but that cannot be possessed as an object; this initially causes Teresa anxiety about her own salvation—she cannot be objectively certain—an anxiety that would transform into desire and confidence without ever being resolved as possession. Salvation is thus a present, contemporary reality—never simply a future, eschatological reality, though it is open to a future and already rooted in a history. This same open temporality of salvation, its ambivalence or polysemy, marks the New Testament, where salvation is presented as coming in the past, in the present, and in the future.[2]

At the heart of this temporal dilation, *salvation is best understood as a contemporary event, rooted in the past and open to an eschatological unfolding.* The eschatological contemporaneity of salvation in Teresa's thought leads her to transgress the temporal framework in her view of heaven,[3] of glorified bodies,[4] interactions with the dead who seem more alive than the living;[5] the end is not far. This bursting of the temporal framework is also apparent in Teresian teaching through the conversion of how she looks at life and death, in a Pauline movement;[6] the end (*telos*) is already present, and death is no more desired than the pursuit of life. Furthermore, even in a strictly personal context, salvation as incarnation cannot be summed up in a single moment, or even a set of moments, of conversion. Salvation is not captured primarily in a chronicle of successive moments whose milestones mark out a history of salvation, but as a today—certainly dependent on the past—unfolding in an incarnate, existential dimension. In this sense, salvation is neither atemporal nor inscribed in a single moment of a temporal continuum. Moreover, it shatters this eventual continuum by opening the way to eternity, a way indicated by the heart of the salvific experience that is the trinitarian indwelling.

Salvation as incarnation, then, carries with it a dynamic of growth. Salvation is not a simple disjunctive reality, as if there were a strict alternative between "saved" and "damned." Rather, it opens a space for development. Salvation grows, deepens, because it is fundamentally relational, of a relationship between human beings and God. The growth of salvation means it is able to integrate the resistances (interior or exterior) it may encounter, even at the risk of decay or extinction. In our analysis of the two impulses of incarnational movement, leading first to the foundation of Saint Joseph and then to a series of further foundations, we saw that the latter instance, beginning some five years after the first, did not include any sign of resistance in Teresa, while for the earlier foundation of Saint Joseph, her interior resistances were notable and only overcome thanks to a vision of Christ.[7] In other words, growth in her relationship of friendship with God—which is how Teresa describes prayer,[8] and which is at the heart of salvation—resulted in Teresa overcoming her internal resistances and also marks a "growth" of the movement of salvation in her.

Understood in this way, salvation is more a dynamism than a static state. In the present, the believer—such as Teresa—is not just "on the way" to being saved (as if it were only a future). Rather, there is a "more and more" aspect to salvation, or—to avoid a quantitative register and adopt a qualitative one—"better." A salvation marked by growth can also account for the "degrees" that it includes, even (as Teresa came to see in a vision) in the reality of heaven.[9] This growth, perceived from the point of view of the subject, transcribes the fruitfulness at work, both for the transformation effected in the individual and by the exterior fruitfulness of that whose life is inhabited by a divine host. Such a conception of the (possible) growth of incarnate salvation also underlines the risk of destruction; inscribed in the fragility of life, salvation can also diminish and die. The early Teresian vision of hell illustrates this possibility—which is not presented as realized—while Teresa would later write that some people refuse the salvation offered by refusing to see or hear.[10]

The growth of salvation and its fruitfulness ultimately demonstrate that salvation is oriented toward exteriorization, both collectively and individually. Salvation is in this at work. Collectively, this exteriorization of salvation can be read in a community that grows in a visible manner—the monastery of the primitive rule being the paradigm (but not the sole example) in Teresian teaching. Another aspect of this operational dimension of salvation lies in its apostolic character. The works that it prompts, in whatever form they appear, express to the world, in a visible way, the reality of a salvation already lived, present, and active.

Salvation Is Welcoming the Indwelling of God

Teresa's "last testament"[11] shows us that in the evening of her life, the imaginative visions had ceased, there would be no further words or foundations, but that God was continuously present, offering her through divine indwelling a down payment on the eschatological fullness of salvation. Many years earlier, in the context of the creation of the monastery of Saint Joseph, in the vision that confirmed the project and its supernatural significance, she had seen Saint Joseph guarding one door, Our Lady another, and Christ dwelling in the center, walking with the sisters. Located at the beginning and the end of Teresa's apostolic career, these two instances of salvific presence point in different ways to *the same reality that is inscribed at the heart of salvation: the indwelling of God.* This indwelling, now inverted, is also found in her vision of heaven as the place of God inhabited by human beings. The indwelling *of* God at the heart of salvation emerges as the welcoming of another. It shows salvation to be a temporal continuity and allows for a multiplicity of salvific places, since God's indwelling is unlimited, requiring only a welcome.

Teresa's conception of *salvation as indwelling* reveals the Johannine foundations[12] of her thought, since the Fourth Gospel, which she quotes at key moments, highlights this dimension of reciprocal "abiding" between Christ and the Father, and with the disciples, in the mode of desire and hope. At the same time, in the Prologue of the Gospel of John, the Word becomes flesh in order to come and dwell in our world, inscribing indwelling as a prolongation of the Incarnation. Salvation is therefore fundamentally *welcoming God,* with whom one enters into relationship.

The notion of divine indwelling expresses well this welcoming of the very person of God, who is present not only through divine emanations, but also through created grace or gifts. The presence of God in the human being—by grace—is made possible by attentiveness to God—by listening or vision—that invites to free up a space that God can occupy. It is in the crucible of this space, by constantly renewed attentiveness, that a progressive assimilation to God, despite one's dissimilarity, is made possible through the conformation of one's own will to God's. Teresa thus understood, like Paul, that "it is no longer I who live, but it is Christ who lives in me" (Gal 2:20).[13] The presence of God in the human being by indwelling is thus the very heart and principle of salvation. This indwelling reveals the intimacy and the partnership of the human being with God, emphasizing the welcome that one can offer to God—a human potentiality that is the fruit of divine initiative.

Such a welcome is the fruit of an encounter, of a visitation from God. The dimension of receptivity is illustrated in the figure of Mary at the moment of the annunciation, and it is expressed in Teresa's teaching, which sees at the heart of the movement of salvation the moment of *deshacer,* where everything seems to crumble, but in order to open a space for welcoming a new other and to humble the human person in a way that makes her receptive to the gift of God. The dimension of welcoming expresses well the need for God's offer of salvation to be received by the human person. This offer, broadly made, calls for a response not only in words, but in words given flesh. The reception of the offer of salvation means a reconfiguration of the person who receives it and, by this fact, of their actions.

The notion of indwelling also makes it possible to account for the continuity between a salvation already at work and its unfolding in eternal life. This is the presence of God in the person that leads, finally, to the presence of the person in God. Thus, in the *mise en abîme* that is the trinitarian inhabitation in the human person, established as reciprocal indwelling, a reversal of the horizon arises eschatologically. Indeed, while the first place of dwelling is today the human person—called to welcome the offer of God—at the end of time it will be rather that the human person lives in God, according to the Pauline hope that the dead will be *in* Christ (e.g., 1 Thess 4:16) or *in* God in the infinite horizon.

The entire offer of God and of salvation to the human person is not exhausted in the historical act of the Incarnation, but what abides, eternally, of God's salvation is an "indwelling." God comes to the human person and dwells there specifically; this place and this movement already constitute salvation, a salvation that is open to a horizon of eternity. This dimension is the center and the heart of the soteriological process driven by the Spirit.

The meaning of salvation, for Teresa, is therefore trinitarian indwelling. But this concept of salvation is a challenging one. An understanding of salvation as consummated and ongoing, the trinitarian indwelling is a dwelling that is not of the order of possession; Teresa compares it to a sum of money that has been promised to a person but not yet received.[14]

By its positive orientation toward God and its infinite teleological aim, trinitarian indwelling contrasts with other concepts of salvation. Redemption understands salvation as a buying back; it is present, for instance, as a presumption in Teresa's vision of hell, in that she writes that she saw "the place His [God's] mercy had freed me from."[15] Redemption is a helpful concept of salvation, but it is not the most prominent in Teresian thought.[16] Salvation as indwelling is also distinguished from the concept of divinization (or deification),[17] which also illustrates a teleological aim, since the latter emphasizes more the endpoint—"becoming" God—while in the concept of indwelling, salvation is the dwelling of God in the human person. Finally, salvation as an indwelling is also distinguished from the soteriological concept of justification, a central concept in Teresa's day because of the theological controversies between Protestants and Catholics. Justification is rooted in a more formal and "juridical" conception of the relationship between God and the human person, although it developed beyond this original concept. Such a background is somewhat foreign to Teresian thought, which involves more affective relationships of friendship and gift. Where Teresa will agree with the theory of justification—even Lutheran—is in its keen awareness of the gratuitousness of the divine gift of salvation that calls for humble thanksgiving.[18]

Between Incarnation and Passion: Toward an Incarnational Salvation

At the heart of the mediation of Christ who is the bearer of salvation, two poles emerge. On one hand, an incarnational pole centered on the coming into the flesh of the Son of God, and on the other hand, a paschal pole built around the death and resurrection of Christ. We have noted the presence of these two poles in Teresian thought.[19] If the paschal pole is discursively present—in the cross, in particular—the incarnational pole is more dominant, notably in Teresa's insistence on the sacred humanity of Christ, but especially in the form of an incarnational dynamic. That being said, even in contemporary theology, the relative importance of each pole in theological elaboration is an ongoing topic of reflection, as is the relationship between them.

The fathers of the Church, especially the Greek fathers, reserved a special place for the incarnation in their soteriological reflection, so much so that it was once common to make reference to a "Greek" theory of soteriology, which would have strong incarnational accents, as opposed to a "Latin" theory that would emphasize the full accomplishment of the mission of Christ on the cross. While it is recognized today that circumscribing these divergent patristic approaches in such a radical way is inaccurate,[20] it remains true that key elements of patristic theology place more emphasis on the incarnational dimension than does much contemporary theology, still marked with the seal of the paschal event.

The relative eclipse of the Incarnation by Christ's death and resurrection in contemporary theology can probably be explained by the phenomenal character that is peculiar to each. At the human level, the Incarnation marks the appearance of God in human form. But this entry was discreet, since it was hidden for years, required growth, and was only understood retrospectively. The Incarnation is often understood as "given" (or happening) to Jesus Christ, since his free choice in this process is not apparent. Louis Panier maintains that this "forgotten birth" in contemporary Christologies is due to the "historical" character of Christ's death and resurrection, and the detailed accounts we have of it, while Christ's birth and childhood are described in literary accounts that are marked by supernatural events and Old Testament allusions, making it difficult, if not impossible, to distinguish history from interpretation.[21]

Furthermore, in contrast to the discretion of the Incarnation, the paschal event of Christ's death on the cross and resurrection is vivid. It comes at the end of a public ministry of Jesus Christ that plays out over time and culminates in his conscious acceptance of martyrdom. Then the resurrection emphasizes for believers the ratification by the Father in the Spirit of what had been accomplished by Christ in the Spirit. Without forcing assent—yesterday and today—the death and resurrection is more visible and accessible than the Incarnation. Moreover, the link between this summit of Calvary and the conscious action of Jesus Christ challenges a contemporary civilization marked by the centrality of individual consciousness.

Teresa invites us to reconsider the incarnational pole of soteriology without minimizing the importance of the paschal event. The latter is properly understood as the completion of the process begun with the Incarnation. Teresa offers a new understanding of the relationship between these two poles. An effort to articulate such an understanding would begin by noting that if the death and resurrection of Christ is the central experience or event of Christianity—and therefore, of salvation—then the Incarnation is the first or foundational experience. From the point of view of Christ himself, the Incarnation is the foundation of his human experience. The coming into the flesh of the Word and the continual union of the divine and the human in the person of Jesus Christ are the foundations of his existence. To be sure, the death/resurrection of Christ is a unique and absolute event in his existence. It bears a significance that goes beyond its purely historical moment, revealing the divine power of life and standing as the central experience of Christianity and the summit of the Incarnation. The endpoint is already in germ in the beginning, but the summit reveals it in fullness. Between the incarnational and paschal poles, an inseparable link is clear.

An incarnational soteriology also draws attention to the Spirit's role in the Incarnation of the Word of God and in the unfolding of Christ's life up to the cross and resurrection, as well as at work in human beings. The mystery of salvation is not reduced to a simple step emanating from becoming human, but as an incarnational movement lived and exemplified by Christ, who offers himself as a path of universal salvation, perhaps even without a face. The incarnating Spirit thus marks out a path of salvation and even, more fundamentally, the very path of what it means to be Christian.

THROUGH THE SPIRIT...

Given the abundant witness of the Scriptures, tradition, and the faith of the church that Christ is the Savior of humanity, the question arises: What role does the Holy Spirit play in salvation? While Teresa speaks repeatedly and at great length about Christ, her approach to the Spirit is more circumspect. While Christ is undoubtedly the face of God, his experience, and therefore the imitation of him, is present at a distance for the believer. This difficulty is expressed in a desire for God—oriented toward him—and calls upon the Holy Spirit as an image of God in movement. With additional consideration of the Father, a trinitarian conception of God in the work of salvation unfolds as a Father who is origin and will, a Son who is Face and Word, and the Spirit who is unity and movement. Thus, from the perspective of salvation, a primordial and specific role is attributable to the Spirit, alongside the mediating work of Christ.[22] The Spirit's own mediation is one of movement and in this sense visually transparent while being powerfully active. This kinetic role of the Spirit in the work of salvation is evident in the experience of rapture,[23] but especially in other experiences, changes, and growth attributable to the Spirit's action.

As *incarnator* of salvation, the Spirit plays a role in the salvation of human beings parallel to the Spirit's role in the Incarnation of the Son. This is not a simple repetition of the same work *ad nauseam*; the Spirit's own movement aims constantly to bring to light something new, like a growing, fertile life. The incarnational movement prolongs creation itself. This common work of the Spirit in the Son and in believers is articulated sacramentally in the double epiclesis of the eucharistic prayer of Mass, prayed first over the offerings of bread and wine and then over the faithful.[24]

In the following pages, we explore the figure of the triune God in the work of salvation, in relation to its echo in the human being. The dimension of the effacement, or kenosis, already identified as part of the pneumatological dynamics of *deshacer*, constitutes the focus of our reflection, which then concludes with a theological reprise of the notion of the Holy Spirit as incarnator of salvation.

The Father: Source and Will

In the life of the Trinity, the Father is the figure of the will. In Teresian teaching, there is a *communion* of will between the Father and the Son through the adoption by Christ of the Father's will; their will is one.[25] The Father is thus presented as both the origin and the end, since he is the source from which the action of the Son arises and the end toward which the perfect fulfillment of this will tends. This communion of will, which also extends to the Spirit, thus leads the Son to leave the bosom of the Father in order to become a slave by obedience, following the movement of the Christic hymn of the letter to the Philippians to which Teresa refers.[26]

As a result, the following of Christ (*sequela Christi*) can be understood *mutatis mutandis* to be the following of the Father by union with the Father's will through the path that is Christ.[27] Knowing and welcoming the will of the Father leads the person who listens to him on the path of service.[28] In the horizon of an incarnate salvation, one's works demonstrate one's will. This is what Teresa hears during a locution of Christ, when she wanted to do something in the service of God and she wondered, seeing how little she was capable of, why the Lord wanted her works. The answer she heard was, "To see your will."[29] The will, which cannot be seen, is revealed by the actions it inspires.

While the Father is the source of the divine will common to Christ, it is not because he dictates it. His role as origin of the will is found in a hiding of his own face. This posture is consonant with that of the Gospel of John, where Jesus speaks extensively about his Father, even though the Father's actions are less visible in John than they are in other Gospels.[30] It is through the word of Jesus that the Father makes himself present, and this word speaks their union. In fact, in the Teresian corpus, one finds several moments when Teresa addresses the Father, but there is never a dialogue;[31] if Teresa turns to and receives the Father, it is first of all through Christ. The actantial silence of the Father in Teresa's work ought not therefore be seen as an absence; by the communion of will, the word of Christ is the word of the Father; Christ both receives and shares this will and calls the disciple to do the same.

The Son and the Sons/Daughters: Kenosis and Face

The economic relationship at work between the Father, the Son, and the Spirit, such as it is seen both in Teresa's writings and in Scripture and tradition, suggests a form of mutual kenosis, an effacement for the benefit of the other and a fundamental orientation toward the other. For the Father and the Spirit, this effacement is seen in the visible concentration of everything in Christ—as we see in certain christological hymns of the New Testament (e.g., Eph 1:3–14 and Col 1:15–20)—even though Christ refers constantly to the Father, recognizes himself to be led by the Spirit, and puts his trust entirely in them at the moment of his death. The Divine Persons thus relate to one another in the unity of self-effacement for the benefit of the other. The effacement that can be expressed as kenosis emerges with regularity and vigor in Teresa's relationship to God. She says she is "undone" (*deshacerse*) and recognizes herself as *ruin* (wretched) at the very moment God visits her and configures her to himself. The disciple is called to share in the kenosis of Christ, who is the face of God.

The kenosis of the Son reveals to the world the kenosis of God. In fidelity to the will of the Father, the movement outlined in the life of Christ is that of a kenosis crowned by an exaltation. This dynamic emerges with clarity in the christological hymn that Saint Paul includes into his letter to the Philippians (Phil 2:5–11).

The movement that emerges is one of self-diminishment that sees Christ putting aside the divine glory that was his in order to enter deeply into human experience, choosing the path of service and gift, to the point of reaching the most abject and unjust condition, that of being crucified. This path of self-diminishment is not, however, primarily a path of suffering. The fidelity of the Son to the Father and his love for humanity are expressed in the total character of the self-diminishment that was his, not through the magnitude of his suffering. However, it is through death on the cross that the radical self-diminishment of God in Jesus Christ becomes visible. Through this twofold self-diminishment, a dynamic of kenosis is deeply inscribed in the existence of Christ.

Kenosis leads in Christ to an empty space, where a face—his face—can appear. This face will be reception before being presentation. Christ is the face of God. Through Christ's life, God is revealed. Teresa referred constantly to the "sacred humanity" of Christ, a humanity with a Johannine tonality, his body indwelt by the Spirit and "always glorified."[32] It is in response to the summit of the self-diminishment in anthropological terms—death—that the ultimate face of Christ emerges. By the crowning of his life on Calvary and in his resurrection, the end of Jesus's earthly journey sealed his loyalty and founded a new relationship to existence; death and sin do not have the last word, but life. The power of the triune God is vividly revealed in the resurrection of Christ by the Father in the Spirit, by the opening to a new and transformed life, by the affirmation that the victory of death, which seems obvious, is a deception. It is at the heart of weakness, as Saint Paul himself puts it, that the power of God is most vividly manifested (2 Cor 12:9).

A path can be traced from Christ's ontological kenosis to his anthropological kenosis in the Incarnation and resurrection, which respectively present the face of God in humanity and his glorified Face. The literal kenosis of death, an anthropological kenosis, allows a new incarnation. In this, the very body of Christ becomes the sign, even the matrix, of a movement of incarnation of divine origin that not only creates in empty space, *ex nihilo*, but can restore the life of one who had been killed. The redoubling of the kenosis calls for a redoubling of incarnation. The resurrection is a renewal of the Incarnation in which life is more than restored; it is increased and subsumed. The resurrection is not an identical repetition of the divine act of incarnation—that would literally be a reincarnation—but the same movement of life is at work there that expresses its power this time in a vivid manner. The power of incarnation that emerges in the resurrection defies time and death in order to make visible in time the eternal, universal scope of the movement at work.

The renewal of life in Christ apparent in the post-Easter appearances in his spiritualized body redoubles and confirms the first incarnation and ties together the ontological kenosis and kenosis of the Incarnation, and the anthropological kenosis (death) and resurrection, a link that places them in a relationship of continuity, even of reiteration. This incarnational redoubling at the beginning and the end of the human existence of Christ establishes the incarnational movement as the central motive of the Christic journey. Moreover, this reiteration transforms the *event* of the Incarnation into an incarnational *movement* and suggests in itself the potential opening to others in the figure of the disciple.

The only Son is "the firstborn within a large family" (Rom 8:29). The disciple of Christ is invited to follow her master in the same movement that marks the entry into the way of salvation that is intimacy with God. The kenotic self-diminishment of the Christian, in the image of the face of God who is Christ, is not validated first of all by the extent of her suffering. Jesus, by inviting her to follow him, invites the disciple to take up the cross and follow him (Matt 16:24).[33] This is not, first of all, the cross of crucifixion or the cross of martyrdom, but the movement of self-diminishment that it implies. The heart of discipleship is primarily the adoption of the very movement of self-diminishment that Christ embraced, the self-diminishment that led him to the cross. Where will this self-diminishment lead the disciple? One need simply welcome God, that his Word may take flesh.

The Incarnating Spirit

The kenotic dimension necessary for the face of God to take flesh—Christ himself reflected in the faces of believers—is the Teresian *deshacer* that constitutes the central part of a process imputed to the Spirit. From a Teresian perspective, kenosis is inscribed in the horizon of life and not in annihilation, opening in the disciple space for a new life that no longer fears death. In chapter 4, we noted Teresa's adoption of the Pauline perspective of a life in Christ as one of diminishment, following in the way of service. The goal is not self-diminishment, but a life that is like the life of God.

The Nicene-Constantinopolitan Creed, reflecting the Lukan account (Luke 1:35) espoused by Teresa, already points to the particular role played by the Spirit in the coming in the flesh of the Word of God: *Et incarnatus est de Spiritu Sancto.* This coming of the face of God *de Spiritu Sancto* inaugurates in a visible way an economic complementarity, even an inseparability, of the Son and the Spirit in the work of salvation. This complementarity will blossom in a salvific, incarnational thrust that we find in the Eucharist, but also in this movement that sees God dwelling in—and in doing so, transforming—the human being. The discreet character of the pneumatological action calls for discernment in order to understand clearly the Spirit's role.

Within the Trinity, the Spirit is a bond, a relationship between the Father and the Son. Between God and humanity, the Spirit actualizes this bond. In the dynamic of a trinitarian outpouring, François-Xavier Durrwell presents the Spirit as the "begetting of the Son,"[34] that is, the very *movement* of begetting, since it is the Father who begets as origin within the Trinity. The neologism we introduce in this work, *incarnator*, attributed to the Spirit, underlines the Spirit's active role in this movement, which the term *incarnation* could pass over in silence as a purely passive one, or even as a result. As incarnator, the Spirit is the one who incarnates, without being origin, and the one through whom the Son becomes incarnate. Like the Father, whose effacement in the figure of Christ we have noted, the Spirit is present in a discreet way.

A spirit whose only face is another, the Holy Spirit is not easily grasped. The Spirit's discreet action suggests the elusiveness of God. The creed of the Council of Nicea, before the revision made by the Council of Constantinople in 381, after having spoken at length about the Father, then about the Son, called for Christians to believe "in the Holy Spirit"—and nothing more. This initial silence as to what can be said dogmatically about the Spirit is indicative of the Spirit's manner of being in the world. Rather than a deficiency, Christoph Theobald sees at the heart of this brief article an "empty space" that should be understood as a sort of "guideline" with regard to representation in dogma when it comes to the Holy Spirit.[35] The Spirit resolutely takes its place alongside the Father and the Son in the creed—there is indeed a Trinity—but the definition escapes. In fact, the Spirit is what eludes and escapes. Being the one who incarnates in the crucible of self-diminishment, the Spirit leaves a space empty in a definition of his own self.

In the more substantial Nicene-Constantinopolitan Creed, the gift of life, through begetting and incarnation, is attributed to the Spirit: "I believe in the Holy Spirit, who is Lord and giver of life…."[36] Giving life is the creative act par excellence that brings into existence what was not and might not have been. This outbreak of life through the action of the Spirit expresses the creativity of God. It is this creativity of God that underpins the Spirit's role as incarnator and also exceeds it, inviting us to a great attention in order to recognize the Spirit's action and presence.

While the Spirit is seen at times through the life of Jesus Christ—in Christ's words or actions—it is when Christ becomes invisible that the Spirit becomes more visible, even though it is the Son who imparts the Spirit rather than being guided by him. This action of the Spirit is particularly concrete in the Acts of the Apostles. With Pentecost (Acts 2), the Spirit is presented as the source of an irruption of words addressed in all languages and touching the hearts of many people. Under the guidance of the Spirit, the believing community opens itself to a new life: the encounter of Philip with the Ethiopian eunuch leading to the latter's baptism (Acts 8:26–40), although he was not Jewish, or the magnificent vision presented to Peter from heaven, opening the door of the church to non-Jews (Acts 10:9–16). This Spirit of newness helps the community to discover what is essential within it and reminds it that even though Christ is gone, God dwells in it and guides it.

By the Spirit's way of being, the Spirit is revealed as the image of God par excellence in his *dynamic* relationship to human existence beyond the Image that is Christ. The Spirit comes to surprise humanity without ceasing, inviting people to take unexpected paths. In the Teresian journey of the creation of Saint Joseph, two people represent well these new openings that the Spirit brings. The first is Father Salazar, the superior of a young priest who served as Teresa's confessor, who encouraged the priest to "let the spirit of the Lord work" in her, rather than to lead her on "so confining a path."[37] In doing so, situating himself to the side of the one who leads, he expresses the fact that the priest needed to step aside in leading Teresa so that the elusive Spirit could pick up where he left off. Another "surprise" of the Spirit comes in the person of Father Ibáñez who, consulted on the initial project of Saint Joseph, wanted to discourage Teresa and her companion.[38] Not only did he come to change his mind and to have a hand in the birth of the monastery, but he himself subsequently wished to enter into greater intimacy with God by withdrawing for more than two years to an isolated monastery of his order.[39] Teresa's account does not specify in this second case that the reversal is the work of the Spirit, but it suggests that it was supernatural, as much by its suddenness as by the subsequent personal and apostolic fruits it bore. In doing so, the Spirit does not shape a person in his own image, but rather shapes one who is open in the image of God.

Thus, while avoiding the pitfall of possessiveness, the Spirit continually offers to come and *dwell* in the human being to animate her. But this leads to a posture of humility by the person; though one can welcome God through the Spirit into oneself, still one can never possess the Spirit or even recognize the Spirit's face entirely. Seeing and hearing the triune God happens through Christ. The space of an infinite search unfolds because the God who cannot be depicted remains supremely active. The elusive character of the God who gives himself calls us to hospitality. Like Abraham welcoming the three divine visitors (Gen 18), it is to this fundamental anthropological attitude that the human being is invited in search of God.

...IN THE HUMAN BEING

A Pneumatological Way of Being Christian: See—Incarnate—Tell

Noli me tangere. The encounter between Mary Magdalene and the risen Christ (John 20:11–18) has been depicted over and over in Christian art. Seeing Jesus, being called by name by him, the elusiveness of intimacy and distance, then the sending to the disciples—Mary is *apostola apostolorum*—the details of the story reflect the contemporary disciple's own relationship with God in Christ.

Noli me tangere. The movement of the Spirit is also elusive. In search of the salvific action of the Spirit, we have been able to discover at the heart of the Teresian corpus a pneumatological, incarnational movement that accounts for the action of God and the movement of configuration that calls to the believer. From the point of view of the Spirit, this salvific movement is one of *displacement*—even of release—then of *deshacer*—an emptying that opens a space—and finally of *inspiration*—which fills the open space superabundantly and brings fruitfulness.[40]

From the human point of view, this journey, always to be undertaken anew, begins with the use of the spiritual senses oriented toward God, looking and listening to him; it is by this path that a way of openness to the other can be traced. Then it is in the welcoming and the incarnational unfolding of the One who is received that this movement is rooted. It is the place of the established covenant, of indwelling. Finally, this welcoming of a God who pushes us to reach beyond once again commits us to action, to an irrepressible word directed toward others, word and action that are then marked with the seal of this new, inhabiting, inspiring presence, without being possessed. Such a structure, clear in Teresa's work, is not limited to the singularity of her experience. On the contrary, this structure can be universalized and in fact reveals the essential pneumatological structure of being Christian, and even of being *human.*[41] This structure can be understood in an anthropological movement in three stages: see—incarnate—tell.[42]

This triple movement in the human being is bound up with the movement of the Spirit that we have already considered:

Human being: see—incarnate—tell

Holy Spirit: displacement—*deshacer*—inspiration

The Spirit brings about in the human being *displacement* in order *to see, kenosis* in order to open a space where God can become *incarnate*, and *inspiration* in order that the person in turn becomes *speech*. When seen in its human expression, the movement is similar to that of Christ himself. While the "moment" of seeing can only be applied to Christ obliquely, with reference to the trinitarian life, the moment of incarnation is crystal clear in the Incarnation of the Son. As for the moment of "telling," it is accomplished, of course, in Christ's preaching, but more broadly as a moment radically turned toward others, culminating in the witness (*martyria*) of the cross. The "telling" of the one who is the Word of God is thus revealed as acting and speaking beyond words.

This soteriological movement in the human being is revealed in the Teresian corpus through the confluence of two elements. First, the central place of the dynamic of incarnation. A locution of Christ provides the second heuristic element, as he told Teresa (and which we considered above): see and tell.[43] In this formula is summarized the upstream and downstream of a movement of salvation that has incarnation at its center. Openness to what is presented by God is articulated in a call to see. Because the enjoyment of God is not the last word of salvation for the human being in this earthly life, an invitation to share what has been seen follows. By combining these two dimensions, we can clearly recognize the global perspective of the soteriological movement from the point of view of the human being, according to Teresian thought.

In analyzing Teresa's personal journey, the features of this soteriological movement are easily seen. It is literally by *sight*—in a vision—that her path of conversion begins and develops, much aided by listening—namely, locutions. The vision of Christ with angry eyes surprised her; the sight of a statue of the scourged Christ caused her deep sorrow; the vision of hell opened up a path of apostolate; the visions and locutions of Christ comforted and guided her. A work of *incarnation* developed in parallel; she was gradually formed in the image of the One she contemplated. This work was laborious at first; Teresa did not hide her long years of divided desires.[44] When she fully consented to the welcoming of God, her transformation was radical.[45] Various dimensions of this indwelling of God in Teresa were spectacular, including the mystical betrothal and marriage[46] or the grace of transverberation.[47] But more profoundly, an internal formation occurred, a simple "abiding" of God in silence and peace, when her will conformed to God's and she wanted only to serve him in life and death. Finally, Teresa's journey culminated in an exit from herself directed toward others through a "telling." Teresa spoke, wrote, created, and founded. This incessant activity was not her doing, nor a logical consequence of what preceded it. From this, conformation to God was born, on his initiative—through a number of collaborators—a strong desire to participate in the salvation of others by sparing no effort, no sacrifice. This Teresian "telling," which resounds even up to our own day, carries, under the inspiration of the Spirit, both what has been seen and the weight and the work of consented incarnation. In this sense, Teresa's teaching is deeply rooted in the existential path that she traveled.

Along with Teresa's journey, a brief look at the example of the first disciples of Christ, as set out in the Gospels, allows us to appreciate the universal relevance of the structure we have set out. We look to the disciples for good reason; they have accomplished in full the anthropological itinerary of being Christian under the movement of the Spirit and in imitation of Christ, and in this they have value as models.

Seeing. The call of the disciple comes via sight or hearing. Some of them *see* Jesus and begin to follow him. Others are *called* directly by him: "Follow me" (Matt 4:19; 9:9; Mark 1:17; 2:14; John 1:43). Two disciples *hear* the invitation to "come and *see*" (John 1:39). Before this moment, it is upon hearing John the Baptist speak of Jesus as "the Lamb of God" that John and Andrew set off after him; wanting to see where he was living, and presumably to share the space, they are invited to go and see. What they found was a mobile "inhabiting," since "the Son of Man has nowhere to lay his head" (Matt 8:20) and was about to embark with them quickly on a journey to Jerusalem (see John 2). If "seeing" is the first necessary step in a deepening process, it doesn't automatically make one a disciple. Many who see or hear Jesus don't stop to join him. Others oppose him. Even those who come into direct contact with him do not always offer an immediate and positive response; some agree to go further (e.g., Zacchaeus, in Luke 19:1–10) while others turn back (the rich man in Matt 19:22). Not all those who experience in their bodies the effects of hearing or seeing, such as through a cure, choose to go farther or accompany him. Having said that, without consistently leading a response of welcome—refusal being much more common in the Gospels—"seeing" is undoubtedly the doorway. It is notable that the Acts of the Apostles illustrates the end of the process, on one hand offering a portrait of the first Christian community, men and women transformed by fraternal charity, by whom others are called through *seeing* them (see Acts 2:46–47; 4:32–35; also see John 13:35), and on the other hand, people called by *hearing* what the apostles proclaim (e.g., Acts 2:14–41).

Incarnating/inhabiting. After one becomes open, a long and slow work of companionship then begins for the disciple. This means getting to know Christ, seeing him, listening to him, questioning him, walking with him, and letting oneself be seen, challenged, called, and disturbed by him. It means growing in intimacy, over a presence that teaches and configures. This "inhabiting" is marked by an integral experience of welcoming. And this welcoming transforms. This moment concerns first of all the disciples (*mathètai*), the twelve who follow Jesus wherever he goes. But they are not alone; women also accompany them (Luke 8:1–3), while other people rapidly move through the process of seeing and telling, like the man Christ healed and then sent off to tell his friends what had happened (Mark 5:18–20). "Incarnating" is for the disciple a moment of knowledge, of deepening, and of transformation.

Telling. There is a *provisional* telling in the early parts of Jesus's ministry, when he sends his disciples, who had become apostles, into the world (Luke 9:1–6; Mark 6:6–13; Matt 10). They were commissioned to proclaim to others what they had learned from Jesus. But a *complete* telling had to wait for the experience of their confrontation with death and resurrection, not only that of Jesus, but also that of the faith of the disciple—in doubt and loss, only to be rediscovered and transformed. For Judas, doubt led faith to its death, while the experience of the disciples of Emmaus is one of a loss—they were "looking sad" (Luke 24:17)—that becomes a vigorous renewal—"they got up and returned to Jerusalem" (Luke 24:33). For many disciples, according to the tradition of the church, this integral journey of faith through death led them to witness to martyrdom. The word of the risen One who sends and energetically invites the disciple to "tell" is not added to the other words; there is no new teaching. Everything has been said, and it is the apostles' turn now to be sent without him, but with God present under the mode of the Holy Spirit (John 20:22; Acts 1:8). "Go tell my brothers," "Go, teach!"—the initial interior movement of "Come, see" is now resolutely turned outward, toward others (see, e.g., Matt 28:10, 19–20; Mark 16:15; John 20:17). With the physical departure of him with whom they had communed, the Holy Spirit invited the disciples to bear witness to him in their lives. Christ's *pro nobis*—pushed to its height on the cross—finds an echo in this last point of the incarnational movement picked from God that pours out in a telling addressed to others. Such a movement, which would stop only in a dwelling within an individual, would resist the inspiration of the Spirit, who pushes to make something new, to be creative, and to go toward others.

We find this itinerary of seeing—incarnating—telling summarized in the opening verses of 1 John, where the author describes his intention:

> We declare to you what was from the beginning, what we have heard, what we have seen with our eyes, what we have looked at and touched with our hands, concerning the word of life—this life was revealed, and we have seen it and testify to it, and declare to you the eternal life that was with the Father and was revealed to us—we declare to you what we have seen and heard so that you also may have fellowship with us; and truly our fellowship is with the Father and with his Son Jesus Christ. We are writing these things so that our joy may be complete. (1 John 1:1–4)

This magnificent text sings with beauty. First "what was from the beginning" is invoked, *Life,* before any discourse or manifestation. Then, this eternal life, announced in the Greek by the neutral relative pronoun *ho* (this), is made manifest (*phainô*) by its Word; it is given to be heard, seen, contemplated, touched; it took flesh and became body. It is also through the body that the Word of life is received: through the eyes, the hands. But the physical welcome is not limited to reception; it involves witnessing and announcing this life to others. Thus comes the third moment, this "to you" (*hymin*) to whom the text is addressed. The author reiterates the entirety of the story by saying "we declare to you what we have seen and heard," but specifying its purpose: fellowship, or communion (*koinônia*). The movement of welcoming and announcing aims to form a body, a body marked by a fullness of joy. The author's journey, which began with sight and concluded with telling, ultimately seeks to bring about participation in the movement of incarnation of the Word who is Life.

While our presentation of the pneumatological, salvific structure as received by the human being is sequential, it still must be understood as a continual interaction of its various stages. The seeing, which is first, mustn't stop, any more than the deepening of the inhabiting through *deshacer* can stop. Finally, the telling will constantly be refined with more effectiveness and truth, nourished by contemplation and a growing presence of God in oneself.

This succinct dive into an evangelical rereading of the Teresian structural model suggests its relevance in allowing us to grasp on the human level the pneumatological movement of salvation.

An Anthropological Structure for Reading the Action of God beyond Borders

By pushing a little further, we can ask in an exploratory way the question of the potential fruitfulness of the pneumatological salvific structure inscribed in the human being within the framework of a reflection on God's universal work of salvation. Indeed, Catholic theology's renewed—and positive—look toward other religions, in particular since the Second Vatican Council's declaration *Nostra aetate* and the interreligious meetings of Assisi, has prompted new reflections on the way in which the salvation of non-Christians happens. Faced with the objective problem of people who know nothing about Christianity, one growing edge of theological exploration has been with regard to the role of the Spirit who, as the invisible and active presence of God, sets a horizon for the work of God outside Judeo-Christian borders.

Although modeled on the Christian vision, the pneumatological movement of salvation that we have noted in the human being can also be understood without reference to the person of Christ. It is then always an anthropological movement impelled by the Spirit. However, a "telling" that has no other connection with the Word except through the one who inspires it—the Spirit—is, a priori, at the very least disconcerting. There is a tension between, on the one hand, a faceless and potentially universal movement and, on the other, the face of God acting as revealer of the movement of salvation and of the whole Trinity. Considering the proximity, even the indissociability, of the Spirit and the Son, the link between a "faceless" pneumatological movement—which it always is—and a Face that can only be sketched involuntarily because it is unknown, generates many questions. Indeed, the Spirit takes part in the divine work of salvation—we can even say that the Spirit saves—but not independently of Christ. The completeness of salvation is necessarily trinitarian. How can there be any "seeing" without a face to see, any "incarnating" without a form to take, or any "telling" without reference to Christ? Is the passage through the trinitarian Spirit sufficient to guarantee this bond? Considering that the Spirit is indeed the Spirit of the Father and of the Son, and keeping in mind the revealed face of God who is Jesus Christ—as a normative criterion—the pneumatological movement of salvation can effectively serve as a standard to identify an action of God outside the framework of Christianity, an action that has already been carried by the trinitarian Spirit and therefore, in germ, by the whole Trinity.

This theological elaboration of the pneumatological standard and the christological criterion seeks to reconcile two axioms of Christianity: the inescapable and indisputable character of Christ as the Face and Revelation of God—a fundamental element of Teresian thought—and the certainty that God works through the Spirit in every human being, even outside the visible contours of the church. Recognition of the presence of the pneumatological movement of incarnation in the human person could thus acknowledge that God works in people sometimes in ways that do not (yet) bear visible fruit. This work happens in the depths of hearts and consciences. For the Christian observer, the fruits may be compared in their observability with the Christic criterion of the revealed face of God.

Such an action by one of the Divine Persons is not without precedent. In this study, we have rarely mentioned the Father, although we have recognized him as the origin, particularly of the will. This relative obscurity does not in any way affect the Father's action or the recognition of it. In the incarnational movement inspired by the Spirit, where Christ plays the role of the essential Face, the Spirit seems to be obscured and can be overlooked in theological reflection. But in places where Christ does not appear in a conscious manner, the first role could therefore belong to the Spirit, although he acts discretely.

Giving due attention to the Spirit as we have here is not intended in any way to confuse or replace the role of the Son. The Spirit does not become the face of God. The Spirit has a distinct role, as incarnator of salvation, but since the latter is not pushed to its absolute Face that is Christ, the movement itself acquires a more marked relief. In the multitude of faces and words that then serve as models or outcomes, Christ, the Face and Word of God, remains the absolute criterion of the revelation of God, but without excluding the goodness, even the properly divine character—by gift—of partial images. Following Congar's injunction that any good pneumatology must keep its christological reference,[48] the same logic can be adopted here—any good pneumatological soteriology must keep its christological (and also *patro*logical) reference, even in the case where the figure of Christ is not explicitly present.

The need to look for the proper action of the Spirit in people while keeping a reference to Christ at hand applies not only to non-Christians, since it concerns all human beings. Even for a Christian, the reality of "personal" salvation is recognized not only through a clear verbal profession of faith in Jesus Christ, but by seeing how that faith is concretely incarnate in one's life as a way of salvation and salvation already in germ. Even for the saints, the pneumatological movement of salvation is seen through the resemblance of their "faces," the witness of their lives, to the one face of God. The relationship between the Spirit and Christ, outside of confessed Christianity, thus once again sheds light on the creative tension in the work of the Trinity.

CONCLUSION

The Spirit opens and inspires. The Spirit pulls free and displaces. The intent of this research was precisely to pull free the salvific work of the Spirit as it appears in Teresa's writing, both her experience and her doctrine. It is a pulling free in order to find the presence and the action of the Spirit in the intersections of discourse and action, underneath conventional formulas, images, or silences.

Our examination of the work of Saint Teresa of Avila has allowed us to identify, through the progressive displacements she experienced, a movement of the Spirit. We recall her numerous and obvious geographic displacements. In childhood she desired to die as a martyr among the Moors, then underwent the trial of the illness that led her to the countryside and then close to death upon her return to the monastery of the Incarnation. During the work of founding Saint Joseph monastery, she lived a short exile in Toledo, then came back to prepare the little house that would become the monastery before leaving it for a while once it was founded. Her final displacement to Saint Joseph, into a strict cloister, was an invitation to stability, but this was followed by an ongoing call to found and guide many Carmelite monasteries throughout Spain. What Teresa experienced was a call and a desire for a withdrawn life that was lived, surprisingly, in perpetual movement.

While the geographical displacements are visible, the interior displacements are decisive as well. There was the mystical displacement of leaving her own body in the experience of rapture, the affective displacement from anxiety to peace and joy, and especially interior displacement pushing her from attentiveness to herself and her own concerns to attending to God's plan for her, a transition that Teresa long resisted. It was through sight—of Christ—that this displacement was initiated, within the framework of a movement of encounter supported by prayer that she conceived as an encounter with a friend.

This pulling free opened up space for displacement to the unexpected, the surprise of a new project in a new place. Such openness allows for exploration and avoids circumscribing and closing off the action of God. Embracing this movement, we were attentive in this research not to presume to solve a question, even as we contributed to its exploration.

The Spirit's emptying and opening within a person, *deshacer,* creates a space for indwelling. This means first passing through a kind of death. For Teresa, this emptying was multifaceted. It took a long time for her to be willing to abandon her frivolous relationships. Faced with the greatness of the gift of God, Teresa became acutely aware of her unworthiness. A deep suffering always preceded a salvific desire and underlined its strength and vigor. The Saint Joseph project almost did not see the light of day, and its closure even seemed at one point to be inevitable. The establishment of Saint Joseph was accompanied by a prolonged absence from the place by Teresa. Finally, after numerous foundations, tensions with ecclesiastical authorities forced Teresa into silence for many months and threatened all of her work. It is thus continually at the risk of death, in the fragility of a continuous welcome, that the work of salvation impelled by the Spirit was to develop in her.

Undergoing a long-term *deshacer* was decisive in this—undergoing the experience of distance from God and also undergoing a deepening of her images of God. Indeed, Teresa's fidelity to the images of her experience of God—in particular, those of dwelling and place—can be seen in various texts spanning several years. This constant reflection on the given images allowed a deepening of understanding while at the same time emphasizing their inadequacy by resisting objectification; they remain marked by a space that cannot be completely filled.

In the empty space created by this process of opening, a presence emerges, a dwelling by the God who saves. Something is present that speaks without being graspable, in the singularity of a relationship with God. Something of God and God's action is revealed in his inhabitation of flesh. The incarnational dimension of salvation is clear in the Teresian insistence upon the "always glorified" flesh of Christ, as he presents himself in her visions.[49] The face of God, for Teresa, is thus Christ in his humanity, signifying this already supernatural presence of a God who chooses the fragility of dwelling in the flesh.

The dwelling of God in the human being is, for Teresa of Avila, the very essence of salvation. In this, her fundamental soteriological orientation joins her christological orientation, but also her vision of prayer as an encounter of friendship between the human being and God. Recognized by the church as a master of spirituality, Teresa puts at the heart of prayer the mutuality, gratuitousness, and reciprocity of friendship. It is not dissimilarity, the immensity of the gift, or the fruits of prayer that prevail; it is the friendly relationship with this God whom we know loves us.[50] The same orientation is found in the case of salvation, since it is neither the situation from which we are saved, nor the way it happens, nor what we are transformed into that count; the heart of salvation is nothing more or less than an intimate encounter with God who inscribes in a deep and permanent way his inhabitation in the human being, a trinitarian indwelling that provides the human person with a new and fundamental orientation.

This proximity in distance revealed by *deshacer* and the indwelling challenges human existence. A breath is transmitted, at the risk of death, a breath of life. This breath, when welcomed, will be shared. It is through the presence of God in the hearts of human beings that salvation erupts into the fragility of the present and the future.

The Spirit inspires and prompts us to speak. Armed with tongues of fire, the Spirit pushes human beings to tell, to speak, to write. The Feast of Pentecost, the feast of the Holy Spirit, is thus the inauguration of the profusion of words. In the long discourses of Peter, Stephen, and Paul, and the daring evangelization by the apostolic community under the guidance of the Spirit, even unto the testimony of martyrdom, one sees the spoken word as the fruit of an encounter with God passing through a process of personal appropriation in each flesh. The Acts of the Apostles offers in this sense the story of the companionship of the apostles with the Spirit of God who inspires and prompts them to speech directed toward others.

Teresa's *Foundations* unfolds in a similar vein as Teresa vigorously recounts the providential circumstances of her foundation of several monasteries. It is a story of expansion, with its obstacles and its advances, its opponents and its collaborators, but also a testimony of the action of God that Teresa perceived in her life, pursuing at a collective level the personal impulse seen in her *Life*. *Foundations* gradually leads to its climax, while even the process of writing the book was marked by the hiccups of history, telling the story of an invitation welcomed by Teresa to establish a monastery that became an invitation to found several more.

The Teresian parallels with scriptural texts have already been noted. The self-understanding that Teresa tries to achieve through her work passes through the sieve of the inspired and living Word—Christ himself is, for her, a "living book."[51] Sometimes this happens through commentary on the biblical text[52] or by appropriating it, and sometimes it is by allowing her own story to reflect or be shaped by the one that is told in Scripture.[53] The contemporary reader, after the example of the reader Teresa, is invited to find the Spirit in Teresa's account through the incarnate Word who still speaks today to ears that listen. The living relevance of the Teresian text is found here, in its capacity to be heard as a singular word that always calls out and displaces, allowing to sense, despite the distance and fragility, the inspiration of the very Breath of God.

At the heart of Teresian thought, as at the heart of this research, the Spirit is revealed, discreetly but powerfully, as the incarnator of salvation.

Table of Correspondence for the "Spiritual Testimonies"

The classification system of the "Spiritual Testimonies," called "Cuentas de conciencias" or "Relaciones" in the Spanish editions, is not universal, and the dates of many are disputed. We provide here a table of correspondence between the English translation used (Saint Teresa of Avila, *Collected Works*, vol. 1, rev. 2nd ed. [Washington, DC: Institute of Carmelite Studies], 1987), and two major Spanish editions: Editorial de Espiritualidad (5th ed., 2000), the edition used as reference by the author, and the Editorial Monte Carmelo (16th ed., 2011). All the Spiritual Testimonies cited in the book are included.

Date (according to EDE)	Cuentas de conciencias (EDE)	Relaciones (MtC)	Spiritual Testimonies (ICS)
October–December 1560	1	1	1
(July–August?) 1562	2	2	2

continued

Date (according to EDE)	Cuentas de conciencias (EDE)	Relaciones (MtC)	Spiritual Testimonies (ICS)
Avila, 1563	3	3	3
Toledo, 1570–71	10	13	10
Salamanca, April 8, 1571	12	26	22
Salamanca, April 15–16, 1571	13	15	12
Saint Joseph, Avila, May 29, 1571	14	16–17	13
Medina del Campo, June 30, 1571	15	18	14
Medina del Campo or Avila, July 1571	16	19	15
Avila, July 22, 1571	18	21	17
Place uncertain, 1571	21	24	20
Avila, January 19, 1572	22	25	21
Avila, May 1572	23	31	27
Avila, November 18, 1572	25	35	31
Avila, 1572	26	36	32
Beas, 1575	28	38	34
Écija, May 23, 1575	30	40, 5–8	36, 5–8
Écija, May 23, 1575	31	39	35
Seville, July 22, 1575	33	42	37
Seville, August 28, 1575	36	47	42
Seville, 1575	39	49	44
Seville, 1575	41	54	49

Table of Correspondence for the "Spiritual Testimonies"

Date (according to EDE)	Cuentas de conciencias (EDE)	Relaciones (MtC)	Spiritual Testimonies (ICS)
Seville, 1575	42	56	51
Seville, 1576	47	61	56
Seville, 1576	49	45	40
Seville, 1576	50	51	46
Seville, 1576	51	52	47
Seville, 1576	52	53	48
Seville, February–March 1576	53	4(b)	58
Seville, February–March 1576	54	5	59
Date and place uncertain, 1575–76?	60	33	29
Date and place uncertain	63	30	26
Date and place uncertain	64	28	24
Date and place uncertain	65	29	25
Palencia, May 1581	66	6	65

Notes

TRANSLATOR'S NOTE

1. [Translator's note: This final, brief section of textual remarks was prepared by the English translator; they replace similar textual remarks by the author that appear in the original, French edition of this book, explaining his choices regarding the French translation of the quotations from Teresa's works that appear in the book.]

INTRODUCTION

1. For a classic exposition of the theme of grace (both positive and systematic), see Charles Baumgartner, *La Grâce du Christ* (Tournai: Desclée, 1963). For an ecumenical (Catholic-Lutheran) introduction to the question of grace and salvation from a historical perspective, see Otto Hermann Pesch and Albrecht Peters, *Einführung in die Lehre von Gnade und Rechtfertigung* (Darmstadt: Wissenschaftliche Buchgesellschaft, 1981). For classic texts in French, see esp. two works by Michel Rondet: *Gratia Christi: Essai d'histoire du dogme et de théologie dogmatique* (Paris: Beauchesne, 1948) and *Essais sur la théologie de la grâce* (Paris: Beauchesne, 1964), the latter of which collects a series of articles.

2. The following lines of general observation draw from two general works of theological anthropology: Luis Ladaria, *Mystère de Dieu et mystère de l'homme*, vol. II: *Anthropologie théologique*

(Paris: Parole et Silence, 2011; original Spanish edition *Introducción a la antropología teológica* [Estella: Editorial Verbo Divino, 1993], but citations below will refer to the French edition) and Otto Hermann Pesch, *Frei sein aus Gnade: Theologische Anthropologie* (Freiburg: Herder, 1983).

3. It is properly a divine self-communication (*Selbstmitteilung Gottes*), to use the expression popularized by Karl Rahner and widely used since.

4. And so Ladaria titles chapters 10 and 11 of his work "Grace as a new relationship with God" and "Grace as a new creation." See Ladaria, *Mystère de Dieu et mystère de l'homme.*

5. Ladaria, *Mystère de Dieu et mystère de l'homme*, 502. Ladaria notes his preference, among various images of participation in the divine life, for that of filiation (501).

6. Otto Hermann Pesch, "Grâce," in *Nouveau dictionnaire de théologie*, ed. Peter Eicher, 2nd ed. (Paris: Éditions du Cerf, 1996), 382. It is interesting to note that in this succinct definition, the emphases present in Pesch's masterly work are clear. E.g., in his final book, he understands grace as the love of God (*Liebe Gottes*) to be at the heart of the biblical vision (see Pesch, *Frei sein aus Gnade*, 287, followed by a "meditation on the love of God," 288–306).

7. Eva-Maria Faber, "Grâce," in *Dictionnaire critique de théologie*, ed. Jean-Yves Lacoste, 3rd ed. (Paris: PUF, 2007), 601.

8. This definition comes close to the heart of the definition of salvation as understood by Pesch in the Bible and the tradition of the church, namely, a "relationship between God and the human being oriented towards salvation" (*Gottesverhältnis des Menschen zum Heil*): Pesch, *Frei sein aus Gnade*, 281–83.

9. Responding to certain criticisms of Latin theology for considering only created grace, Yves Congar wrote, "The Western theologians knew that there is no created grace without uncreated grace, since grace is that gift with which God himself is given or rather, it is what God gives when he gives himself" (Yves Congar, *I Believe in the Holy Spirit*, 3 vols., trans. David Smith [New York: Seabury Press, 1983], II:84). He had, however, previously noted that "Catholic theologians speak of 'grace.' In doing so, they run the risk of objectivizing it and separating it from the activity of the Spirit, who is uncreated grace and from whom it

cannot be separated" (II:68–69). Our definition rightly emphasizes the inseparable nature of gift.

10. Exodus offers an archetypal concept of collective salvation, the salvation of a people.

11. Paul Robert, *Le Nouveau Petit Robert* (Paris: Dictionnaires le Robert, 1993), 2273. [Translator's note: The *Petit Robert* is typically considered the standard single-volume dictionary of the French language. Notably, for English readers, the first definition of *salvation* offered by the *Merriam-Webster's Collegiate Dictionary* (11th Edition), one of the most standard for American English, bears the same sense: "a deliverance from the power and effects of sin."]

12. See "Joint Declaration on the Doctrine of Justification" by the Lutheran World Federation and the Catholic Church (1999), no. 26.

13. On the other hand, Rowan Williams argues that the emphasis on the purely juridical dimension of justification is rather an expression of Lutheran thought that developed after Luther himself (Rowan Williams, "Justification," in Lacoste, *Dictionnaire critique de théologie*, 748).

14. Council of Trent, *Decree on Justification* (January 13, 1547).

15. The theological debate on the understanding of salvation as justification reached an important degree of resolution in the "Joint Declaration on the Doctrine of Justification."

16. Joseph A. Fitzmyer, "Pauline Theology," in *The New Jerome Biblical Commentary*, ed. Raymond E. Brown, Joseph A. Fitzmyer, and Roland E. Murphy (Englewood Cliffs, NJ: Prentice Hall, 1990), 1397–1402. One could also add to this list the image of forgiveness (*aphesis*).

17. Already in the nineteenth century, Jacques Paul Migne's publication of critical editions of works of Latin and Greek fathers had provided wider access to these texts.

18. Jean-Pierre Jossua, *Le Salut, incarnation ou mystère pascal: Chez les Pères de l'Église de saint Irénée à saint Léon le Grand* (Paris: Éditions du Cerf, 1968). The book's introduction is enough to make clear the turning point that it represents.

19. Michel Fédou thus underlines the ante-Niceans' particular interest in trinitarian theology, as opposed to Arianism or the formulas adopted (later) at the Council of Nicea: Michel Fédou,

"La redécouverte des anténicéens et ses enjeux pour la théologie trinitaire," in *Les sources du renouveau de la théologie trinitaire au XXe siècle*, ed. Emmanuel Durand and Vincent Holzer (Paris: Éditions du Cerf, 2008), 72.

20. Their approaches vary enormously, e.g., on the question of the adoption of a "human nature" by Christ (ontologically, in solidarity, and so on).

21. Jossua reminds us that it is anachronistic to speak of any systematic soteriological "theory" before Anselm, even among the great scholastics of the thirteenth century (Jossua, *Le Salut*, 5).

22. On this, see esp. Francis Xavier Durrwell, *Christ Our Passover: The Indispensable Role of Resurrection in Our Salvation* (Liguori, MO: Liguori Publications, 2004; orig. French ed. 1950).

23. E.g., in medieval art that depicts a crucified Christ crowned.

24. Bernard Sesboüé, *Jésus-Christ l'unique médiateur: Essai sur la rédemption et le salut*, 2nd ed. (Paris: Desclée de Brouwer, 2010).

25. Sesboüé defines the descending movement as a movement that "goes from God to humanity through the humanity of Jesus," then the ascending movement as that which "goes from humanity to God, since in Jesus, the Son par excellence, humanity completes its passage into God," while emphasizing that "these two movements are founded on the human-divine person of Jesus, who has perfect solidarity with God and with humanity" (55).

26. One important example, among others, of this new approach was the series "Jésus et Jésus-Christ," launched by the publisher Mame-Desclée in 1977. An emblematic example is the work of René Girard, on the question of the scapegoat and sacrifice, which, while being rooted in the humanities, has repercussions for theological discourse.

27. The Congregation for the Doctrine of the Faith criticized, among other things, the use of Marxist paradigms to understand the social situation. See the Instruction on Certain Aspects of the Theology of Liberation, *Libertatis nuntius* (August 6, 1984), section VII.

28. While liberation theology first developed in the Latin American context, other currents were subsequently inspired by it: African theology, feminist theology, and more.

29. See Second Vatican Council, Decree on the Missionary Activity of the Church *Ad gentes* (December 7, 1965), no. 11.

30. Second Vatican Council, Declaration on the Relation of the Church with Non-Christian Religions *Nostra aetate* (October 28, 1965), no. 2.

31. *Nostra aetate*, no. 1. Subsequently, other texts of the magisterium contributed to the pursuit of reflection in this field, including Pope John Paul II's encyclical *Redemptoris missio* (1990). In addition to the documents, various gestures by recent popes have illustrated the new approach to religious pluralism, the most striking being the interreligious prayer event in Assisi in 1986.

32. Jacques Dupuis, *Toward a Christian Theology of Religious Pluralism* (Maryknoll, NY: Orbis, 1997).

33. A "notification" by the CDF, received by the author, accompanies editions published after 2001.

34. One can get a good idea of these developments in two important works on the renewal of trinitarian theology in the twentieth century, both edited by Emmanuel Durand and Vincent Holzer and published by Éditions du Cerf: *Les sources du renouveau de la théologie trinitaire au XXe siècle* (2008) and *Les réalisations du renouveau trinitaire au XXe siècle* (2010).

35. Karl Rahner, *The Trinity*, trans. Joseph Donceel (London: Burns and Oates, 1970). This work was originally published as the article "The Triune God as the Transcendental Ground of Salvation History" in *Mysterium Salutis*, then later published in book form.

36. Rahner, *Trinity*, 22.

37. Rahner, *Trinity*, 76–77, on "the common activity *ad extra* and appropriation."

38. Rahner, *Trinity*, 24–33: "The Incarnation as an 'Instance' of a More Comprehensive Reality."

39. In French-language theology, see, e.g., François-Marie Humann, *La Relation de l'Esprit-Saint au Christ: Une relecture d'Yves Congar* (Paris: Éditions du Cerf, 2010); Rémi Chéno, *L'Esprit-Saint et l'Église: Institutionalité et pneumatologie: Vers un dépassement des antagonismes ecclésiologiques* (Paris: Éditions du Cerf, 2010); and Jean-Miguel Garrigues, *Le Saint-Esprit sceau de la Trinité: Le Filioque et l'originalité trinitaire de l'Esprit dans sa personne et dans sa mission* (Paris: Éditions du Cerf, 2011).

40. Congar, *I Believe in the Holy Spirit.*

41. See, e.g., François-Xavier Durrwell, *Holy Spirit of God: An Essay in Biblical Theology*, trans. Benedict Davies (London: Geoffrey Chapman, 1986).

42. Paul Evdokimov, *L'Esprit Saint dans la tradition orthodoxe* (Paris: Éditions du Cerf, 1970). Drawing extensively from the patristic tradition, Evdokimov succinctly and sensibly presents the Eastern way of approaching the Holy Spirit, which is distinguished from a Western understanding that starts from a consideration of the nature of the one God (*De Deo uno*) before approaching the persons of the triune God (*De Deo trino*).

43. Jürgen Moltmann, *The Spirit of Life: A Universal Affirmation*, trans. Margaret Kohl (Minneapolis: Fortress, 1992).

44. [Translator's note: In this paragraph and the next, the author refers several times to the French word *expérience* and the concept it represents, comparing it to the related German and Spanish words. Because of its similarity of the French word with the English *experience*, the same point can be made through references to the English. For that reason, the author's references to the French word have been replaced in these two paragraphs by references to the English.]

45. Sylvie Robert, "Vocation actuelle de la théologie spirituelle," *Recherches de Science religieuse* 97 (2009): 65. Robert continues, "This encounter takes place in the context of a personal history, transforms the subject, and traces a singular path that unfolds according to the various dimensions of time: the moment of significant experiences, which always have an unexpected character, something new or renewing; the continuity of the experiences, which prompt one to consider the same aspects, attitudes, and struggles within oneself, but with greater depth each time; the permanence of the wisdom acquired. This encounter prompts words: all spiritual experience leads, at some point and in some way, to expression, whether it is directed to God or to third parties. It is an encounter with God that happens through some kind of mediation—pedagogy, the accompaniment or teaching of a more experienced guide, biblical or liturgical texts, a group, in short, a tradition. It engages the whole Christian mystery, but in an individual way, with an original structure: a 'core' insight becomes a gateway to the mystery of God and a center around which the

whole of one's faith is organized, thus prompting a structuring of one's existence that unifies one's entire being and life. It creates a particular modality of bonds, offering the most singular, rigorously non-transferable experience that one can experience but that at the same time brings one into communion with others, both specific people and all humanity."

46. For a good overview of the issues, see Michel de Certeau, "Mystique," in *Encylopédie Universalis* (Paris: Encyclopaedie Universalis France, 1968), 11:521–26.

47. François-Régis Wilhélem, drawing on Marie-Eugène de L'Enfant-Jésus's work *Je veux voir Dieu*, also tends to distinguish mystical life from mystical experience in order to raise the value of ordinary Christian life and to avoid the suggestion that such value is based on extraordinary experiences (Wilhélem, *Dieu dans l'action: La mystique apostolique selon Thérèse d'Ávila* [Venasque: Éditions du Carmel, 1992], 16–17n7). While the goal is laudable—and fair—it is not the path we are taking. On the other hand, if we equate mystical experience with a common experience of encounter with Christ, we must add the adjective "para-mystical" to speak of experiences that are out of the ordinary (this is the approach of Antonio Mas Arrondo, *Teresa de Jesús en el matrimonio espiritual: un análisis teológico desde las séptimas moradas del Castillo interior* [Avila: Institución Gran Duque de Alba, 1993], 456).

48. Teresa's own spirituality was very marked by spiritual, even mystical, experiences. Because of this, a definition of *mysticism* that does not include experience, even an experience of an extraordinary kind, would lack necessary relief, particularly in the Teresian context. Denys Turner, on the contrary, having the *mysticism* of the Middle Ages above all in mind, does not so closely connect mysticism and personal experience (Denys Turner, *The Darkness of God: Negativity in Christian Mysticism* [Cambridge: Cambridge University Press, 1995], 2). The rootedness of our research in the sixteenth and twenty-first centuries determines our conceptual choices.

49. Christoph Theobald, "La 'théologie spirituelle': Point critique pour la théologie dogmatique," in *Le christianisme comme style* (Paris: Éditions du Cerf, 2008), 1:390.

50. On systematic theology, see Olivier Riaudel, "Systématique (théologie)," in Lacoste, *Dictionnaire critique de théologie,* 1367–68.

51. Karl Rahner, *Foundations of Christian Faith,* trans. William V. Dych (New York: Seabury Press, 1978).

52. The Dominican theologian Melchior Cano, in his *De loci theologicis* (1563), does not include spiritual experience among the "*loci theologici*" (cf. Christoph Theobald, "La théologie comme discernement de la vie authentique: Sur une manière ignatienne de faire de la théologie," in *Le Christianisme comme style,* 1:414).

53. Denys Turner observes that until the middle of the fourteenth century, lists of the most important authors for spirituality and for theology would have been mostly the same, but that thereafter, the ways diverge; so that "almost none of the important authors for the history of western Christian theology would appear on the list of 'mystics,' and almost no mystic made any significant contribution to development of the theology proper" (Turner, *Darkness of God,* 214–15). For an understanding of the pivotal moment of the thirteenth century (around Thomas Aquinas and his successors) as regards the relationship between theology and spirituality, see Gilles Berceville, "Entre logique et mystique: La théologie universitaire," in Jean-Yves Lacoste, ed., *Histoire de la théologie* (Paris, Seuil, 2009), 225–82.

54. On this question, see, e.g., the differentiated positions of a spiritual theologian and a dogmatic theologian: Robert, "Vocation actuelle de la théologie spirituelle," 53–74; Theobald, "La 'théologie spirituelle,'" 389–411.

55. Robert, "Vocation actuelle de la théologie spirituelle," 64.

56. In his theological work, Balthasar draws not only from the contributions of spiritual authors (including Adrienne von Speyr), but also from literature, alongside more conventional sources such as the fathers of church or the Bible.

57. On the relationship of distance or proximity to a text, see Robert, "Vocation actuelle de la théologie spirituelle," 68–69.

58. Our inquiry will be theological in the sense that the action of God is presupposed; it differs in this from a purely literary analysis, although certain tools are used in common. See the reflections of Patrick Goujon on the subject, as part of his work

on Surin (discussed in Robert, "Vocation actuelle de la théologie spirituelle," 68).

59. "After the Scriptures, the many rich documents of the greatest Christian mystics are theological sources that are as interesting, if not more so, than many of the other documents in the living tradition of the church" (B. J. Duque, "Función del místico en la teología y en la Iglesia hoy," *Revista de Espiritualidad* 29 [1970]: 305–6, cited by Maximilian Herraiz, "Teresa de Jesús, Maestra de experiencia," *Monte Carmelo* 88 [1980]: 275).

60. "Teresa of Jesus" (*Teresa de Jesús*)—not to be confused with Thérèse of the Child Jesus (the "little" Thérèse, of Lisieux)—is the formal name of Teresa of Avila in Spanish. Because the name "Teresa of Avila" is the one most commonly used in French [translator's note: and also in English], we will identify her by this name here.

61. Joseph Doré, "Présentation," in Michel de Goedt, *Le Christ de Thérèse de Jésus* (Paris: Desclée de Brouwer, 1993), 5.

62. These include Teresa of Avila and Catherine of Siena in 1970, Thérèse of Lisieux in 1997, and Hildegard of Bingen in 2012.

63. Along with John of the Cross, Teresa even entered the "Bibliothèque de la Pléiade" series in the fall of 2012. [Translator's note: The "Bibliothèque de la Pléiade" is an editorial collection published in France by Éditions Gallimard that provides reference editions of the complete works of classic authors in a pocket format. Initiated in 1931, it is still in print and publishing new volumes today.]

64. She frequently consulted with clergymen to make sure that she was theologically and spiritually on the right track.

65. Eulogio Pacho, *El apogeo de la Mística Cristiana: Historia de la espiritualidad clásica española 1450–1650* (Burgos: Editorial Monte Carmelo, 2008), 1041.

66. Tomás Álvarez, "Jesucristo en la experiencia de Santa Teresa," *Monte Carmelo* 88 (1980): 343.

67. See Pacho, *El apogeo de la Mística Cristiana,* 1042, 1044.

68. Secundino Castro, "Aproximación al pensamiento religioso de Teresa de Teresa," in *Teresa de Jesús, mujer, cristiana, maestra* (Madrid: Editorial de Espiritualidad, 1982), 63–80, at 69.

69. De Goedt, *Le Christ de Thérèse de Jésus,* 150. See also Secundino Castro, *Cristología teresiana* (Madrid: Editorial de Espiritualidad, 1978), 58–59.

70. Castro, "Aproximación al pensamiento religioso de Teresa de Teresa," 69.

71. See Teresa of Avila, *The Way of Perfection* (hereafter, *Way*), 17:2. (On the citation of Teresian texts in this book, see the "Textual remarks" section at the end of this introduction.) See also Wilhélem, *Dieu dans l'action,* 185, and 16–17 on the link between "mystical life," mystical graces, and the perfection of Christian life. Waltraud Herbstrith also judges that although "Teresa was convinced that any human being could encounter God in contemplation, she knows, on the other hand, that this experience is not in itself salvific, because Christ linked salvation not to sight and not to palpable experience, but to faith" (Waltraud Herbstrith, *Teresa von Ávila: Lebensweg und Botschaft* [Munich: Verlag Neue Stadt, 1993], 86).

72. Wilhélem, *Dieu dans l'action,* 17n7. In Teresa's writings, see, e.g., *The Interior Castle* (hereafter, *Castle*) I:2:17; III:2:10.

73. See *Way*: prologue.

74. Efrén de la Madre de Dios and Otger Steggink, *Tiempo y vida de Santa Teresa,* 3rd ed. (Madrid: La Editorial Católica, 1996), 925.

75. Manuel Diego Sánchez, *Bibliografía sistemática de Santa Teresa de Jesús* (Madrid: Editorial de Espiritualidad, 2008).

76. Several of Tomás Álvarez's studies have been collected in the three volumes of *Estudios teresianos* (Burgos: Editorial Monte Carmelo, 1995–96).

77. Juan Luis Astigarraga, *Concordancias de los escritos de Santa Teresa de Jesús,* 2 vol. (Rome: Editoriales OCD, 2000).

78. Tomás Álvarez, ed., *Diccionario de Santa Teresa,* 2nd ed. (Burgos: Editorial Monte Carmelo, 2006).

79. E.g., Aurora Egido, *El águila y la tela: Estudios sobre San Juan de la Cruz y Santa Teresa de Jesús* (Palma: José J. de Olañeta and Edicions Universitat de les Illes Balears, 2010).

80. This vein is mainly Anglo-Saxon. Some of these theses are daring and upset the traditional consensus. More generally, it is noticeable that many important monographs in English have been written by female scholars who were not members of

religious congregations. See, e.g., in chronological order, Jodi Bilinkoff, *The Avila of Saint Teresa: Religious Reform in a Sixteenth-Century City* (Ithaca, NY: Cornell University Press, 1989); Deirdre Green, *Gold in the Crucible: Teresa of Avila and the Western Mystical Tradition* (Longmead: Element, 1989); Alison Weber, *Teresa of Avila and the Rhetoric of Femininity* (Princeton, NJ: Princeton University Press, 1990); Carole Slade, *St. Teresa of Avila: Author of a Heroic Life* (Berkeley: University of California Press, 1995); Gillian T. W. Ahlgren, *Teresa of Avila and the Politics of Sanctity* (Ithaca, NY: Cornell University Press, 1996); Elena Carrera, *Teresa of Avila's Autobiography: Authority, Power and the Self in Mid-Sixteenth-Century Spain* (London: Modern Humanities Research Association and Maney Publishing, 2005); Bárbara Mujica, *Teresa de Ávila, Lettered Woman* (Nashville: Vanderbilt University Press, 2009).

81. Felicidad Bernabéu Barrachina, "Aspectos vulgares del estilo literario teresiano y sus posibles razones," *Revista de Espiritualidad* 22 (1963): 359–75. In 1963, the editors of the journal commented in an introductory footnote to this article, "The fundamental point on which it is based, namely the racial Jewish ancestry of Saint Teresa, is still far from being demonstrated." Today, the reality of Teresa's Jewish ancestry through her father's line is universally accepted.

82. Castro, *Cristología teresiana.* Castro continued his reflection in subsequent articles, such as "Aproximación al pensamiento religioso de Teresa."

83. Augusto Guerra, "Presencia del dolor en la oración teresiana," *Revista de Espiritualidad* 40 (1981): 508–9n26; cited by Secundino Castro, "Jesucristo y su misterio," in *Teresa de Jesús, mujer, cristiana, maestra,* 155n55.

84. See n. 64 above.

85. Álvarez, "Jesucristo en la experiencia de Santa Teresa," 335–65.

86. Castro, "Aproximación al pensamiento religioso de Teresa de Teresa," 72–73.

87. See, e.g., Álvarez, "Jesucristo en la experiencia de Santa Teresa," 340ff. (which offers some ancient and contemporary sources); Castro, "Aproximación al pensamiento religioso de Teresa de Teresa," 70; Castro, "Jesucristo y su misterio," 150ff. (which explores Teresa assertions about this); and Antonio Mas

Arrondo, *Teresa de Jesús en el matrimonio spiritual,* 263. We will deal with this issue in greater detail below.

88. Álvarez, "Jesucristo en la experiencia de Santa Teresa," 338; Castro goes in the same direction: "For her [Teresa], there exists today neither the Word nor Jesus of Nazareth, but Jesus Christ: Word–incarnate–risen" (Castro, "Jesucristo y su misterio," 155n55).

89. See Álvarez, "Jesucristo en la experiencia de Santa Teresa," 361; and Secundino Castro, *Ser cristiano según Santa Teresa* (Madrid: Editorial de Espiritualidad, 1985), 93ff.

90. Teresa of Avila, *The Book of Her Life* (hereafter, *Life*) 7:6.

91. Álvarez, "Jesucristo en la experiencia de Santa Teresa," 343.

92. Maximiliano Herraiz clearly underlines this hermeneutic link between Teresa's existential experience and the biblical texts. He concludes that "lived experience is first, and the spiritual understanding of texts that secure it and confirm it follows. Lived experience predisposes her to understanding the word of God. The latter refers to life and penetrates it. A perfect symbiosis. The word explains her life and perfectly describes what is going on inside her" (Maximiliano Herraiz, "Biblia y espiritualidad teresiana," *Monte Carmelo* 88 (1980): 329).

93. Álvarez, "Jesucristo en la experiencia de Santa Teresa," 358. Teresa had to rely mainly on her personal library: vernacular Bibles, works by Saint Francis Borgia, and so on.

94. On the various ways Teresa had access to biblical texts, see Tomás Álvarez, *Cultura de mujer en el siglo XVI: El caso de Santa Teresa de Jesús* (Burgos: Editorial Monte Carmelo, 2006), 373–82. Concerning the *Vita Christi,* Alvarez indicates elsewhere that Ambrosio de Montesino's Spanish translation draws attention to the numerous biblical quotations by means of a distinctive typography. Thanks to this, Teresa could "study and unravel the mysteries of the life of Jesus from his eternal begetting to glorification, as well as his presence in the church, in the Scriptures, until his parousia": Álvarez, "Jesucristo en la experiencia de Santa Teresa," 339. Cf. Ludolph of Saxony, *The Life of Jesus Christ,* trans. Milton T. Walsh, vols. 1–4 (Collegeville, MN: Liturgical Press, 2018–21).

95. Herraiz goes so far as to say that "the 'auditions' [*hablas*] are like a transcription on a personal level of the word of God

once entrusted to the prophets and recorded in Scripture. The link between 'auditions' and Scripture is absolutely clear. God speaks to Teresa using his own biblical word, or at least with a clearly biblical content" (Herraiz, "Biblia y espiritualidad teresiana," 320).

96. Teresa cites certain prominent Pauline texts (Gal 2:20, among others) to explain spiritual marriage (Herraiz, "Biblia y espiritualidad teresiana," 331).

97. A "Pauline" structure of Teresa's conversion and the apostolate becomes clear in the interconnections between the Pauline text, Teresa's life, and Teresa's writing. Tomás Álvarez, e.g., highlighted the link between Paul's journey and that of Teresa, both in their broad articulations and in their relationship to Christ. This relationship with Christ, according to Álvarez, begins with *cristopatía* (relationship to the suffering Christ), continues with *cristonomía* (following Christ), and ends with *cristología* (Álvarez, "Jesucristo en la experiencia de Santa Teresa," 336ff.).

98. Rómulo Cuartas Londoño, *Experiencia trinitaria de Santa Teresa de Jesús* (Burgos: Editorial Monte Carmelo, 2004).

99. One of Cuartas Londoño's objectives is to promote dialogue between spiritual theology and dogmatic theology, the mentioned authors having contributed to overcoming the gap that exists between these two fields (see Cuartas Londoño, *Experiencia trinitaria de Santa Teresa de Jesús*, 28–29).

100. He defines *doxology* as "the acknowledgment of her [Teresa's] experience of divine realities expressed in worship, praise, thanksgiving, and confident intercession, with the attitudes of reverence and joyful welcome of God and of what God has done for her and for all humanity" (Cuartas Londoño, *Experiencia trinitaria de Santa Teresa de Jesús*, 413).

101. Cuartas Londoño, *Experiencia trinitaria de Santa Teresa de Jesús*, 29.

102. Angel María García Ordás, *La persona divina en la espiritualidad de Santa Teresa* (Rome: Éditiones Teresianum, 1967).

103. Cuartas Londoño, *Experiencia trinitaria de Santa Teresa de Jesús*, 197.

104. Cuartas Londoño, *Experiencia trinitaria de Santa Teresa de Jesús*, 197.

105. Wilhélem concludes his book with these words: "This is how 'the Spirit appears in this world under a thousand human

faces on which his hidden presence reflects his power and his grace.' Was it not this same Spirit who made Teresa de Ahumada an accomplished woman, an extraordinary reformer, a brilliant and effective guide on the paths of prayer and action, and at the same time a 'daughter' and a Doctor of the Church?" (Wilhélem, *Dieu dans l'action,* 339 [the internal quotation is from Marie-Eugène de L'Enfant-Jésus, *Je veux voir Dieu* (Venasque: Éditions du Carmel), 1075]). Emmanuel Renault also points, in his final pages, to the Holy Spirit under whose inspiration Teresa lived (Renault, *L'Idéal apostolique des Carmélites selon sainte Thérèse d'Ávila* [Paris: Desclée de Brouwer, 1981], 178).

106. De Goedt, *Le Christ de Thérèse de Jésus,* 171–72.

107. Jesús Castellano, "Espiritualidad teresiana: Experiencia y doctrina," in *Introducción a la lectura de santa Teresa,* ed. Alberto Barrientos, 2nd ed. (Madrid: Editorial de Espiritualidad, 2002), 232.

108. Ignatius of Loyola was also suspected of heresy by the Inquisition due to a charge of sympathy with the *Alumbrados.* He writes of this in his *Autobiography* (section 58). On the *Alumbrados* ("the Enlightened Ones"), see Pacho, *El apogeo de la Mística Cristiana,* 291ff. and 826ff.

109. *Life* 33:5. Notably, these threats did not frighten Teresa; rather, they made her laugh. On the question of Teresa's relationship with the Inquisition, see Enrique Llamas, *Santa Teresa de Jesús y la Inquisición Española,* Bibliotheca Theologica Hispana, series 1.a, vol. 6 (Madrid: Consejo Superior de Investigaciones Científicas, 1972).

110. Castro, *Ser cristiano según Santa Teresa,* 190.

111. Castro, *Ser cristiano según Santa Teresa,* 184.

112. Castro, *Ser cristiano según Santa Teresa,* 190.

113. Michael Strucken, "Trinität aus Erfahrung: Ansätze zu einer trinitarischen Ontologie in der Mystik von Ignatius von Loyola, Teresa von Avila und Johannes vom Kreuz," (PhD diss., Rheinischen Friedrich-Wilhelms-Universität, 1999). The three authors are systematically treated in parallel (except John of the Cross, who is absent from the autobiographical part) by theme. The unity of this work is found both in subject matter treated by each of the authors and by their context in the sixteenth-century Spain.

114. Giuseppe Ferraro, *Lo Spirito Santo, Cristo, il Padre,* vol. II: *nella dottrina di santa Teresa d'Ávila e santa Teresa di Lisieux e della beata Elisabetta della Trinità* (Rome: Edizioni OCD, 2007). Ferraro's first volume is on John of the Cross, while the second deals with the Christology and the pneumatology of the female authors of Carmel.

115. José Cristiano Garrido, "Experiencia teresiana de la vida de gracia," *Monte Carmelo* 75 (1967): 345–91.

116. Teresa of Avila, *Spiritual Testimonies* (hereafter, *Testimonies*) 14 and 40. Garrido, "Experiencia teresiana," 351.

117. Garrido, "Experiencia teresiana," 352.

118. Garrido, "Experiencia teresiana," 357.

119. Garrido, "Experiencia teresiana," 356.

120. Miguel Maury Buendía, "Puntos clave en la interpretación teológica de la experiencia teresiana de la gracia," *Monte Carmelo* 95, no. 2 (1987): 283–302.

121. Buendía, "Puntos clave en la interpretación teológica," 284.

122. Buendía, "Puntos clave en la interpretación teológica," 291.

123. Jean-Marie Laurier, *Marcher dans l'humilité: Thérèse d'Ávila et la théologie de la justification* (Toulouse: Éditions du Carmel, 2003).

124. Laurier treats both at length: Luther on pp. 17–73 and Trent's Decree on Justification on pp. 75–131.

125. Laurier, *Marcher dans l'humilité,* 252–53.

126. Laurier, *Marcher dans l'humilité,* 265.

127. See, among others, Renault, *L'Idéal apostolique des Carmélites,* 8, 154, 171–72.

128. Renault was later followed along this path of study by Wilhélem.

129. We should note that there will also be references to the specific Carmelite monastery *named* Incarnation, where Teresa lived for a period of time.

130. This choice is very different from that of Cuartas Londoño, who puts Teresa in dialogue with the most outstanding figures of twentieth-century theology throughout his study.

131. E.g., Laurier. Most works on Teresa's prayer are of this nature, following the pedagogical and sequential path of *The Way*

of Perfection or *The Interior Castle* or the overall historical framework of the *Life*.

132. E.g., this is the case (as the title itself indicates) with Arrondo, *Teresa de Jesús en el matrimonio spiritual*.

CHAPTER 1

1. This account is found in *Life* 32–36.

2. Teresa writes of this foundation in *The Book of Her Foundations* (hereafter, *Foundations*):1–3.

3. After Avila (1562) and Medina del Campo (1567) came the foundations of the monasteries of Malagon (1568), Valladolid (1568), Toledo (1569), Pastrana (1569), Salamanca (1570), Alba de Tormes (1571), Segovia (1574), Beas (1575), Seville (1575), Villanueva de la Jara (1580), Palencia (1580), Soria (1581), and Burgos (1582), in addition to the monasteries of Caravaca (1576) and Granada (1582) founded by her companions.

4. This is the text we have now, divided by Teresa into forty chapters, including a brief summary of their content at the beginning of each chapter. This document was intended for Father John of Avila—a spiritual master who was canonized in 1970 and declared a Doctor of the Church in 2012—from whom Teresa sought confirmation to allay her fears. On the history of the text of Teresa's *Life*, see Teresa of Jesus, *Obras completas*, 7th ed., Biblioteca de Autores Cristianos (Madrid: La Editorial Católica, 1982); introductions and notes by Efren de la Madre Dios and Otger Steggink (hereafter: *Obras* [BAC]), 25–28. It is likely that the final document of 1565 incorporates older elements, since Teresa alludes to an account of the founding of Saint Joseph that she was ordered to produce in 1562 by Father García de Toledo, OP (*Foundations*, prologue:2).

5. Those readers were, first of all, her fellow sisters, her confessors, clergy she consulted (by her choice or in response to accusations); they later included a wider reading audience of nobles or ecclesiastics who had made a copy of the text before it was widely distributed.

6. *Obras* (BAC), 28. See *The Collected Letters of St. Teresa of Avila*, 2 vols., trans. Kieran Kavanaugh (Washington, DC: ICS

Publications, 2001, 2007) (hereafter, *Letters*), 415:1 (November 19, 1581). Elsewhere, Teresa speaks of the "big book" (*libro grande*) or the book of "my soul" (*mi alma*).

7. In response to a command from her confessor in Salamanca, Father Jerónimo de Ripalda, SJ (*Foundations*, prologue:2; *Obras* [BAC], 517).

8. For the history of the text, see *Obras* (BAC), 517–19.

9. Four chapters (37 to 40) complete the *Life*, including chapter 38, which will be the subject of analysis in our next chapter.

10. For Teresa, *Foundations* constitutes the continuation of her description of the foundations subsequent to that of Saint Joseph treated in the book of her *Life*, since her confessor had seen this first account and considered it useful that it should be continued for later monasteries (see *Foundations* prologue:2). We can therefore surmise that if Teresa's confessor had access to the text of the *Life*, it was because she herself had a copy of it, and that she therefore had it available at the time she wrote the first chapters of *Foundations*, hence a great continuity of style.

11. The monastery of Medina, founded in 1567, was followed in 1568 by Malagon, then Valladolid, then others at an approximate rate of one monastery per year.

12. In addition to founding many monasteries, note also the important works that she wrote during this phase of maturity: *The Book of Her Life, The Way of Perfection*, and *The Interior Castle.*

13. *Life* 32:1. This happened in August (see Teresa of Jesus, *Obras completas*, ed. Alberto Barrientos, 5th ed. [Madrid: Editorial de Espiritualidad, 2000]; introductions and notes by Enrique Llamas, Teófanes Egido, Daniel de Pablo Maroto, José Vicente Rodriguez, et al. [hereafter: *Obras* (EDE)], 214n2) or at the beginning of September 1560 (see Teresa of Avila, *Oeuvres complètes*, vol. 1, trans. Mother Marie du Saint-Sacrement [Paris: Éditions du Cerf, 1995] [hereafter: *Oeuvres* (Cerf)], 248n1).

14. *Life* 32:1. Father Ribera, Teresa's contemporary and first biographer, interprets this by saying that it is the place that Teresa would have deserved if she had continued on the lukewarm path she had long walked (*Obras* [EDE], 214n2). This interpretation is plausible, but it is not the only one possible. One could argue, on the contrary, that her being shown what she "merited" by her sin demonstrated the free gift of salvation by God.

15. Three times in *Life* 32:3, Teresa mentions something that "the Lord wanted" (*quiso el Señor*).

16. *Life* 32:1. Teresa will recall this vision of hell several times thereafter, a sign of its lasting imprint (see *Life* 38:9; 40:1).

17. *Life,* 32:1, 3. This is a rare olfactory element in Teresa's descriptions, making clear the all-encompassing sensory character of this vision.

18. She notes that doctors had told her that the physical pain she experienced was "the worst that can be suffered on earth" (*Life* 32:2).

19. *Life* 32:2–3. Teresa writes that being burned by a real fire amounts to very little compared to being burned by this interior fire (*Life* 32:3).

20. *Life* 32:2. One cannot hope for any consolation there (see *Life* 32:3).

21. Teresa writes of "the soul's agonizing: a constriction, a suffocation, an affliction so keenly felt...that I don't know how to word it strongly enough" (*Life* 32:2).

22. Teresa asserts this when she reports seeing another dreadful vision after this that was less frightening and without the pain (*Life* 32:3).

23. *Life* 32:6. Because, she wrote, they were already members of the church by the baptism.

24. [Translator's note: This sense is not reflected in the English of Kavanaugh/Rodriguez in *Life* 32:6, which says the pain "flow[ed] from" the experience of the vision.]

25. *Life* 32:6. Teresa often uses this expression of dying several deaths, even of "suffering a thousand deaths" to emphasize a point she is making.

26. [Translator's note: Kavanaugh/Rodriguez translates this instance of the verb as "I was anxious to...."]

27. In 1432, Pope Eugenius IV approved a mitigation of the Rule, relaxing the abstinence from meat and the obligation of silence.

28. *Obras* (EDE), 252n3.

29. *Obras* (EDE), 252n4.

30. The question of income, which was of major importance in the sixteenth century, was a subject of constant attention for Teresa, as it was for other reformers of the time (e.g., Ignatius of

Loyola, founder of the Society of Jesus). The challenge was both economic and spiritual: Should a monastery have stable sources of revenue (which introduces a pressure to admit only women who bring with them a significant financial endowment, thus running the risk of a community becoming rich and comfortable), or should it trust entirely in the grace of God (which would always raise concerns among ecclesial authorities regarding the sustainability of the enterprise)? Teresa's position on the subject evolved over the years.

31. For nuns coming from wealthier backgrounds, the rooms of the monastery of the Incarnation were large and comfortable. Visitors to this monastery can still see this today.

32. Although no image (something normally implied by the word *vision*) as such is mentioned by Teresa, this is the word she uses to speak of this experience with Christ (*Life* 32:12).

33. In Spanish "*habla*"; these are words spoken by Christ to Teresa. Considering this phenomenon from the point of view of the transmitter, one could speak here of a *locution*; the word *audition* emphasizes its reception by Teresa. [Translator's note: The use of the word *audition* (that is, something *heard*) as a mystical experience is rare in English works of spirituality. The word *locution* (something *said*) is almost always used to describe the experience referred to here. Because the author distinguishes between the two in this work, and because that distinction becomes significant in at least one instance (in Teresa's vision of the Holy Spirit, which has an important place in chapter 2, she *hears* the beating of the wings of the dove she sees; since what she hears is not words, it would be problematic to refer to this as a locution), this translation will reflect the author's distinction between *locution* and *audition.*]

34. This sort of statement comes up again and again in her account of this episode, highlighting the clarity of Teresa's perception of the expression of the divine will.

35. *Life* 33:1. Her confessor would later give her permission to proceed with the project, even without discussing it with her superiors (*Life* 33:11).

36. *Life* 33:4. See also *Life* 32:4.

37. *Life* 33:14. We will consider this vision in some detail later.

38. *Life* 33:16; 35:6, 8.

39. *Life* 34:17. This will be analyzed later.

40. *Life* 35. A *beata* was one who wore the Carmelite habit but lived a life of prayer outside the community.

41. *Life* 36:3. This illness enabled Teresa to carry on outside the sight of others her preparatory work regarding the house purchased for use as the future monastery. Her brother-in-law recovered as soon as her business in this regard was completed.

42. *Life* 36:2. Peter of Alcántara, a Franciscan priest, was canonized in 1669.

43. *Life* 36:5–6. Teresa always mentions these two elements together, although sometimes in a different order.

44. This will also be the case for subsequent foundations (see, e.g., *Foundations* 3:9).

45. *Life* 36:5. Teresa was legitimately present in the house since she had to take care of her brother-in-law (who had just recovered) there. She had consulted theologians and knew that this project would be beneficial for the order. Due to the impossibility of founding this monastery under the obedience of the Carmelite general, Teresa was all the more attentive to ensuring obedience to God by listening to the legitimate authorities as a guarantee that it was indeed God's undertaking.

46. Speaking a bit later of the persistent opposition to this foundation, Teresa says explicitly that it was the devil that "stirred up" so much opposition against "a few poor little women" (*Life* 36:19; see also *Life* 36:20, 22). Teresa is not stingy with references to the devil in her work; there are more than six hundred instances (see Astigarraga, *Concordancias,* 720–29).

47. About a year after the founding of the monastery, in August 1563 (*Obras* [EDE], 256n28).

48. *Life* 36:29. In the original, Teresa begins her sentence in the singular but ends it in the plural.

49. *Life* 33:14–15. It occurred on August 15, 1561, at the Dominican convent in Avila. This vision marks the end of chapter 33. Chapter 34 opens with the account of her departure for Toledo, with Luisa de la Cerda.

50. In her writing, Teresa refers regularly to herself as *ruin* (small and weak) and *baja* (low). It is often on precisely such

foundations, on such weakness, that God builds. We can think of the experience of Paul (2 Cor 12:9–10) or the prophets.

51. Audition (in Spanish, *habla*) is the most common way Christ presented himself to Teresa, in a very clear way and often when she was receiving Communion.

52. *Life* 33:12, for Saint Joseph and the words of Christ; *Life* 33:13, for the appearance of Saint Clare on August 12, 1561. Teresa comments that her great devotion to this saint made her desire more strongly the perfection of her monastery's poverty.

53. The Virgin here echoes the promises of Christ expressed in a previous vision (see *Life* 32:11), which confirmed the divine origin of Teresa's efforts to found a monastery. This reminder, in this place, underlines the importance of this vision.

54. After losing her sight (*ver*) and hearing (*oír*), they were gradually restored when Teresa was dressed in white clothing—first sight, then hearing.

55. This is one of the moments of dialectic between life and death that colors the Teresian approach to salvation and the apostolate.

56. Or "I heard"; it is possible that this is, strictly speaking, an audition (this is the interpretation chosen by some translators). Auditions are often introduced by *Díjome el Señor* ("the Lord said to me") or the equivalent.

57. *Life* 34:10. This passage has been touched up in the original edition so as not to give rise to an accusation of too great a confidence about her own salvation, which might have been understood to contradict the doctrine of the very recent Council of Trent. See *Obras* (EDE), 235n9, which refers to session 6, chapter 9 of the Council of Trent.

58. *Life* 34:19. Previously, Teresa described at length the events surrounding her conversations with Father García de Toledo.

59. *Life* 34:17. Teresa understood from this vision that her friend was making great spiritual progress.

60. Glory designates both the ultimate attribute of God (see *kabod* in the Old Testament, *doxa* in the New) and at the same time the potential gift given to believers who enter into intimacy with God (see, e.g., Rom 8:30).

61. The (glorified) body of the risen Christ is both similar to his mortal body (it can be recognized: Matt 28:17) but also different (it is not always recognized at first: John 20:14). It is not a ghost (Luke 24:43), but it is not bound by the laws of nature (Luke 24:36–37). In the Teresian context, the glorified body appears mainly as a visual element of presence whose material reality is not accentuated, but which reveals a state of proximity to God. This presence in the form of a glorified body also includes words.

62. *Life* 36:21. Saint Peter reminds her of the advice, which he had already given to her in his lifetime, not to accept an income so as not to lose the spirit of poverty. At that time, Teresa considered the relenting to the wishes of others on this question in order to soften their opposition to the new monastery. This appearance restored her conviction to hold a hard line in this matter.

63. This tension between life and death is recurrent in Teresa, as we will see below.

64. *Life* 33:8. Teresa notes in *Life* 33:7 that in the Society of Jesus, obedience was such that a Jesuit did not want to do anything against the will of his superior. The change of superior therefore led her confessor to a new way of directing her.

65. *Life* 33:11. This permission was important to Teresa since she could not apply to those in charge of her congregation to obtain it. However, as Teresa wanted to remain obedient even though she had to keep her religious superiors in ignorance, the support of her confessor (and of her confessor's rector) was paramount.

66. In *Life* 33:7–10, the noun *spirit* appears eight times, and the adjective *spiritual* is used twice. [Translator's note: In Kavanaugh/Rodriguez, the noun appears seven times and the adjective three, because in one instance, *ímpetus de espíritu*—literally, "impulses of the spirit"—is translated "spiritual impulses."] We will discuss Teresian anthropology in chapter 3.

67. The operational dimension of the Spirit is emphasized in Teresa's remarks about the rector, regarding his manner of instructing Teresa's confessor to let the Spirit act (*obrar*) (*Life* 33:8) and in the consideration he gives to the effects (*efectos*) of this action (*Life* 33:10) in order to understand whether they have their origin in God.

68. Teresa also spoke previously of the "heat" that the Lord had given to her soul to "digest" new knowledge (*Life* 32:8)—a form of wisdom.

69. See, e.g., *Life* 33:13–14, where she describes two visions, one that happened when she was going to Communion, the other during the elevation of the host at Mass (and preventing her from seeing it). Apart from the importance of the Blessed Sacrament, which we've already noted, this theme is not developed in the pages under study.

70. We will analyze these links in the next chapter.

71. *Life* 32:1–3 (see esp. paragraph 3).

72. In five chapters, she mentions the *casa* 31 times and the *monasterio* 40 times (although not always in reference to Saint Joseph).

73. *Life* 33:12. The Lord tells her "to enter as best you can."

74. Like the Spirit of God does to the spirit (*espíritu*) of the human person.

75. Hence the title of Teresa's masterwork, *The Interior Castle*, or *The Book of Dwelling Places*.

76. This is a trace of her Jewish cultural heritage—through her father—since in Castile during this period, *illiteracy* was valued as a sign of blood purity, the Jews being understood as having a special predilection for literature. On Teresa's culture, see Álvarez, *Cultura de mujer en el siglo XVI*.

77. Álvarez, "Jesucristo en la experiencia de Santa Teresa," 359.

78. Several studies have considered Teresa's relationship with Scripture and the word of God—and even with the words of the Lord. See, e.g., Román Llamas, *Biblia en Santa Teresa* (Madrid: Editorial de Espiritualidad, 2007).

79. *Life* 32:11–12; cf. Luke 1:26–38.

80. Familial references to Saint Joseph as "my true father" (e.g., *Life* 33:12) or to Saint Joseph and the Virgin Mary together (e.g., *Life* 33:14) reinforce this domestic imagery.

81. Having learned that in the past Carmelite monasteries did not accept income (*Life* 35:2), Teresa wanted to follow this practice, and this concern kept coming up since it was a matter of debate and opposition.

82. *Life* 33:13. The confirmation of poverty is Teresa's interpretation of the help promised by the saint in the vision.

83. *Life* 35:1–2; on a *beata*, see n. 40 above.

84. *Life* 34:6–17 for these conversations, 34:17 for this "Magnificat." For the gospel, see Luke 1:46–55. We have already mentioned these talks in the analysis of the "language of the Spirit" in *Life* 34:17.

85. *Life* 34:1–2. This was Doña Luisa de la Cerda.

86. One might also recognize a Johannine dimension (see John 1:10–11) in the refusal of many people (provincial, devotees, authorities, and so on) to support Teresa's efforts.

87. Secundino Castro points out that in Teresa's spiritual vocabulary, the verb *deshacer* is one of great expressiveness, indicating a sense of creatureliness, smallness, in the face of the visions of the Lord (Castro, *Cristología teresiana*, 63). [Translator's note: In his French original, when referring to the threat to the monastery, the author translates Teresa's *deshacer*, a verb that will have a prominent place in his consideration of Teresa's thought below, as "to destroy," writing that the authorities wished to "destroy" the new monastery. However, the Kavanaugh/Rodriguez English translation opts for the more canonical "to suppress," suggesting the authorities wanted to suppress, or formally close down, the monastery.]

88. This number and the reference to Christ and the twelve apostles were inscribed in the first *Constitutions*. See *Oeuvres* (Cerf), 253n7.

89. In the tradition of the church, one frequently finds a distinction made, in a schematic way, between theological works that emphasize, in the work of salvation, the incarnational aspect (the Son of God taking human nature to save all humanity) or on the redemptive aspect (Christ dying on the cross for the redemption of the sins of humanity). Both elements are part of the history of salvation, but Teresa's massive recourse to the Lukan structures of the story of the Incarnation further highlights the incarnational dimension.

90. In *Life* 33:14, e.g., at the time of the vision of Our Lady and Saint Joseph. In *Life* 38:9, in a vision that will be analyzed in the next chapter, this same characteristic of suddenness—and

quickness—will be found in an important vision where the Holy Spirit is central.

91. One might offer by analogy the Christ–Spirit relationship, in the sense that the Spirit actively prepares the revealing of the face of God, but also has the mission of working unseen in the background (see, e.g., Luke 1:35; 3:22; 4:1).

92. These are sometimes very explicit, such as when the Lord gave her specific directions on how to obtain Roman documents. While her previous efforts had been unsuccessful, the latter worked (*Life* 33:16).

93. E.g., in *Life* 36:29, even though the foundation was at that point accomplished, she calls herself *ruin y baja* [translator's note: "terrible and lowly," suggesting being of poor quality and little use, or as Kavanaugh/Rodriguez translates it, "wretched and dreadful"].

94. It is therefore not a desire *for self*, either in its origin or in its goal.

95. On the contrary, when Teresa was forbidden to work on the foundation project, it was Father Ibáñez, along with Doña Guiomar de Ulloa, who continued to help move it forward.

96. According to Teresa's account, Father Ibáñez requested permission to move to one of his order's monasteries, so that he could develop his prayer life more effectively. He was recalled from this way of life two years later in order to respond to pastoral needs, after having benefited greatly from this deepening of his prayer life (see *Life* 33:5).

97. Teresa saw in the monastery's survival against such opposition a sign of God's approval (*Life* 36:25).

98. During the vision of *Life* 32:11, which confirms the project.

99. The installation of the Blessed Sacrament, but also the final vision of *Life* 36:24.

100. *Foundations* 1:1–6. This picks up from where Teresa left off at the end of chapter 36 of her *Life* (*Life* 36:26).

101. *Foundations* 1:1–2. She even describes them as "angelic souls" (*Foundations* 1:6).

102. As we have seen, the monastery of Saint Joseph had been placed under the jurisdiction of the bishop of Avila due to the opposition of the provincial to its foundation (*Life* 32:15; 33:1).

103. Despite the human difficulty of the project, even more than the father general's desire that other monasteries should be founded, Teresa kept in mind the words the Lord has spoken to her (*Foundations* 2:4, cf. *Foundations* 1:8) and proceeded with confidence.

104. *Foundations* 3:14–15. Teresa also found the first two discalced Carmelite friars, including Saint John of the Cross.

CHAPTER 2

1. Chapters 37 to 40 are the last of the book.

2. *Life* 37:1. Tomás Álvarez mentions Father García de Toledo and probably Father Domingo Báñez among those responsible (Teresa of Jesus, *Obras completas*, 16th ed. [Burgos: Editorial Monte Carmelo, 2011] [hereafter, *Obras* (MtC)], 389n3).

3. The summary heading for chapter 38 that Teresa provides reads, "Deals with some great favors [*grandes mercedes*] the Lord granted her by showing her certain heavenly secrets, and with other great visions and revelations that His Majesty wanted her to see. Tells of the effects they had on her and of the great profit her soul derived from them." The summary heading for the next chapter, 39, notes that she "continues on the same subject, telling of the great favors the Lord granted her."

4. E.g., *Life* 38:26.

5. E.g., *Life* 38:3, 22.

6. E.g., *Life* 38:2.

7. See, e.g., *Life* 38:1, 27, 28. In addition, Teresa frequently uses in her descriptions the verb *parecer* ("to seem"): *Life* 38:1, 10, 11.

8. Thus, an intellectual vision (*visión intellectual*) does not have the same weight as an imaginative vision (*visión imaginaria*), although Teresa often assigns in its account a certainty value specific to each vision. The "locutions" (*hablas*) seem less subject to doubt. The intellectual vision is one in which Teresa sees without seeing, or even sees in a more interior way, "with my soul's eyes" (*con los ojos del alma*) (*Life* 38:23), while in the imaginative vision a particular image is given. Teresa is careful to describe with as much accuracy as possible the different nuances of these phenomena.

9. [Translator's note: While the English verbs are somewhat different in Kavanaugh/Rodriguez, they are identical in Teresa's original Spanish.]

10. See *Testimonies* 59. In this text, written ten years after (1576) the composition of her *Life*, Teresa explains the distinctions between *arrobamiento, arrebatamiento, suspención, ímpetu,* and *vuelo de espíritu.* In *Life* 20:1, all these phenomena were simply grouped under the figure of ecstasy (*éxtasis*) and contrasted collectively with union.

11. *Arrebatamiento* is much less common than *arrobamiento* in the Teresian corpus, with the former term having only 8 occurrences, compared to latter's 108 (Astigarraga, *Concordancias,* 219, 221–22). [Translator's note: In Kavanaugh/Rodriguez (*Testimonies* 59:9), *arrebatamiento* and *arrobamiento* are "rapture" and "transport," respectively.]

12. A term of Ignatian spirituality. See Ignatius of Loyola, *Spiritual Exercises,* section 317.

13. See, e.g., the disturbance recounted in *Life* 32:7–9, which began slowly with a few questions.

14. This is also the case in *Life* 20:1; 38:5; 40:1; *Castle* VII:3:12 (Astigarraga, *Concordancias,* 219).

15. *Life* 38:2. See also *Life* 38:3.

16. She does this in *Life* 38:1, but also again in *Life* 38:10.

17. *Life* 38:1. Saint Paul, speaking in the third person in 2 Cor 12:2–4, recalls having been "caught up to the third heaven," noting that he does not know how, and having heard "ineffable things, which no one may utter." The Teresian narrative is very similar to this, even in its uncertainty.

18. *Life* 38:1. In *Life* 32:1, at the beginning of the vision of hell, we find a similar formula: "*quería el Señor*" ("the Lord wanted").

19. Chronologically, the vision of heaven happened before the foundation of the second monastery, in Medina del Campo.

20. It was at this point that Teresa began to consider "everything earthly" to be "like dung" (*Life* 38:3).

21. *Life* 38:4. [Translator's note: In Kavanaugh and Rodriguez, "dominion."]

22. Which Teresa had previously greatly feared (*Life* 38:5).

23. *Life* 38:5. The "good things" Teresa refers to are, she suggests, freedom and rest.

24. *Life* 38:7. In the face of this fear, Teresa's assurance is always placed in the mercy of God and in the recognition of the efforts he has already made to provide her salvation.

25. This attitude of interior freedom (or, in Ignatian language, "indifference") is one of the characteristics of the text of the "Principle and Foundation" that opens the *Spiritual Exercises* of Saint Ignatius of Loyola (section 23). Through her Jesuit confessors, Teresa certainly had access if not to the text itself, at least to the spirit of it.

26. She is referring to the *Vita Christi* by Ludolph of Saxony, who was commonly known as "the Carthusian" (*el Cartujano*). [Translator's note: The English translation is Ludolph of Saxony, *The Life of Jesus Christ*, trans. Milton T. Walsh, vols. 1–4 (Collegeville, MN: Liturgical Press, 2018–21).] We find the text to which Teresa alludes in part 4, chapter 84.

27. *Life* 34:17. Analyzed in the previous chapter.

28. *Obras* (MtC), 402n17.

29. *Life* 34:17. On the terminology of the *perder/ganar* as graphic representation of one's entry into ecstasy, see *Obras* (MtC), 359n42.

30. According to a dictionary from Teresa's time, the Spanish word *gozo* comes from the Latin *gaudium*. The difference between *gaudium* and another Latin word, *laetitia*, lies in the fact that *gaudium* is not externally visible, while *laetitia* is. (See Sebastian de Covarruvias Orozco, *Tesoro de la Lengua Castellana o Española* [Madrid: Melchior Sanchez, 1674], 2nd part, fol. 37ff.)

31. Teresa does say that "the glory" in this vision (of the Holy Spirit) was "extraordinary" (*Life* 38:11). But she does not dwell on this aspect.

32. This is often his first words during the post-Easter appearances (Luke 24:36; John 20:19, 21, 26).

33. In Teresa's post-Pentecost context, the gift of peace and the presence of the Spirit are already concomitant.

34. Teresa read the section concerning the text of the Pentecost, which also speaks of the presence of the Holy Spirit among those who are beginners, proficient, and perfect in prayer (*Vita Christi*, part 4, chapter 84). This chapter comments on the crucial passages in which the evangelist speaks of the relationship between the Son, the Father, the Spirit, the disciples,

the dwellings of heaven, and love, themes also approached by Teresa in chapter 38 of her *Life*. As the chapter on the Pentecost Sunday Gospel (beginning with John 14:23) is found in the same volume as the commentary on the Pentecost event, it is safe to conclude that Teresa consulted it at the same time. Even if this were not the case, the Johannine echoes of Teresa's reflections are worth highlighting.

35. Ludolph of Saxony, *Vita Christi*, vol. 4, chap. 84. Each of the quoted passages in the following paragraphs are from this chapter. [Translator's note: At the time of the preparation of this translation, the fourth volume of the English translation (Ludolph of Saxony, *The Life of Jesus Christ*, vol. 4, trans. Milton T. Walsh (Collegeville, MN: Liturgical Press, 2021) was not yet available. The passages quoted here have therefore been translated directly from the French excerpts provided by the author.]

36. See, e.g., *Life* 38:17. More broadly, large sections of the *Life*—e.g., chapters 10 to 22—depart from the narrative flow to introduce long digressions of a less strictly autobiographical character or in an order other than strictly chronological.

37. *Obras* (EDE), 269n7.

38. *Obras* (EDE), 269n8.

39. *Life* 38:14. A paragraph later, she recounts that she was given to see "great things" about the Society of Jesus as a whole (*Life* 38:15).

40. Moreover, Teresa recounts a vision of the suffering Christ, with a nail driven into his hand, at the beginning of chapter 39 (*Life* 39:1).

41. In *Life* 38:16–17, Teresa uses the verb *deshacer* (literally, "to unmake," "to deconstruct") three times to talk about her condition. We pointed out in the previous chapter of this book how strong this expression is in her writing. [Translator's note: As can be seen in this paragraph and the next, Kavanaugh/Rodriguez varies the English translation of these three instances of the word, depending on the context, rendering them respectively as "consuming," "reduces me to nothing," and "humbled."]

42. *Life* 36:16. The same verb *deshacer* is used for the potential "suppression" of the monastery.

43. Teresa repeats "how vain" (*y cuán vanos, y cuán vanos*) twice here in the manuscript. What some scholars take to be a

redundancy (*Obras* [EDE], 271n11) others perceive to be an "emphatic" repetition (*Obras* [MtC], 406n30). It is, however, a fairly common mistake in Teresa's writing for her to repeat a word.

44. *Life* 32:1, where there are three occurrences of the verb *meter.*

45. His being "put" (*metido*) in a place raises the question of who is the one who *puts.*

46. "I went about in the presence of that majesty of the Son of God" (*Life* 38:17).

47. From the adjective *esculpido/a,* used twice in *Life* 38:16–17.

48. *Life* 38:18. Here the verbal form is *imprimido.*

49. *Life* 38:18. Cf. *Vita Christi,* part 4, chapter 84.

50. *Life* 38:21. A body inhabited by the Spirit.

51. One can see this in the christological hymn of Phil 2:6–11, or, in a narrative tradition, the birth at Bethlehem.

52. *Life* 38:19. This is similar to the meaning of *deshacer.*

53. In *Life* 38:20, Teresa tells here the story of the peasant who had found in his field a great treasure, one worth more than he could handle, and not knowing what to do with such a large treasure, he died of grief. If the same treasure had been given to him in smaller portions over time, he would have lived happily. By analogy, the Lord of great majesty gives himself to humanity in the Eucharist.

54. This vision was analyzed in the previous chapter.

55. *Life* 38:25. One could make a connection with the request of the rich man in the netherworld asking Abraham that Lazarus be sent to his brothers to warn them (Luke 16:19–31).

56. *Life* 38:27. Teresa indicates that she could not doubt the validity of this vision. Further confirmation came when she subsequently learned of the "edifying" circumstances of the death, in tears and humility (*Life* 38:27).

57. This splendor corresponds with the glory that Teresa mentions often in connection with such apparitions, whether they are those of Christ or those of people raised to heaven (e.g., *Life* 38:30).

58. *Obras* (EDE), 276n14.

59. Translating *imaginarias* as "imaginative" (as opposed to "intellectual" visions) conveys the presence of an *image* in them; it is not intended to have the connotation of nonreality suggested by the word *imaginary*.

60. *Life* 38:28. So these two are intellectual visions. Teresa emphasizes, though, that the intellectual visions are "as certain as the imaginative visions."

61. *Life* 38:30–31. The Jesuit would be Alonso de Henao, which would situate these events in April 1557 (*Obras* [MtC], 412n43). Regarding the identity of the Carmelite priest, the note suggesting it in the French translation published by Éditions du Cerf (*Oeuvres* [Cerf], 316n12) is contradicted by the following note (317n13). He should therefore be understood to be Father Diego Matías. The identification of several of the protagonists in Teresa's accounts is provided by marginal notes by Father Jerónimo Gracián, a relative of Saint Teresa. (On Gracián, see Álvarez, *Dicionario de Santa Teresa*, 908ff.)

62. *Life* 38:32. The other two were Saint Peter of Alcántara and the Dominican Father Pedro Ibáñez.

63. See, e.g., the fact that the Lord called Teresa to pray for the salvation of a specific priest (*Life* 38:23).

64. These chapters of the Gospel of John are commented on in the section of the *Vita Christi* on the Feast of Pentecost—the text Teresa was reading, as we mentioned. It interprets the verse of John on the many dwelling places in the Father's house with Saint Augustine, indicating that there are "various forms of participation in the beatitude in the glory of heaven" (*Vita Christi*, part 4, chapter 57). In the marginal notes printed in the Spanish edition, this passage is summarized, "There is only one glory in heaven, but the forms of participation in it are diverse."

65. Tomás Álvarez, rather than emphasizing the Johannian notion of place, which he does not refer to, suggests that the notion of difference between the different degrees of glory reference 1 Cor 15:41 (*Obras* [MtC], 413n48).

66. *Vita Christi*, part 4, chapter 84.

CHAPTER 3

1. See her letter to her brother Lorenzo de Cepeda of January 17, 1577 (*Letters* 177:19). The book was in the hands of the Inquisition.

2. According to some specialists, the hermeneutic structure of nuptiality suggests the influence of Saint John of the Cross, who was confessor of the monastery of the Incarnation at the time Teresa was prioress there, from 1571 to 1573 (Pacho, *El apogeo de la Mística Cristiana,* 1026; Rómulo Cuartas Londoño, *Experiencia trinitaria de Santa Teresa de Jesús,* 150–51). It was also during this time that she experienced the grace of spiritual marriage (*Testimonies* 31).

3. Taking up the expression of *Life* 34:17 noted in chapter 1. Teresa uses similar expressions elsewhere, e.g., in *Meditations* 1:4 ("language [...] spoken by the Holy Spirit") and 1:8 ("what the Holy Spirit means").

4. *Letters* 177:10 (January 17, 1577). The possible source of this quotation in the work of Saint Augustine could not be identified.

5. Castellano, "Espiritualidad teresiana," 235.

6. Saint Paul called Christ "*to eikôn [tou] theou*" (1 Cor 11:7; 2 Cor 4:4; Col 1:15). Teresa's visions of God are all Christic. Even the (trinitarian) vision of the Son within the Father (*Life* 38:17, analyzed in the previous chapter) focuses all its attention on the Son.

7. In the first portrait of Teresa, painted by friar Juan de la Miseria in 1576, the artist included on the right side of the image, at the level of the head, a dove, in reference to the Holy Spirit and the supernatural inspiration of the writer. This detail was then taken up in subsequent portraits of Teresa (Tomás Álvarez, *Estudios teresianos,* I: *Biografíae historia* [Burgos: Editorial Monte Carmelo, 1995], 49; see also Jean de la Croix, "L'iconographie de Thérèse de Jésus, docteur de l'Église," *Ephemerides Carmeliticae* XXI, 1–2 [1970]: 219–60).

8. We will come back to the idea of inspiration a little later.

9. Teresa was canonized quite soon (less than forty years) after her death.

10. María de Toledo, Duchess of Alba, reported that her husband constantly carried with him an image of the Holy Spirit that

had been painted according to the directions of Teresa, following a vision. The Holy Spirit appeared in it as "a handsome young man, surrounded by flames or flaming volcanoes." To those who were astonished at such a representation of the Holy Spirit, Teresa had the habit of answering, "Why could we not paint the Holy Spirit with a human form, since one paints the eternal Father in this way, even though he did not become a human?" (Lafuente, *Obras de Santa Teresa*, vol. 6 [Madrid, 1881], 297, cited by García Ordás, *La persona divina en la espiritualidad de Santa Teresa*, 96–97n167.)

11. In doing so, Teresa echoes an ancient tradition that even represented the Father in the guise of the Son (illustrating the "christomorphism" of the Christian representation of God), since the Father also, like the Spirit, did not have a role as the face of God. On the history of the representation of God, see François Boespflug, *Dieu et ses images: Une histoire de l'Éternel dans l'art*, 2nd ed. (Montrouge: Bayard, 2011). The depiction of the Holy Spirit as a young man evokes Andreï Rublev's famous icon of the three visitors, symbolizing the Trinity.

12. Jesús Castellano prefers to group them as fire and water (Castellano, "Espiritualidad teresiana," 235). The water reference, e.g. in the fourth mansions, would emphasize the outpouring of the Holy Spirit like a torrent of living water evoked in John 7:37–39 as flowing from the bosom of Christ, in analogy to "baptism in the Holy Spirit." If the metaphor of water is very present in Teresa's work, its application to the Spirit can only be made analogically. However, there is no direct textual support for the relationship Castellano proposes. In contrast, the bird metaphor applied to the Spirit is well established in the Teresian corpus.

13. *Life* 38:12. The dove also appears in flight over Teresa herself (*Life* 38:10).

14. *Testimonies* 13:4.

15. In the gospel accounts, the figure of the dove is not necessarily visible phenomenologically to all those present in the scene, in the same way the Teresian visions are "seen" with the interior eyes.

16. As we have already noted, the Spanish verb *entender* can mean both "to hear" and "to understand."

17. One can think of the images of fire that represent the Holy Spirit in the New Testament (Acts 2:3; Matt 3:11; Luke 3:16). Teresa uses it, e.g., in *Meditations* 1:4 and 5:5 (in both cases, she writes that the Holy Spirit "enkindles" us in love). The enkindling of Teresa herself by the fire of the Holy Spirit is celebrated in the contemporary Carmelite liturgy: "Lord our God, who set ablaze in a marvelous manner the heart of our holy Mother Teresa by the fire of your Holy Spirit..." (*Misal del Carmelo Teresiano* [Valencia: 1973], 33, cited by Castellano, "Espiritualidad teresiana," 235n129).

18. *Meditations on the Song of Songs* 5:5

19. *Soliloquies* 7:2.

20. Either directly in connection with the Holy Spirit (*Testimonies* 36:7–8 [in the context of the vow of obedience to Father Gracian]; *Life* 24:5; 40:24; *Letters* 121:1 (September 9, 1576); *Castle* VI:7:6), or putting God (*Señor, Dios, Majestad*) and light in dialogue (e.g., *Life* 2:10; 5:6; 7:6; 21:7; 28:16 [in connection with confession]; 36:9; *Foundations* 10:13–14; 15:16; 23:10; 29:24; etc.).

21. *Testimonies* 36:7.

22. Eulogio Pacho, "La iluminación divina y el itinerario espiritual según Santa Teresa de Jesús," *Monte Carmelo* 78 (1970): 365–75.

23. Cuartas Londoño emphasizes that the Holy Spirit helps to understand Scripture (Cuartas Londoño, *Experiencia trinitaria,* 234–35).

24. *Testimonies* 59:11; *Life* 18:7; 20:1, 24; *Castle* VI:5:1; VII:3:12.

25. On ecstasy in the Carmelite school and in particular in Teresa of Avila, see Tomás Álvarez, "L'extase chez Sainte Thérèse d'Ávila," in *Dictionnaire de spiritualité ascétique et mystique,* vol. 4 (Paris: Beauchesne, 1960–61), col. 2151–60.

26. Miguel Ángel Díez, "Gozo," in Álvarez, *Diccionario de Santa Teresa,* 303–7. This article considers the mystical dimension of joy; the other aspects of it are considered by Álvarez in the article "Alegría" in the same volume.

27. *Life* 38:11. We considered this vision in chapter 2.

28. *Testimonies* 36:5; *Foundations* 17:1,5; 24:7,12; 26:1. [Translator's note: What Kavanaugh/Rodriguez renders in English in each of these passages as "Pentecost" are in Teresa's original Spanish "*Pascua del Espíritu Santo.*"]

29. *Testimonies* 36.

30. *Life* 24:5. Tomás Álvarez notes that in the liturgy this hymn is specific to Pentecost, but that it was ordinarily recited throughout the year by believers (*Obras* [MtC], 240n12). The French translators of the Cerf edition hastily conclude that this grace took place during the octave of Pentecost of 1556 or 1557 (*Oeuvres* [Cerf], 180n6). But there is nothing to suggest this assumption is certain.

31. Thus, Teresa indicates in *Castle* VI:5:9 that the soul and the spirit "are one" (*una misma cosa*), while at the same time noting their distinction with the metaphor of the sun and its rays. Likewise, she indicates that while "the soul and the spirit...are both one," still there is a "division" (*división*) in the soul, with one part always enjoying quietude, like Mary compared to her sister Martha (*Castle* VII:1:10–11).

32. *Life* 20:14; *Castle* IV:1:10; cf. *Meditations* 4:5; *Soliloquies* 16:3.

33. In scholastic anthropology marked by Aristotelianism, the human being is composed of vegetative, sensitive, then rational faculties, freeing for the soul a space in two planes: sensitive and rational, also called lower and higher parts of the soul. Rhine-Flemish mystics, on the other hand, use a tripartite anthropology for the soul that leaves a specific place beyond the rational faculties for the essence of the soul, sometimes called the *apex spiritus*. This structure envisioned by Rhine-Flemish anthropology has no direct equivalent in scholastic anthropology. Mino Bergamo adds that "Saint Thomas undoubtedly distinguishes the essence of the soul from its powers, but he does not represent this essence as one of the planes of the structure of the soul, but rather as the common substrate of all parts of this structure" (Mino Bergamo, *L'Anatomie de l'âme: De François de Sales à Fénelon* [Grenoble: Jérôme Millon, 1994], 53). Bergamo notes, however, that the anthropological structure of the Rhine-Flemish mystics is much less systematized than that of scholastic theology, even within the corpus of an author (like Tauler, for example).

34. Teresa thus notes that in the seventh mansions, "there is no more thought of the body than if the soul were not in it, but one's thought is only of the spirit" (*Castle* VII:2:3). This reflection comes in the context of explaining the difference between

spiritual marriage and other graces, such as spiritual union or spiritual betrothal.

35. *Castle* VI:5:1; see also *Testimonies* 59:11.

36. Thus Teresa emphasizes that in such a "flight of the spirit," it is not possible to resist, since the spirit is raised as by a huge giant who lifts up a bit of straw (*Castle* VI:5:2), in such a way that it is difficult to say whether the spirit still inhabits the body, so different is everything (*Castle* VI:5:7).

37. This is the project of books IX through XIV of *De Trinitate.*

38. This intimacy between the spirit and the Spirit is palpable, e.g., in the episode of the encounter—narrated in *Life* 33:9–10—between Teresa and Father Dionisio Vázquez, who was rector of the Jesuit college of San Gil in Avila. Teresa felt "in [her] spirit [*espíritu*]" that this soul was going to understand her and felt great joy (*gozo*) about that. She recognized in him a "special gift from the Lord for discerning spirits [*conocer espíritus*]." This priest never doubted that Teresa was inspired by "the spirit of God [*espíritu de Dios*]," since he took care to be attentive to the effects induced concretely in Teresa's soul.

39. *Castle* VII:2:3.

40. *Castle* VII:2:3, as when Christ offers his peace to the disciples just before giving them the Spirit (John 20:19–22).

41. *Castle* VII:2:7.

42. *Castle* VII:2:7.

43. *Castle* V:2:8. In *Castle* III:1:5, a first avian allusion is made when speaking of herself as a bird with broken wings.

44. *Castle* V:3:1. [Translator's note: Kavanaugh/Rodriguez renders this word "little moth," noting in a footnote, "For Teresa the little moth is equivalent to the little butterfly; she uses these images interchangeably."]

45. Of thousands of letters that Teresa composed during her life, and especially during her founding career, about 476 letters remain extant, whole or in part.

46. "May the Holy Spirit be with your honor" or "May the Holy Spirit be with your ladyship" or "May the Holy Spirit always be in your soul" (see *Letters* 2; 5; 17; 18; 19; 21; 22; 24; 25; 26, etc.). By comparison, Ignatius of Loyola, Teresa's contemporary, whose thousands of letters have come down to us, made reference only to Christ in the openings of his letters. The remarkable epistolary

presence of the Spirit alongside Christ in Teresa's letters is therefore notable.

47. E.g., Astigarraga does not include these mentions of the Holy Spirit in his concordance of Teresa's writings.

48. Secundino Castro, *Ser cristiano según Santa Teresa* (Madrid: Editorial de Espiritualidad, 1985), 190.

49. For a vocabulary of these phenomena written at a time of great maturity, see *Testimonies* 59, which dates from February/ March 1576.

50. E.g., *Life* 24:5.

51. Teresa uses this expression in *Life* 23:1.

52. Castellano, "Espiritualidad teresiana," 232.

53. This, in fact, was precisely the judgment offered to her by two learned men whom she had consulted (*Life* 23:14).

54. *Life* 23:16. The priest was Father Diego de Cetina, who was Teresa's confessor for a short time.

55. *Castle,* epilogue:2. That being said, since the Lord of the castle is the triune God, the Holy Spirit should not be excluded too quickly from this function.

56. *Castle* IV:1:1; V:1:1; V:4:11; VI:1:1.

57. *Castle* V:4:11.

58. We will see a little later the role of the Holy Spirit evoked by the metaphor of the silkworm that grows "by the heat of the Holy Spirit" (*Castle* V:2:3).

59. "The 'dilation of the heart' brought about by the prayer of quietude is certainly not reducible to any spiritual feeling or sense; but it is accompanied by a powerful decentering which, in the fifth mansions, pulls the soul from itself and allows it to say in a whole new way, 'It is no longer I who live; it is Christ who lives in me'" (de Goedt, *Le Christ de Thérèse de Jésus,* 139; see also 210).

60. *Testimonies* 14 and 40.

61. This episode is recounted in *Testimonies* 36. The favor given to Teresa on the vigil of the Feast of Pentecost is reported in *Life* 38:9–11.

62. *Life* 11:14–15; 28:18; 33:11; *Foundations* 2:4,6; 27:11; *Way* 1:2; *Castle* I:2:7; etc.

63. The word *ruin* comes up repeatedly in her writing (e.g., *Life* prologue:1; 1:1; 5:1, 3, 5, 10; 7:2, 3, 16, 22; etc.). [Translator's

note: *ruin* is translated in Kavanaugh/Rodriguez most often as "wretched," sometimes as "miserable" or "bad."]

64. See, e.g., the "protestation" (*protesta*) at the beginning of *The Way of Perfection*, where Teresa implores her readers (theologians) who would read it to examine it carefully and to correct any errors they may find.

65. This is confirmed by the Lord as well, who instructed her to write down what he said to her, "for even though it may not benefit you, it can benefit others" (*Testimonies* 48).

66. Literally, *deshacer* means "to un-do," "to un-make," or, as the *Diccionario de la Lengua Española Plus* (Barcelona: Editorial Norma, 2003), says in its first definition of this verb, both transitive and pronominal, "to destroy something already made" (250).

67. Perhaps a comparison could be made with the "*nada*" of John of the Cross? The Teresian spiritual doctrine does not, however, in general, have the kenotic character of the latter.

68. *Life* 36:15. [Translator's note: The Kavanaugh/Rodriguez translation of *deshacer* in this context as referring to the potential "suppression" (formal closing) of the monastery, rather than to its "destruction," does not convey the same level of violence or harshness that the author is referring to here.]

69. "The Lord spoke these words to me: 'It [the soul] detaches itself [*deshácese*] from everything, daughter, so as to abide more in me'" (*Life* 18:14).

70. *Life* 38:19–21.

71. *Castle* V:2:1–9.

72. *Castle* III:1:8.

73. *Castle* IV:2:10. See the theology of Jean-Marie Laurier on the role of Teresian humility as a way of salvation: Laurier, *Marcher dans l'humilité.*

74. *Castle* V:2:7.

75. *Castle* VII:3:1.

76. *Castle* VII:3:2.

77. Wilhélem, *Dieu dans l'action,* 186n10.

78. E.g., *Testimonies* 16.

79. See, among others, *Testimonies* 65.

80. This grace is recounted most particularly in *Life* 29:13.

81. Cuartas Londoño, *Experiencia trinitaria,* 221; Cuartas Londoño refers here to John of the Cross.

82. Castellano, "Espiritualidad teresiana," 235n129.

83. *Life* 29:13.

84. For a general overview of semiotic terminology, see Groupe d'Entrevernes, *Analyse sémiotique des textes: Introduction: Théorie—pratique* (Lyon: Presses universitaires de Lyon, 1979).

85. *Meditations*, prologue:3.

86. E.g., in the way one of Teresa's companions first uttered the idea of founding a monastery of discalced Carmelites (*Life* 32:10) or in the way Father Pedro Ibáñez came around to lending his support to the project (*Life* 32:17).

87. *Life* 23:16.

88. *Life* 23:16.

89. *Life* 23:17.

90. "My soul began to improve noticeably," Teresa wrote (*Life* 23:18).

91. *Life* 38:3.

92. *Castle* VI:1:2.

93. *Meditations* 1:10.

94. *Meditations* 6:7.

95. *Meditations* 5:5.

96. *Meditations* 5:2. See also the descriptive heading that Teresa provides for chapter 5: "Continues to deal with the prayer of union and tells of the riches the soul acquires in it through the mediation of the Holy Spirit. Tells of the soul's determination to suffer trials for the Beloved."

97. The full verse is worth noting: "The Holy Spirit will come upon you, and the power of the Most High will overshadow you."

98. The evangelist indicates the angel came (*eiselthôn*) to Mary and spoke (*eipen*) to her, that Mary was troubled by his words (*epi tô logô*), and that the angel left her (*apèlthen ap'autès*) at the end of their encounter. It is clearer here that Mary *heard* the angel than it is that she *saw* him. There is, however, a relationship between sight and hearing as a medium of reception.

99. *Life* 38:17.

100. One could theoretically add the other senses as well—taste, touch, smell—but the latter have such a small place in Teresa's writing that they do not have the status of paradigms like sight and hearing. Teresa herself links these latter in *Soliloquies* 11:2,

where she speaks of the soul of the sinner whose eyes are covered with mud and ears plugged.

101. See *Castle* VII:1:2 and VII:2:2.

102. *Castle* V:4:4.

103. *Testimonies* 58:20.

104. It is a theme that is dear to Teresa. Her christocentrism has been the subject of numerous studies, including Castro, *Cristología teresiana.*

105. Let us recall the force with which Teresa rejects certain spiritual advice according to which it would be necessary at a certain stage of the spiritual life to leave behind the figure of Christ (*Life* 22).

106. See, e.g., *Testimonies* 21, where it is the Father who speaks.

107. *Castle* VI:3:18. The question of whether or not to capitalize the first letter of *Espíritu* in this sentence—that is, whether it is a reference to the Holy Spirit or to the human spirit of the praying subject—is disputed. The Spanish edition published by Editorial de Espiritualidad does not capitalize it, while that of Monte Carmelo does. In her French translation, Marie du Saint-Sacrement does not. At the anthropological level, as mentioned above, the spirit is in the human person as the superior part of the soul, but it is not so much a place of diction—a place that speaks—as a place of reception of the Lord who, in the Spirit, can speak. In our opinion, Teresa is saying that it is the Holy Spirit (God) who speaks and who, by this presence, causes other thoughts to stop. This interpretation agrees with the other references to a voice of God that is imposed in a clear manner on the soul already familiar with it through long experience (see, e.g., *Castle* VI:2:3). [Translator's note: In the English of Kavanaugh/Rodriguez, the word is not capitalized.]

108. See, e.g., *Castle* II:1:2–3; *Castle* VI:4:11; *Meditations* 3:13; *Soliloquies* 11:2; *Testimonies* 20.

109. *Castle* II:1:3; VII:1:3.

110. *Life* 38:3.

111. In *Soliloquies* 8, Teresa laments that in the past the man who was blind from birth at least knew that he wanted to see and the Lord healed him (see John 9; Luke 18:41), whereas today, "there is no desire to see" (*Soliloquies* 8:2). This blindness—"our blindness" (*nuestra ceguedad*), Teresa writes, including herself

in the common lot—characterizes the "real sinners"; it is by the blood of the Son that she implores the mercy of God (*Soliloquies* 8:3). See de Goedt, *Le Christ de Thérèse de Jésus,* 200.

112. *Life* 9:1.

113. *Castle* II:1:2.

114. "I don't know in what way or how they heard their shepherd's whistle. It wasn't through the ears, because nothing is heard. But one noticeably senses a gentle drawing inward, as anyone who goes through this will observe, for I don't know how to make it clearer" (*Castle* IV:3:3).

115. *Castle* VI:2:3.

116. *Castle* VII:1:6. Cf. Acts 9:18.

117. *Castle* VII:1:6. Cf. John 14:23.

118. *Life* 7:6.

119. The Word of God being both word and gesture—that is, it is "performative"—the word of the one in whom God is present will tend toward actualizing it (see *Castle* VII:4:6 for Teresa's insistence on the concrete incarnation of love in works [*obras*], or *Castle* VI:3:5 on the performative nature of God's utterances: they "effect what they say").

120. In *Testimonies* 14, Teresa writes of "how a sponge absorbs and is saturated with water; so, I thought, was my soul which was overflowing with that divinity and in a certain way rejoicing within itself and possessing the three Persons." She takes up the same image in *Testimonies* 40. In addition, the metaphor of wax and a seal, that she uses in *Castle* V:2:12, suggests the idea of God forming the human being to be like himself.

121. *Castle* V:2:3.

122. See, e.g., *Life* 38:20–21.

123. *Castle* VII:1:7. In classical theological terms, one can speak of a kind of divinization.

124. See in particular *Life* 32:6; *Foundations* 1:8; *Testimonies* 3:8; *Way* 1:2.

125. Renault notes, concerning Teresa prior to her radical conversion, "When one considers the energy deployed by Teresa and the variety of means used by her (example, speech, reading, and prayer) to share with others the good that she had discovered, one can only admire such zeal in a nun still very young and in such bad state of health, even if this apostolic activity was

limited to the narrow circle of those she knew and to a limited subject of spiritual doctrine: prayer" (Renault, *L'Idéal apostolique des Carmélites,* 16).

126. She writes in *The Way of Perfection,* "I was a woman and wretched and incapable of doing any of the useful things I desired to do in the service of the Lord" (*Way* 1:2), a complaint she repeats elsewhere in various forms. Daniel de Pablo Maroto does not hesitate to write that Teresa is "above all offended by the absence of women in ecclesiastical tasks...and [by] the prejudices of theologians against contemplatives." He concluded that *The Way* "conceals a very significant social and feminist protest" (*Obras* [EDE], 651n3).

127. Renault, *L'Idéal apostolique des Carmélites,* 103.

128. On the importance of the word and of preaching in Teresa's thought, see Renault, *L'Idéal apostolique des Carmélites,* 60, 102–3.

129. Congar, *I Believe in the Holy Spirit,* I:167, III:165–71.

130. "Glorification" is one of the ways Saint Paul speaks of salvation, along with, e.g., justification and sanctification. See Fitzmyer, "Pauline Theology," 1397–1402.

131. *Life* 29:4. This point is emphasized by all Teresiologists: Álvarez, "Jesucristo en la experiencia de Santa Teresa," 362; Castro, *Ser cristiano según Santa Teresa,* 93, 97–98, 111; Arrondo, *Teresa de Jesús en el matrimonio spiritual,* 460. Castro writes, "Teresa has always understood the being of Jesus in his dual reality. For her, there is today neither the Word, nor Jesus of Nazareth, but only Jesus Christ: Word-incarnate-risen" (Castro, "Jesucristo y su misterio," 155n56).

132. See, e.g., *Meditations* 2–3.

133. *Castle* II:1:9; V:1:12; VII:2:3, 6.

134. *Castle* VII:2:11.

135. *Testimonies* 13.

136. Here Teresa, strangely, uses the word "reliquary" (*relicario*).

137. *Testimonies* 13:4.

138. *Testimonies* 13:5.

139. The Spanish use the word *forma,* which can also be translated as "form," to designate the sacred host.

140. *Life* 38:10, 12.

141. Several examples are found in *Life* 38:26–31.

142. Sometimes even in terms of the physical age that the body *appears* to have, despite the age at which the person died (see *Life* 38:27).

143. *Life* 36:20. In this apparition, the "great glory" (*gran gloría*) of Peter's glorified body seems to be reflected on Teresa, indicated by the fact that she says seeing him "gave me a powerful feeling of glory."

144. *Foundations* 28:36.

145. Teresa indicates that Catalina also said other things to her, but that there was no reason to write them down (*Foundations* 28:36).

146. *Meditations* 5:5.

147. Respectively, *Meditations* 5:2 and 5:3.

148. "so sovereign a union of spirit with spirit" (*Castle* VII:4:10).

149. *Castle* VII:2:7. Teresa is referring to John 17:20–23.

CHAPTER 4

1. Despite its magnitude, the excellent Teresian encyclopedia edited by Tomas Alvarez, *Diccionario de Santa Teresa,* does not have a thematic article on salvation (*salvación*) in Teresa's thought.

2. Castellano, "Espiritualidad teresiana," 217. Castellano notes Teresa's strong awareness of being saved by Christ, because of, among other reasons, the liberation she experienced in her second conversion. Castellano goes so far as to describe Teresian mysticism as "soteriological mysticism" (*mística soteriológica*), which is bold.

3. *Castle* VI:7 (descriptive heading); *Soliloquies* 17:6; *Poetry* 19 (Astigarraga, *Concordancias,* 2469). She uses the word twice more, but in the name of a monastery, *San José del Salvador,* in the town of Beas (see *Foundations* 22).

4. *Way* 1:3; *Soliloquies* 3:1 (Astigarraga, *Concordancias,* 2347).

5. *Poetry* 2 (Astigarraga, *Concordancias,* 2347) [Translator's note: Although in this instance, Kavanaugh/Rodriguez translates it as "Redeemer."]

6. More affective titles like "Beloved" (*Amado*), "Spouse" (*Esposo*) are widely used alongside more neutral names like "Christ" (*Cristo*) or "Jesus" (*Jesús*).

7. For a detailed account of the evolution of Teresa's personal conception of salvation, see Renault, *L'Idéal apostolique des Carmélites*, 13–46.

8. *Life* 3:5–6.

9. *Life* 7:3.

10. *Life* 7:6.

11. *Life* 8:5.

12. *Life* 9:1

13. *Life* 3:6; *Castle* VI:1:7; VI:3:17; VI:7:4; *Testimonies* 26.

14. See, e.g., *Castle* III:1:1; VI:11:7; VII:2:9; *Life* 40:24.

15. *Castle* VII:4:3.

16. See *Castle* VI:7:3.

17. This was the case until the very end of her life. At her last hour, after having received the viaticum, Teresa declared that "it is by the blood of Jesus Christ that she would be saved," and she further asked his sisters "to help her get out of purgatory" (Efrén de la Madre de Dios and Steggink, *Tiempo y vida de Santa Teresa*, 935, citing the deposition of María de San Francisco of the *Proceso de Medina* of 1610, Biblioteca Nacional de Madrid, ms. 12.763, p. 108).

18. The noun *salvación* appears less than twenty times throughout her corpus (Astigarraga, *Concordancias*, 2468). That being said, there are other ways to express the concept of salvation.

19. See *Life* 5:6; 7:4; 8:4; *Foundations* 10:5; *Castle* III:1:1.

20. This dynamic is also seen in the expression *ir al cielo* (going to heaven).

21. E.g., there are 173 occurrences of "the cross" (*cruz*) throughout the Teresian corpus (including 42 times in her letters), but often in the sense of generic trials (Astigarraga, *Concordancias*, 634–36).

22. Although in *The Interior Castle*, it is in the seventh mansions that the cross is most present.

23. *Soliloquies* 2:2; 8:3.

24. *Soliloquies* 10:1.

25. *Poetry* 19.

26. *Poetry* 26.

27. *Poetry* 19.

28. *Poetry* 19.

29. *Poetry* 19.

30. *Poetry* 20; 30. See also *Poetry* 29.

31. *Poetry* 20. See also *Poetry* 21. This call to embrace the cross or to embrace Christ is also present in her letters: e.g., *Letters* 21:2 (October 18, 1569); 201:2 (July 2, 1577).

32. *Poetry* 20. The Teresian origins of this poem is called into question by the editors of *Obras* (EDE), see 1178n41.

33. There are 311 occurrences of *gracia* in the Teresian corpus. However, 73 of them are found in the expression *caer en gracia* (to please, to be nice) and 57 relate to the expression *dar gracias* (to give thanks): (Astigarraga, *Concordancias,* 1227–31).

34. *Life* 34:10; *Way* 40:2; *Castle* I:2:2; VII:1:5; *Testimonies* 20; 25:1, 3; 29:1; 52. Half of the occurrences, then, are found in *Testimonies.*

35. *Testimonies* 20; 29:1.

36. The latter is depicted as powerless (*Testimonies* 20).

37. Sometimes she speaks in the first person, and at other times she relates the fears of her sisters (e.g., *Life* 34:10; *Testimonies* 52). In *Way* 40:2, Teresa indicates that if we are certain that we love, we can also be certain that we are in a state of grace, thus making love the measure of the reception of salvation.

38. It is found mainly in her letters, which suggests its informal, oral character.

39. The *doxa tou theou* represents the divine attribute par excellence, being so strongly associated with God that it came to represent God's personal presence. This strong personal identification between glory and God is also present in Teresa's thought, e.g., in *Life* 28:10, where she notes that the devil, even when he tries to falsely represent himself before her as Christ in the flesh, cannot counterfeit the glory that marks such a vision when it comes from God.

40. The word *gloria* appears 309 times in the Teresian corpus, of which the expression *gloria a Dios* accounts for 81 (Astigarraga, *Concordancias,* 1212–16).

41. E.g., "being in glory" (*estar en la gloria*) (*Testimonies* 65:9). For the opposition between hell (*infierno*) and glory, see *Life* 8:7.

42. As in the case of Peter of Alcántara (*Life* 36:20), a Franciscan priest who was, as we have noted, later canonized by the

church, who even converses with Teresa, as a sort of image of Christ (*Life* 38:13); and also a Jesuit priest (*Life* 38:30).

43. She emphasizes the dynamic—even ascensional—dimension with verbs like *llevar* and *levantar* (*Life* 34:17).

44. A state expressed by *con my gran gloria* (e.g., *Life* 34:17; 38:13).

45. E.g., *Way* 30:5; 40:9.

46. *Life* 19:1; 37:2; 39:23.

47. In all, ninety-three occurrences in the Teresian corpus.

48. *Life* 6:6 (twice); 6:7; 6:8; etc.

49. There are only nine occurrences (eight distinct ones), which is one-tenth the number of occurrences of the adjective *glorioso*.

50. *Life* 29:4; see also *Way* 34:9, where *glorificado* is not directly associated with a noun, but simply with the pronoun referring to Jesus.

51. *Life* 22:6; *Testimonies* 13:5.

52. *Life* 28:2, 3, which also includes the glorified Christ.

53. *Life* 36:20 (Peter of Alcántara); *Foundations* 28:36, an intellectual vision of Catalina de Cardona.

54. See, e.g., *Life* 32:6 (*pena*); *Foundations* 1:7.

55. *Life* 32:1–3. Analyzed in chapter 1.

56. See, e.g., *Testimonies* 20: the soul is powerless, like a person bound and blindfolded, unable to move or hear, in great darkness.

57. *Testimonies* 20.

58. *Castle* V:2:10. Teresa expressly mentions heretics and Moors, although it is the loss of Catholics that is the most distressing. See also, e.g., *Castle* VII:4:3 on this torment, which includes some fear about her own salvation.

59. *Testimonies* 20.

60. *Meditations* 7:8.

61. *Meditations* 7:5.

62. *Meditations* 7:6. Teresa often gives the verb *aprovechar* ("to take advantage of," "to make profit from," "to progress") so strong a meaning in her writing that some translators render it as "to save." [Translator's note: This is the verb that Kavanaugh/Rodriguez renders in this passage as "helped."]

63. *Foundations* 1:6.

64. Renault, *L'Idéal apostolique des Carmélites*, 101.

65. *Castle* V:2:13.

66. After the first definition of *trabajo* as "labor" or "work," a second follows: "We call *trabajo* anything that causes a difficulty, a loss, or a damage to one's body": Covarruvias Orozco, *Tesoro de la Lengua Castellana o Española*, fol. 50ff.

67. *Castle* VII:4:5.

68. *Castle* VI:1:2.

69. In *Testimonies* 32:1, Teresa relates an audition from the Lord: "Do you think, daughter, that merit lies in enjoyment? No, rather it lies in working and suffering and loving." The Lord continued by making reference to the example of Saint Paul.

70. *Castle* VII:4:12.

71. *Castle* VII:4:6.

72. *Testimonies* 32:1. The Son himself is the first witness of this.

73. *Castle* VII:3:6. The sharing of suffering goes in both directions of the relationship; Teresa notes that the Lord told her that by her *desposorio* (espousal) with him, he shared with her all the trials (*trabajos*) and sufferings (*dolores*) that he underwent (*Testimonies* 46).

74. *Castle* VII:4:8.

75. Saint Paul also takes up the concept of servant/slave (*doulos*) of God that comes with being an apostle (see, e.g., Rom 1:1; Gal 1:10; Phil 1:1; Titus 1:1).

76. *Castle* VII:4:4.

77. An important meditation of the *Spiritual Exercises* of Saint Ignatius of Loyola takes up this theme of proximity in work and trials with the militant Christ. See Ignatius of Loyola, *Spiritual Exercises*, sections 91–98.

78. See de Goedt, *Le Christ de Thérèse de Jésus*, 177–78; also, in the same volume, the Introduction by Joseph Doré, 8.

79. *Castle* VII:2:1.

80. *Testimonies* 31.

81. *Testimonies* 31.

82. The question of one's honor (*honra*) was very sensitive in Teresa's time, which is why she often talks about it (see, e.g., *Life* 11:2; 16:7; 20:26; 21:9; 27:13; 37:10; *Way* 2:5; 7:10; 12:5; etc.). When she was young, her family, being of paternal Jewish origin, had to

have the legality of their right of nobility (*hidalguía*) proven by a trial. "Points of honor" were frequently invoked and Teresa called her nuns to a greater simplicity in these matters. This distance from the world's understanding of honor also translated into a rejection of the superabundance of titles (see, e.g., Teresa's letters to Don Teutonio de Braganza (*Letters* 69:1 [July 3, 1574]; 226:19 [January 16, 1578]), but also to her acceptance into her monasteries of poor novices, including those without a dowry, and even of a black slave (see *Letters* 198:5 [June 28, 1577]).

83. *Soliloquies* 2:2.

84. 1 John emphasizes the concrete exterior character of the incarnate Logos: "We declare to you what was from the beginning, what we have heard, what we have seen with our eyes, what we have looked at and touched with our hands, concerning the word of life" (1 John 1:1).

85. It is interesting to note that the association between the monastery (here, Saint Joseph) and (terrestrial) paradise is common in monastic patristic and medieval literature (see Joseph F. Chorpenning, *The Divine Romance: Teresa of Avila's Narrative Theology* [Chicago: Loyola University Press, 1992], 68).

86. Teresa declares at the beginning of *The Interior Castle*, "The soul of the just person is nothing else but a paradise where the Lord says He finds His delight." (*Castle* I:1:1, referring to Prov 8:31).

87. *Castle* I:2:1.

88. *Castle* VII:1:3.

89. Georges Didi-Huberman, "Puissances de la figure: Exégèse et visualité dans l'art chrétien," in *L'Image ouverte: Motifs de l'incarnation dans les arts visuels* (Paris: Gallimard, 2007), 211.

90. Didi-Huberman, "Puissances de la figure," 228. Huberman uses the mystery of the Incarnation—Word made flesh—as a starting point of his reflection on the image.

91. This monastery can be compared to Teresa's previous home, Incarnation monastery, which, because of the freedoms taken with enclosure, among other things—before the Council of Trent tightened regulations—seemed to Teresa to be more of a "path to hell" for the weak (*paso para caminar al infierno*) than a remedy for their weaknesses (*Life* 7:3).

92. *Life* 40:21.

93. *Life* 32:10.
94. *Life* 36:5.
95. She says so at the end of her *Life* (40:22) and again at the beginning of *Foundations* (1:1–6).
96. *Way* 28:1–2.
97. *Castle* VII:4:6. See also *Meditations* 7:3.
98. *Castle* VII:4:9.
99. It is interesting to note that spiritual rhetoric in the seventeenth century described the "interior" space of the soul in precisely this kind of terminology: the interior is vast, large, airy. We see this, e.g., in the work of Jean-Joseph Surin. See Bergamo, *L'Anatomie de l'âme*, 9–10.
100. *Castle* VII:1:5.
101. *Castle* II:1:11.
102. *Castle* VII:3:11.
103. *Life* 32:10.
104. *Foundations* 2:3.
105. Teresa was very attentive to the presence of the right conditions before moving forward to found a new monastery. She chose to move ahead with a new foundation after she perceived that it was indeed the desire of God, which was expressed, among other things, by the meeting of certain necessary conditions.
106. See *Soliloquies* 2; de Goedt, *Le Christ de Thérèse de Jésus*, 202–3.
107. A little over 450 letters or fragments have come down to us that testify to the magnitude of the Teresian epistolary monument. The total number of letters written by Teresa was certainly several thousand and probably somewhere between 10,000 and 25,000, according to estimates by Luis Rodríguez Martínez and Teófanes Egido (*Obras* [EDE], 1195).
108. In chapter 2, we saw the centrality of the vision of the Trinity at the very heart of the movement of chapter 38 of the *Life*, linking Spirit, Eucharist, Trinity, and salvation.
109. *Life* 1:8.
110. *Life* 1:1–2.
111. *Life* 1:3.
112. *Life* 1:4.
113. *Life* 1:4.
114. *Life* 1:4.

115. *Life* 1:5.

116. *Life* 1:6.

117. *Life* 1:7.

118. *Life* 1:8.

119. Renault, *L'Idéal apostolique des Carmélites,* 29.

120. *Life* 32:6. Eulogio Pacho, however, places this awareness only in the next phase, through the visit of Father Maldonado and the subsequent foundation of the monastery of Medina del Campo (Pacho, *El apogeo de la Mística Cristiana,* 1039). However, Teresa was aware, even before the foundation of Saint Joseph, of the Lutheran threat.

121. The "Lutherans" (*luteranos*) that Teresa referred to were French or German Protestants (mostly Calvinists). See *Life* 32:6; *Foundations* 3:1; 18:5; *Way* 1:2; 35:3; *Castle* epilogue:4; *Testimonies* 3:8, 26.

122. Renault is too categorical when he asserts that "in the initial project of the foundation of Saint Joseph monastery in Avila, there is no trace of apostolic intention" (Renault, *L'Idéal apostolique des Carmélites,* 33). In fact, the root of Teresa's commitment to salvation is located within the Saint Joseph project, which grew out of her experience of the vision of hell, to which she repeatedly refers thereafter. This vision would provide Teresa with both a grief for the souls who suffer such torment and an impulse to work for the salvation of others. It is this movement—then in seed—that will be at the heart of all her apostolic action.

123. *Life* 36:5.

124. Renault, *L'Idéal apostolique des Carmélites,* 33.

125. De Goedt, *Le Christ de Thérèse de Jésus,* 14. See also 205–6.

126. *Testimonies* 14.

127. The collective dimension of salvation, being saved as a people, was predominant in the Old Testament, but in our day only the notion of individual retribution—a sort of "privatization" of salvation—seems to remain.

128. *Life* 38:32.

129. *Life* 37:2.

130. *Meditations* 7:3.

131. Without knowing it, these souls greatly help others (see *Meditations* 6:12).

132. *Meditations* 2:29. In *Castle* VII:1:3, Teresa invites her sisters to pray for souls "as though in a dark prison, bound hands and feet, in regard to doing anything good."

133. *Meditations* 2:29.

134. Wilhélem, *Dieu dans l'action.*

135. Renault, *L'Idéal apostolique des Carmélites,* 107–8.

136. *Life* 38:12.

137. *Castle* V:4:6. Teresa was writing long before the canonization of Ignatius of Loyola; in fact, both he and she were canonized together in 1622.

138. *Testimonies* 3:7.

139. Renault attributes this Teresian conviction to the consciousness of participating in the mystical body, this "invisible but real solidarity such that just one soul become perfect has the power to obtain the salvation of many others" (Renault, *L'Idéal apostolique des Carmélites,* 167).

140. Cuartas Londoño expresses well the centrality of trinitarian indwelling in Teresian thought when he writes that "trinitarian indwelling is in itself salvific grace, source and root, journey and dynamism, purpose and summit of the mystical life, of holiness, of the Christian vocation to participate in the intradivine life" (Cuartas Londoño, *Experiencia trinitaria,* 495).

141. *Poetry* 8.

142. Castellano writes, "Life in Christ is transformed in Teresa's thought into participation in the life of the Trinity. Here we touch the highest summit of Christian life....Teresa reaches these heights after a long spiritual journey. In her autobiography, we have a full series of texts in which Teresa lets us understand that the trinitarian mystery has been glimpsed. There followed an exceptional period of mystical graces during which Teresa saw herself immersed in the Trinity. In *The Interior Castle,* she systematizes this experience [*vivencia*]: this presence of God in the soul serves as its foundation, but the definitive encounter only takes place in the seventh mansions" (Castellano, "Espiritualidad teresiana," 227).

143. *Life* 38:17.

144. *Castle* VII:1:6.

145. That is, *Testimonies* 65, composed in May 1581, a year before Teresa's death.

146. See, e.g., *Testimonies* 13:3.

147. *Testimonies* 13:1 (in an intellectual vision); 14; 21; 29; 42; 49; 51 (in an imaginative vision).

148. *Testimonies* 29.

149. *Testimonies* 13:3 [Translator's note: In Kavanaugh/Rodriguez *imprimadas* is here rendered "fixed"]; see also *Testimonies* 14; 51. In *Testimonies* 42:1, she speaks of the three Persons of the Trinity as sculpted (*esculpidas*) in her soul. [Translator's note: In Kavanaugh/Rodriguez *esculpidas* is here rendered "imprinted."] This metaphor from printing and sculpture is also used in *Life* 38:16–17 (see chapter 2 above). Teresa even adds a reference to painting, which shows that the realm of art seems to be the most apt to evoke the mystery with accuracy.

150. *Testimonies* 21.

151. *Testimonies* 14. In *Testimonies* 49, she says she bears "this company" (*compañía*) in her soul "always" (*siempre*).

152. *Testimonies* 49; 51.

153. *Testimonies* 49.

154. *Testimonies* 49. This is one of the occasions when Teresa uses scholastic terminology in her writings.

155. *Testimonies* 49.

156. *Testimonies* 14.

157. *Testimonies* 13:3; 14.

158. *Testimonies* 42. [Translator's note: Kavanaugh/Rodriguez: they "are one."]

159. *Testimonies* 42.

160. "I see clearly that the Persons of the Trinity are distinct.... Although knowledge is given in a strange manner that these Persons are distinct, the soul understands there is only one God" (*Testimonies* 59:21, 23).

161. *Testimonies* 10.

162. *Testimonies* 21.

163. *Testimonies* 13:1.

164. *Way* 27:7.

165. *Testimonies* 29:2.

166. That is, each Divine Person can be seen and speak.

167. *Testimonies* 29:3.

168. *Testimonies* 59:22.

169. *Testimonies* 59:23.

170. See, e.g., Garrido, "Experiencia teresiana," 377; Efrén de la Madre de Dios, "Doctrina y vivencia de Santa Teresa sobre el misterio de la Santísima Trinidad," *Revista de Espiritualidad* 22 (1963): 771; Arrondo, *Teresa de Jesús en el matrimonio spiritual*, 458. Michel de Goedt argues, at one point, that it is indeed the Holy Spirit who does not speak, but a few lines later, he notes that the Father (also!) has only one Word, evoking the Lord who speaks only through humanity (de Goedt, *Le Christ de Thérèse de Jésus*, 181–82).

171. *Testimonies* 13:1; *Castle* VII:1:6; *Testimonies* 29:3, cited by Castro, *Ser cristiano según Santa Teresa*, 182.

172. *Testimonies* 59:23.

173. Buendía, "Puntos clave en la interpretación teológica," 300.

174. Some Teresian statements may lend themselves to such an interpretation, notably when Teresa aligns the "three Persons [of the Trinity] and...the humanity of Christ" (*Testimonies* 65:3).

175. *Testimonies* 14.

176. *Testimonies* 14. On the difficulty of the intellect to grasp the Trinity, see *Testimonies* 29:2.

177. *Testimonies* 14.

178. *Testimonies* 29:3.

179. *Testimonies* 13:3.

180. *Testimonies* 49; 51.

181. Garrido writes, "The mystical life does not end with the experience and adoration of the trinitarian mystery. On the contrary, by the very fact that the soul is engulfed in the divine life, it experiences the mystery that unites it to the august Trinity and its saving will of divine Incarnation and redemption" (Garrido, "Experiencia teresiana," 380).

182. *Life* 7:6.

183. See *Castle* VII:2:2, 4; V:4:4. The spiritual betrothal (*desposorio*) thus belongs to the sixth mansions.

184. *Testimonies* 31; *Castle* VII:1:2.

185. *Testimonies* 15.

186. *Castle* II:1:8.

187. *Meditations* 3:1. Teresa adds elsewhere that "what gives value to our will is to unite it with that of God so that it does

not want anything other than what His Majesty wants" (Teresa of Avila, *Escritos sueltos,* 2, in *Obras* (EDE), 2032).

188. Wilhélem, *Dieu dans l'action,* 339. He refers here to *Way* 32:12.

189. Renault, *L'Idéal apostolique des Carmélites,* 159.

190. *Castle* VI:3:5.

191. *Testimonies* 47.

192. *Life* 40:5–6.

193. *Castle* VII:1:3, 6.

194. The mystical betrothal, marriage, etc. Wilhélem emphasizes this constant relationship to Christ even in the trinitarian visions of the seventh mansions (Wilhélem, *Dieu dans l'action,* 263).

195. Garrido, "Experiencia teresiana," 383.

196. One thinks of the importance of the "most sacred humanity" of Christ as set out in *Life* 22, for example. In *The Interior Castle,* upon arrival in the central mansion, that of God—which presupposes previously passing through the doors of the other mansions—no door (*puerta*) is necessary, but one finds in the heart of this mansion, appearing beyond by means of the senses and powers, Christ in his humanity who then plays this role of entryway in the most intimate place of the meeting of God and the soul (*Castle* VII:2:3).

197. *Castle* II:1:9, VI:4:10 (in the form of hope).

198. The Lord reveals to the soul "the glory of heaven": *Castle* VII:2:3.

199. *Castle* V:1:2.

200. See, e.g., *Soliloquies* 13:1.

201. *Meditations* 4:8.

202. *Castle* VI:5:9. She speaks in similar terms in *Life* 38:6.

203. *Castle* V:4:11.

204. *Castle* VII:2:1.

205. *Castle* VI:11:11; *Meditations* 4:8.

206. *Poetry* 8.

207. *Castle* V:1:9.

208. *Castle* V:2:5.

209. *Castle* V:2:4.

210. *Testimonies* 14.

211. *Testimonies* 56. Teresa writes elsewhere of this state of being *embebido/a* (plunged, absorbed): *Life* 20:20; 28:9; *Foundations* 6:2, 5, 7, 15; 28:24; *Way* 31:3; 37:4; *Castle* VI:4:8; VII:1:8; see also *Testimonies* 40. In the same vein, Teresa writes in *Life* 40:10 of God like a diamond or a mirror, bigger than the whole world, in which all the actions of the world are reflected.

212. *Life* 32:1–3.

213. *Castle* VI:2:4.

214. *Castle* VI:4:13. On the soul's breathing (or lack thereof), see *Castle* V:1:4.

215. *Castle* VII:1:5. This transient obscuration is peculiar to the prayer of union, in addition to spiritual marriage. Before going into the description of the latter, Teresa had described the soul in a state of grace as a vast interior world where many mansions stand, and not something narrow and enclosed.

216. She notes in July 1571 that this desire to die has ceased (*Testimonies* 17).

217. Thus, in *Castle* VI:11:9, Teresa indicates that "the soul dies with the desire to die." Entering the seventh mansions brings about a change of perspective in this regard.

218. *Soliloquies* 17:3. Teresa also talks about making herself a slave to the Lord, not wanting any other freedom. She will return to the theme in *Castle* VII:4:8.

219. *Testimonies* 17; 37; *Meditations* 7:1. This desire to live for the sake of others is accompanied by a desire to suffer in order that the Lord may be glorified (*Castle* VII:3:6).

220. *Castle* VII:3:1.

221. *Castle* VI:11:11. Teresa also has the vivid expression of being "absent from God" (*ausente de Dios*); see *Testimonies* 59:13; 22:2; 60.

222. *Castle* VII:2:4.

223. *Castle* VII:2:4.

224. *Castle* VII:2:5.

225. Teresa renders it in Latin: *Mihi vivere Christus est, mori lucrum* (Phil 1:21). By presenting here two Pauline texts side by side and then continuing with a few comments on the metaphor of the butterfly, Teresa combines the evocative power of images with doctrinal prudence in appealing, in these delicate matters, to the authority of the apostle.

226. *Castle* VII:2:5.
227. De Goedt, *Le Christ de Thérèse de Jésus,* 202.
228. *Castle* VI:5:3.
229. *Castle* VI:4:15.
230. Teresa speaks of Martha and Mary who must unite to welcome and feed Christ: "His food is that in every way possible we draw souls that they may be saved and praise Him always" (*Castle* VII:4:12).
231. *Castle* VII:4:16.
232. See, e.g., Castellano, "Espiritualidad teresiana," 227.
233. As we have seen for *The Interior Castle.*
234. Under the Greek forms of *monê, oikos,* and *oikia.*
235. See chapter 1.
236. *Way* 34:7, 10–13. Teresa also reports in one of the *Spiritual Testimonies* that the Lord made her understand that after having ascended to heaven, he "never came down to earth to commune with anyone except in the most Blessed Sacrament" (*Testimonies* 13:6).
237. *Way* 33:2.
238. *Way* 33:5.
239. *Way* 34:9.
240. *Way* 34:6.
241. *Way* 34:8. The presence of the eucharistic Christ in the human person is therefore temporally limited, which distinguishes it from other forms of presence that are of longer duration or even permanent.
242. *Way* 34:7–8.
243. Garrido, "Experiencia teresiana," 380.
244. *Testimonies* 44.
245. See in particular *Way* 34:1–2.
246. *Way* 34:1.
247. *Way* 34:1. Teresa dealt with "Thy will be done" in chapter 32 of the same book.
248. *Way* 35:3.
249. *Way* 35:4.
250. *Way* 35:5.
251. *Testimonies* 65.
252. De Goedt uses the same expression. Teresa, of course, did not know at the time that she had only one year left to live; it

was therefore not from a testamentary perspective that she wrote this relation (de Goedt, *Le Christ de Thérèse de Jésus*, 182–83).

253. *Testimonies* 65:1.

254. Pacho, *El apogeo de la Mística Cristiana*, 1040. Further on, he adds, "The disappearance of mystical phenomena with somatic repercussions is the sign of the perfect harmony between body and spirit that is characteristic of spiritual marriage (*Castle* VI–VII). Teresa's mystical life concludes with experiences in which the trinitarian, christological, and ecclesial dimensions merge. This is how she described it a year before her death [in *Testimonies* 65]. She feels seized by calm and rest in the experience of 'these three divine Persons and of the humanity of Christ,' without the weight of difficult mystical phenomena."

255. *Testimonies* 65:2.

256. *Testimonies* 65:4.

257. *Testimonies* 65:3.

258. *Castle* VII:3:12. At this point, the raptures occur very rarely.

259. *Testimonies* 65:3.

260. *Testimonies* 65:5.

261. *Testimonies* 65:7.

262. *Testimonies* 65:5.

263. *Testimonies* 65:6.

264. *Testimonies* 65:5.

265. *Testimonies* 65:6.

266. *Testimonies* 65:7.

267. Ellipses in the original.

268. Teresa speaks here, as often, of her own soul in the third person.

269. *Testimonies* 65:9.

CHAPTER 5

1. See the analyses at the beginning of chapter 4.

2. To stick to the single emblematic verb *sôzô*—in its strict sense of "to save," since this verb can also mean "to heal"—in the Gospels, salvation always inclines toward the future, which is easily explained by the fact that they narrate the life of Christ who was

engaged in the work of salvation (Matt 10:22; 24:13; Mark 13:13; Luke 13:23; John 10:9). This salvation in hope is also expressed in other texts of the New Testament (Acts 2:21; 16:30–31; Rom 5:9–10; 10:9, 13; 11:26; 1 Cor 3:15; 2 Tim 4:18; see also 1 Thess 2:16; 1 Tim 2:4). In addition, salvation is sometimes presented as an accomplished event (2 Tim 1:9; Titus 3:5; see also Rom 8:2: a salvation in hope, etc.) or even as a present reality that is usually the result of a past action (Acts 2:47; 15:11; 1 Cor 1:18; 15:2; 2 Cor 2:15; Eph 2:5).

3. *Life* 32:1.

4. *Life* 36:20; 38:26–31.

5. See *Life* 38:6.

6. See chapter 4.

7. See chapter 1.

8. *Life* 8:5.

9. We considered this vision (*Life* 38:32) in chapter 2.

10. See, e.g., *Life* 38:3; *Meditations* 3:13; *Testimonies* 20.

11. *Testimonies* 65; see the final section of chapter 4 above.

12. See chapter 4 above.

13. See *Testimonies* 51 and 3:10; also *Life* 18:14.

14. *Testimonies* 65:1.

15. *Life* 32:3.

16. We mentioned its various occurrences in chapter 4.

17. The notion of deification (*theôsis*) is anchored in the great patristic tradition, first appearing in Clement of Alexandria, supported vigorously in Athanasius of Alexandria's *De Incarnatione*, and crystallized in the theology of Maximus the Confessor in the seventh century (see Jean-Claude Larchet, *La Divinisation de l'homme selon saint Maxime le Confesseur* [Paris: Éditions du Cerf, 1996]).

18. Jean-Marie Laurier highlights certain connections (among others, the notion of humility) that Teresian doctrine encourages between Tridentine theology and Luther's theology (see Laurier, *Marcher dans l'humilité*).

19. See, e.g., their use, with biblical echoes, in chapters 32 through 36 of the *Life*, as explained in chapter 1 above.

20. On this, see, e.g., the reflections of Pierre-André Liégé in his preface to Jossua, *Le Salut*, xii–xiv.

21. Louis Panier, *La Naissance du Fils de Dieu: Sémiotique et théologie discursive: Lecture de Luc 1–2* (Paris: Éditions du Cerf, 1991), 295–97.

22. See Sesboüé, *Jésus-Christ l'unique médiateur.*

23. See chapter 3.

24. This double epiclesis is most explicit in Eucharistic Prayer III.

25. *Way* 27:4.

26. See *Foundations* 5:17.

27. *Castle* II:1:11; VI:7:6, inspired by (among other passages) John 14:6.

28. *Way* 32:11.

29. *Testimonies* 47.

30. The long discourse of John 14—17 mentions the Father (*patèr*) fifty times. However, the theophanic instances found in the synoptic gospels (e.g., the transfiguration), which make "visible" a divine presence at the heart of the earthly life of Jesus, is not found in the Gospel of John.

31. Words addressed to the Father are found primarily in *The Way of Perfection*, where Teresa comments at length on the prayer the Our Father (*Way* 3:7–8; 27:1; 33:3, 5; 35:4; 39:6), but they appear also in the *Soliloquies* (2:2; 7:1; 14:2).

32. *Life* 29:4.

33. See Michel Gourgues, *Le Crucifié: Du scandale à l'exaltation* (Paris/Montréal: Desclée/Bellarmin, 1989), 147ff.

34. François-Xavier Durrwell, *L'Esprit Saint de Dieu* (Paris: Éditions du Cerf, 1983), 155.

35. Christoph Theobald, *Le Christianisme comme style,* vol. 2 (Paris: Éditions du Cerf, 2007), 776–77.

36. Jürgen Moltmann also started from this fundamental characterization of the Spirit for his project of "integral pneumatology," *The Spirit of Life.*

37. *Life* 33:8.

38. *Life* 32:16–17.

39. *Life* 33:5.

40. See chapter 3 above.

41. It would be interesting to compare the anthropological structure present in Teresa's thought with other theoretical models from, e.g., linguistics, semiotics, or psychoanalysis. The

accuracy and relevance of Teresian thought seem promising to me, so that it is able to enter into dialogue with other systematic proposals. The correctness of Teresian thought in its double consistency of experience and doctrine was, e.g., analyzed from a psychoanalytic point of view by Lucie Cantin, in an article where she compares the case of Jeanne des Anges to that of Teresa, by delivering very relevant analyses (see Lucie Cantin, "La féminité: D'une complicité à la perversion à une éthique de l'impossible," in *Savoir: Psychanalyse et Analyse culturelle* 2, nos. 1–2 (May 1995, titled "La féminité"): 47–89.

42. See chapter 3 above.

43. *Life* 38:3.

44. *Life* 7:17; 8:2.

45. In the account of her life, she notes that this decision brought a passage to a new life, hence a "new book" that begins with *Life* 23.

46. *Testimonies* 31.

47. *Life* 29:13.

48. Congar, *I Believe in the Holy Spirit,* I:167, III:165–71.

49. *Life* 29:4.

50. *Life* 8:5.

51. *Life* 26:5.

52. See the *Meditations on the Song of Songs* or the commentary on the Our Father in the *Way of Perfection.*

53. E.g., the account of the annunciation in the establishment of the monastery of Saint Joseph, or the Acts of the Apostles for the book of *Foundations.*

Bibliography

Only the main works that were consulted in the preparation of this work are included in this bibliography. For a complete (and thematic) bibliography on Teresa of Avila, see

Sánchez, Manuel Diego. *Bibliografía sistemática de Santa Teresa de Jesús*. Madrid: Editorial de Espiritualidad, 2008.

[Translator's note: Where English editions of cited texts are available, these have replaced the foreign editions listed. In the case of the Teresian texts, in addition to the English editions, the French editions have been retained in the list because the author refers at times to notes included in them.]

TERESIAN TEXTS

Teresa of Avila, *The Collected Letters of St. Teresa of Avila*. Vols. 1–2. Translated by Kieran Kavanaugh. Washington, DC: ICS Publications, 2001, 2007.

———. *The Collected Works of Saint Teresa of Avila*. Vols. 1–3. Translated by Kieran Kavanaugh and Otilio Rodriguez. Washington, DC: ICS Publications, 1979–85.

———. *Obras completas*. 7th ed. Biblioteca de Autores Cristianos. Madrid: La Editorial Católica, 1982. Introductions and notes by Efren de la Madre Dios and Otger Steggink.

———. *Obras completas*. Alberto Barrientos, ed. 5th ed. Madrid: Editorial de Espiritualidad, 2000. Introductions and notes by Enrique Llamas, Teófanes Egido, Daniel de Pablo Maroto, José Vicente Rodriguez, et al.

———. *Obras completas*. 16th ed. Burgos: Editorial Monte Carmelo, 2011.

———. *Oeuvres complètes*. Translated by Mother Marie du Saint-Sacrement. Paris: Éditions du Cerf, 1995.

HISTORICAL DOCUMENTS AND ANCIENT TEXTS

Athanasius of Alexandria. *Contra Gentiles and De Incarnatione*. Translated by R. W. Thomson. Oxford Early Christian Texts. Oxford: Clarendon Press, 1971.

Covarruvias Orozco, Sebastian de. *Tesoro de la Lengua Castellana o Española*. Madrid: Melchior Sánchez, 1674.

Ignatius of Loyola. *Spiritual Exercises and Selected Works*. Translated by George E. Ganns. Classics of Western Spirituality. New York: Paulist Press, 1991.

Ludolph of Saxony. *The Life of Jesus Christ*. Vols. 1–4. Translated by Milton T. Walsh. Collegeville, MN: Liturgical Press, 2018–21.

SECONDARY SOURCES

Ahlgren, Gillian T. W. *Teresa of Avila and the Politics of Sanctity*. Ithaca, NY: Cornell University Press, 1996.

Álvarez, Tomás. *Cultura de mujer en el siglo XVI: El caso de Santa Teresa de Jesús*. Burgos: Editorial Monte Carmelo, 2006.

———, ed. *Diccionario de Santa Teresa*. 2nd ed. Burgos: Editorial Monte Carmelo, 2006.

———. *Estudios teresianos*. 3 vol. Burgos, Monte Carmelo, 1995–96.

———. "Jesucristo en la experiencia de Santa Teresa." *Monte Carmelo* 88 (1980): 335–65.

———. (under the name Tomás de la Cruz). "L'extase chez Sainte Thérèse d'Ávila." In *Dictionnaire de spiritualité ascétique et mystique*, vol. IV, col. 2151–60. Paris: Beauchesne, 1960–61.

Astigarraga, Juan Luis. *Concordancias de los escritos de Santa Teresa de Jesús*. Rome: Editorialiales OCD, 2000.

Baumgartner, Charles. *La Grâce du Christ*. Tournai: Desclée, 1963.

Berceville, Gilles. "Entre logique et mystique: La théologie universitaire." In *Histoire de la théologie*, edited by Jean-Yves Lacoste, 225–82. Paris: Seuil, 2009.

Bergamo, Mino. *L'Anatomie de l'âme: De François de Sales à Fénelon*. Grenoble: Jérôme Millon, 1994.

Bernabéu Barrachina, Felicidad. "Aspectos vulgares del estilo literario teresiano y sus posibles razones." *Revista de Espiritualidad* 22 (1963): 359–75.

Bilinkoff, Jodi. *The Avila of Saint Teresa: Religious Reform in a Sixteenth-Century City*. Ithaca, NY: Cornell University Press, 1989.

Boespflug, François. *Dieu et ses images: Une histoire de l'Éternel dans l'art*. 2nd ed. Montrouge: Bayard, 2011.

Buendía, Miguel Maury. "Puntos clave en la interpretación teológica de la experiencia teresiana de la gracia." *Monte Carmelo* 95, no. 2 (1987): 283–302.

Cantin, Lucie. "La féminité: D'une complicité à la perversion à une éthique de l'impossible." *Savoir: Psychanalyse et Analyse culturelle* 2, nos. 1–2 (May 1995, titled "La féminité"): 47–89.

Carrera, Elena. *Teresa of Avila's Autobiography: Authority, Power and the Self in Mid-Sixteenth-Century Spain*. London: Modern Humanities Research Association and Maney Publishing, 2005.

Castellano, Jesús. "Espiritualidad teresiana: Experiencia y doctrina." In *Introducción a la lectura de santa Teresa*, 2nd ed., edited by Alberto Barrientos, 157–281. Madrid: Editorial de Espiritualidad, 2002.

Castro, Secundino. "Aproximación al pensamiento religioso de Teresa." In *Teresa de Jesús, mujer, cristiana, maestra*, 63–80. Madrid: Editorial de Espiritualidad, 1982.

———. *Cristología teresiana*. Madrid: Editorial de Espiritualidad, 1978.

———. *Ser cristiano según Santa Teresa*. Madrid: Editorial de Espiritualidad, 1985.

Certeau, Michel de. "Mystique." In *Encylopédie Universalis*, vol. 11., 521–26. Paris: Encyclopaedie Universalis France, 1968.

Chéno, Rémi. *L'Esprit-Saint et l'Église: Institutionalité et pneumatologie: Vers un dépassement des antagonisms ecclésiologiques*. Paris: Éditions du Cerf, 2010.

Chorpenning, Joseph F. *The Divine Romance: Teresa of Avila's Narrative Theology*. Chicago: Loyola University Press, 1992.

Congar, Yves. *I Believe in the Holy Spirit*. 3 vols. Translated by David Smith. New York: Seabury, 1983.

Congregation for the Doctrine of the Faith. Instruction on Certain Aspects of the Theology of Liberation, *Libertatis nuntius*. August 6, 1984. https://www.vatican.va/roman_curia/congregations/cfaith/documents/rc_con_cfaith_doc_19840806_theology-liberation_en.html.

Council of Trent. *Decree on Justification*. January 13, 1547. In *The Canons and Decrees of the Council of Trent*, 29–46. Translated by H. J. Schroeder. Rockford, IL: Tan Books, 1978.

Cuartas Londoño, Rómulo. *Experiencia trinitaria de Santa Teresa de Jesús*. Burgos: Editorial Monte Carmelo, 2004.

Didi-Huberman, Georges. "Puissances de la figure: Exégèse et visualité dans l'art chrétien." In *L'Image ouverte: Motifs de l'incarnation dans les arts visuels*, 195–231. Paris: Gallimard, 2007.

Dupuis, Jacques. *Toward a Christian Theology of Religious Pluralism*. Maryknoll, NY: Orbis, 1997.

Duque, B. J. "Función del místico en la teología y en la Iglesia hoy." *Revista de Espiritualidad* 29 (1970): 305–6.

Durand, Emmanuel, and Vincent Holzer, eds. *Les Réalisations du renouveau trinitaire au XXe siècle*. Paris: Éditions du Cerf, 2010.

———. *Les Sources du renouveau de la théologie trinitaire au XXe siècle*. Paris: Éditions du Cerf, 2008.

Durrwell, Francis Xavier. *Christ Our Passover: The Indispensable Role of Resurrection in Our Salvation*. Liguori, MO: Liguori Publications, 2004.

———. *Holy Spirit of God: An Essay in Biblical Theology*. Translated by Benedict Davies. London: Geoffrey Chapman, 1986.

Efrén de la Madre de Dios. "Doctrina y vivencia de Santa Teresa sobre el misterio de la Santísima Trinidad." *Revista de Espiritualidad* 22 (1963): 756–72.

Efrén de la Madre de Dios and Otger Steggink. *Tiempo y vida de Santa Teresa*. 3rd ed. Madrid: La Editorial Católica, 1996.

Egido, Aurora. *El águila y la tela: Estudios sobre San Juan de la Cruz y Santa Teresa de Jesús*. Palma: José J. de Olañeta and Edicions Universitat de les Illes Balears, 2010.

Evdokimov, Paul. *L'Esprit Saint dans la tradition orthodoxe*. Paris: Éditions du Cerf, 1970.

Faber, Eva-Maria. "Grâce." In *Dictionnaire critique de théologie*, 3rd ed., edited by Jean-Yves Lacoste, 601–6. Paris: PUF, 2007.

Fédou, Michel. "La redécouverte des anténicéens et ses enjeux pour la théologie trinitaire." In *Les Sources du renouveau de la théologie trinitaire au XXe siècle*, edited by Emmanuel Durand and Vincent Holzer. Paris: Éditions du Cerf, 2008.

Ferraro, Giuseppe. *Lo Spirito Santo, Cristo, il Padre*, vol. II: *nella dottrina di santa Teresa d'Ávila e santa Teresa di Lisieux e della beata Elisabetta della Trinità*. Rome: Edizioni OCD, 2007.

Fitzmyer, Joseph A. "Pauline Theology." In *The New Jerome Biblical Commentary*, edited by Raymond E. Brown, Joseph A. Fitzmyer, and Roland E. Murphy, 1397–1402. Englewood Cliffs, NJ: Prentice Hall, 1990.

García Ordás, Angel María. *La persona divina en la espiritualidad de Santa Teresa*. Rome: Éditiones Teresianum, 1967.

Garrido, José Cristiano. "Experiencia teresiana de la vida de gracia." *Monte Carmelo* 75 (1967): 345–91.

Garrigues, Jean-Miguel. *Le Saint-Esprit sceau de la Trinité: Le Filioque et l'originalité trinitaire de l'Esprit dans sa personne et dans sa mission*. Paris: Éditions du Cerf, 2011.

Goedt, Michel de. *Le Christ de Thérèse de Jésus*. Paris: Desclée de Brouwer, 1993.

Gourgues, Michel. *Le Crucifié: Du Scandale à l'exaltation*. Paris/Montréal: Desclée/Bellarmin, 1989.

Green, Deirdre. *Gold in the Crucible: Teresa of Avila and the Western Mystical Tradition*. Longmead: Element, 1989.

Groupe d'Entrevernes. *Analyse sémiotique des textes: Introduction: Théorie—pratique*. Lyon: Presses universitaires de Lyon, 1979.

Guerra, Augusto. "Presencia del dolar en la oración teresiana." *Revista de Espiritualidad* 40 (1981).

Herbstrith, Waltraud. *Teresa von Ávila: Lebensweg und Botschaft*. Munich: Verlag Neue Stadt, 1993.

Herraiz, Maximilian. "Biblia y espiritualidad teresiana." *Monte Carmelo* 88 (1980): 305–34.

———. "Teresa de Jesús, Maestra de experiencia." *Monte Carmelo* 88 (1980): 269–304.

Humann, François-Marie. *La Relation de l'Esprit-Saint au Christ: Une relecture d'Yves Congar*. Paris: Éditions du Cerf, 2010.

Jean de la Croix. "L'iconographie de Thérèse de Jésus, docteur de l'Église." *Ephemerides Carmeliticae* XXI, 1–2 (1970): 219–60.

Jossua, Jean-Pierre. *Le Salut, incarnation ou mystére pascal: Chez les Pères de l'Église de saint Irénée à saint Léon le Grand.* Paris: Éditions du Cerf, 1968.

Ladaria, Luis. *Mystère de Dieu et mystère de l'homme*, vol. II: *Anthropologie théologique.* Paris: Parole et Silence, 2011.

Larchet, Jean-Claude. *La divinisation de l'homme selon saint Maxime le Confesseur.* Paris: Éditions du Cerf, 1996.

Laurier, Jean-Marie. *Marcher dans l'humilité: Thérèse d'Ávila et la théologie de la justification.* Toulouse: Éditions du Carmel, 2003.

Llamas, Enrique. *Santa Teresa de Jesús y la Inquisición Española.* Bibliotheca Theologica Hispana, series 1.a, vol. 6. Madrid: Consejo Superior de Investigaciones Científicas, 1972.

Llamas, Román. *Biblia en Santa Teresa.* Madrid: Editorial de Espiritualidad, 2007.

Lutheran World Federation and the Catholic Church. "Joint Declaration on the Doctrine of Justification," 1999. http://www.vatican.va/roman_curia/pontifical_councils/chrstuni/documents/rc_pc_chrstuni_doc_31101999_cath-luth-joint-declaration_en.html.

Mas Arrondo, Antonio. *Teresa de Jesús en el matrimonio espiritual: un análisis teológico desde las séptimas moradas del Castillo interior.* Avila: Institución Gran Duque de Alba, 1993.

Misal del Carmelo Teresiano. Valencia: 1973.

Moltmann, Jürgen. *The Spirit of Life: A Universal Affirmation.* Translated by Margaret Kohl. Minneapolis: Fortress Press, 1992.

Mujica, Bárbara. *Teresa de Ávila, Lettered Woman.* Nashville: Vanderbilt University Press, 2009.

Pacho, Eulogio. *El apogeo de la Mística Cristiana: Historia de la espiritualidad clásica española 1450–1650.* Burgos: Editorial Monte Carmelo, 2008.

———. "La iluminación divina y el itinerario espiritual según Santa Teresa de Jesús." *Monte Carmelo* 78 (1970): 365–75.

Panier, Louis. *La Naissance du Fils de Dieu: Sémiotique et théologie discursive: Lecture de Luc 1–2.* Paris: Éditions du Cerf, 1991.

Pesch, Otto Hermann and Albrecht Peters. *Einführung in die Lehre von Gnade und Rechtfertigung.* Darmstadt: Wissenschaftliche Buchgesellschaft, 1981.

Pesch, Otto Hermann. *Frei sein aus Gnade: Theologische Anthropologie.* Freiburg: Herder, 1983.

Pesch, Otto Hermann. "Grâce." In *Nouveau dictionnaire de théologie,* 2nd ed., edited by Peter Eicher, 380–86. Paris: Éditions du Cerf, 1996.

Rahner, Karl. *Foundations of Christian Faith.* Translated by William V. Dych. New York: Seabury Press, 1978.

———. *The Trinity.* Translated by Joseph Donceel. London: Burns and Oates, 1970.

Renault, Emmanuel. *L'Idéal apostolique des Carmélites selon sainte Thérèse d'Ávila.* Paris: Desclée de Brouwer, 1981.

Riaudel, Olivier. "Systématique (théologie)." In *Dictionnaire critique de théologie,* 3rd ed., edited by Jean-Yves Lacoste, 1367–68. Paris: PUF, 2007.

Robert, Sylvie. "Vocation actuelle de la théologie spirituelle." *Recherches de Science religieuse* 97 (2009): 53–74.

Rondet, Michel. *Essais sur la théologie de la grâce.* Paris: Beauchesne, 1964.

———. *Gratia Christi: Essai d'histoire du dogme et de théologie dogmatique.* Paris: Beauchesne, 1948.

Sánchez, Manuel Diego. *Bibliografía sistemática de Santa Teresa de Jesús.* Madrid: Editorial de Espiritualidad, 2008.

Second Vatican Council, Decree on the Missionary Activity of the Church, *Ad gentes.* December 7, 1965. http://www.vatican.va/archive/hist_councils/ii_vatican_council/documents/vat-ii_decree_19651207_ad-gentes_en.html.

Second Vatican Council, Declaration on the Relation of the Church with Non-Christian Religions, *Nostra aetate.* October 28, 1965. http://www.vatican.va/archive/hist_councils/ii_vatican_council/documents/vat-ii_decl_19651028_nostra-aetate_en.html.

Sesboüé, Bernard. *Jésus-Christ l'unique médiateur: Essai sur la rédemption et le salut.* 2nd ed. Paris: Desclée de Brouwer, 2010.

Slade, Carole. *St. Teresa of Avila: Author of a Heroic Life.* Berkeley: University of California Press, 1995.

Strucken, Michael. "Trinität aus Erfahrung: Ansätze zu einer trinitarischen Ontologie in der Mystik von Ignatius von Loyola, Teresa von Avila und Johannes vom Kreuz." PhD diss., Rheinischen Friedrich-Wilhelms-Universität, 1999.

Theobald, Christoph. *Le christianisme comme style*, vol. I. Paris: Éditions du Cerf, 2008.
Turner, Denys. *The Darkness of God: Negativity in Christian Mysticism*. Cambridge: Cambridge University Press, 1995.
Weber, Alison. *Teresa of Avila and the Rhetoric of Femininity*. Princeton, NJ: Princeton University Press, 1990.
Wilhélem, François-Régis. *Dieu dans l'action: La mystique apostolique selon Thérèse d'Ávila*. Venasque: Éditions du Carmel, 1992.
Williams, Rowan. "Justification." In *Dictionnaire critique de théologie*, 3rd ed., edited by Jean-Yves Lacoste. Paris: PUF, 2007.

Index of Authors Cited